BOCOCK, ROBERT
FREUD AND MODERN S

KU-301-472

BF176.B67/

University of Liverpool

Withdrawn from stock

This
date and

Books i
the issue

Books is
followin
returned
payable

S.J.

10 MAY

2.3

11

S.J.S.

25 APR

11am

042851-8

NOT TO BE
REMOVED FROM
THE LIBRARY

Food and Modern Society

Freud and Modern Society

An outline and analysis of Freud's sociology

Robert Bocock

Nelson

[Liverpool University Library stamp]

Thomas Nelson and Sons Ltd
Nelson House   Mayfield Road
Walton-on-Thames   Surrey KT12 5PL

P.O.Box 18123   Nairobi   Kenya

116-D JTC Factory Building
Lorong 3   Geylang Square   Singapore 1438

Thomas Nelson Australia Pty Ltd
19–39 Jeffcott Street   West Melbourne   Victoria 3003

Nelson Canada Ltd
1120 Birchmount Road   Scarborough   Ontario M1K 5G4

Thomas Nelson (Hong Kong) Ltd
Watson Estate   Block A   13 Floor
Watson Road   Causeway Bay   Hong Kong

Thomas Nelson (Nigeria) Ltd
8 Ilupeju Bypass   PMB 21303   Ikeja   Lagos

First published in Great Britain by Thomas Nelson and Sons Ltd, 1976
© Robert Bocock 1976

Reprinted 1978, 1980, 1981

All rights reserved. No part of this publication may be reproduced,
stored in a retrieval system, or transmitted, in any form or by any
means, electronic, mechanical, photocopying, recording or otherwise,
without the prior permission of the publishers.

ISBN 0-17-712090-8
NCN 400-5803-2

Printed and bound in Great Britain at
The Camelot Press Ltd, Southampton

Contents

Introduction

by *Ronald Fletcher*

To devote a volume to Freud in a series on 'The Making of Sociology' might seem, to some readers, very strange. Freud, they might argue, was not only (and very explicitly) a *psychologist*, but also (and equally explicitly) a *clinical* psychologist, whose most immediate preoccupation was that of trying to cure the mental illnesses of his patients. Furthermore, he was a psychologist who insisted on relating his theories as closely as possible to biological and physiological facts. All this, of course, is true. But to adopt this view as one which distinctly marks Freud off from sociology is a basic mistake, and one which shows how sadly subjects which were once seen as being essentially interrelated have been forced into false separation by the current vogue of 'specialization'—necessary and correct when it is soundly conceived, but intellectually disastrous when it is not.

It is worthwhile to recall that *all* the major thinkers who contributed to the making of sociology—from Comte and Spencer to Ward, Giddings, Tönnies, Durkheim, Hobhouse, Weber, Simmel, Pareto (this could be a very long list!)—were, in fact, convinced about the close relationships between biology, psychology and sociology. The same is true of all the major anthropologists. The simple truth is that all these men were critically and creatively participating in the revolution which was taking place in man's approach to his knowledge of nature, and of his own nature and place within it. The geological and biological revolutions were quickly followed by a sociological revolution, within which psychology was given a new context. How it is possible *not* to see Freud within this wider context is a mystery to anyone at all aware of the interrelationships of thought among the human sciences throughout this period. But the importance of Freud, and his relevance to the making of sociology, can be seen in quite specific ways, and some of these are worth noting.

First, he was one of those important theorists who, early in this century, were developing new concepts in their effort towards a satisfactory analysis of 'the psychological aspects of society'. Possessing its own distinctive conceptualizations, his work was of the same kind, for example, as that of McDougall (within psychology) and Cooley and Mead (within sociology) who, concerned to analyse the development of the 'self' in 'society', were also moving towards a satisfactory *social* psychology.

Second, within this area, Freud's system of concepts and ideas—certainly rooted in biology and physiology, and certainly focusing on the development of the *individual personality*—were such, nevertheless, as to emphasize the *associational* context of the growth of the 'self'. This was as powerful an emphasis in Freud as it was in Mead, though not so explicitly articulated.

Freud's account of 'personality development' was, in fact, a theory of *social learning*, which also emphasized the crucial importance (for individual and society alike) of *primary groups*. A comparison of his ideas with those of McDougall, Cooley and Mead (and also those of Westermarck, Durkheim, Pareto, and other theorists offering systems of larger scale) demonstrates their great similarity in emphasizing association, communication, symbolization, and the establishing of sanctions, sentiments, and values in the process of accommodation to the role-constraints and institutionalized patterns of conduct encountered in the social system. They also follow the same sequence in tracing the movement of the individual from the family, through other primary groups, towards the larger and more formal associational structures of society. Freud is as emphatic as Cooley and Mead that the growth of the 'self' is, in important respects, essentially a *social* process. Indeed, many of the 'mental mechanisms' operating *within* the self—repression, identification, idealization, introjection, projection, etc—cannot be understood except in terms of the forms of social relationships experienced. If, incidentally, the name of McDougall is so old-fashioned as to bring blushes to psychologists' cheeks (he is, of course, not at all old-fashioned in this, and the psychologists' blushes should be on their own account) the name of Piaget might be mentioned as an accepted modern theorist whose ideas fit closely with those we have mentioned. To read *The Moral Judgment of the Child* in the company of McDougall, and Cooley, and Mead . . . *and* Freud!—is not only not difficult, but very worthwhile.

Thirdly, however: quite apart from his 'meta-psychological' theories of this kind, Freud also wrote directly on the 'malaise' of modern industrial society. *Civilization and its Discontents* uncovers other dimensions of the same malaise explored in Tönnies' 'Gesellschaft', Durkheim's 'anomie', and Marx's 'alienation'. *The Future of an Illusion* probes the same dilemmas that Weber had in mind when speaking of the 'disenchantment' of the modern world. Sociological dimensions proper are therefore *there*, to be considered, in Freud's work.

A fourth point, too, which may seem small, but has always seemed to be of interest to me, is that Freud—as well as Durkheim, Hobhouse, Westermarck, Cooley, McDougall, and many others—was stimulated towards some of his theories by one book which was, at the time of its appearance and immediately afterwards, of very considerable seminal importance. This was Spencer's and Gillen's study of the aboriginal tribes of Australia. *Totem and Taboo* had its roots in this socio-anthropological investigation just as much as Durkheim's *Elementary Forms of the Religious Life*. Indeed, Freud and Durkheim were opposite sides of the same coin: Freud looking through the individual psyche, Durkheim through the moral community, at the same socio-psychological facts. And both saw the close interdependence of 'society' and the 'consciousness' and 'conscience' of the individual.

Fifthly and finally, some important present-day theorists (whether or not in ways that can be accepted!) have begun to incorporate Freud's concepts into their own systems of analysis. The most prominent of these, perhaps, is Talcott Parsons.

From many points of view, then, it is a salutary thing to consider the ideas of Freud within the making of sociology.

Dr Bocock has already written on the nature of ritual and its place in the complex nature of modern society; he is especially interested in the whole area of the interplay—in both fact and theory—between psychology and sociology; and this study of Freud has grown out of this wider interest. Unlike most volumes in the series, this does not provide a selection of readings, but this is for the obvious reason that Freud's works are already widely available in excellent translation. This book is therefore Dr Bocock's own total study, a critical essay, and very much his own statement. On such a controversial subject-matter—especially, too, since he relates it not only to the theorists mentioned above, but also to writers like Fromm, Marcuse, and the Frankfurt School—theorists very controversial in their own right!— his work is bound to present grounds for disagreement. But this does not matter. To bring Freud firmly into the forefront of our consideration in seeking to clarify all the dimensions that have gone into—and are still going into—the making of sociology, is contribution enough, and his book is a very welcome addition to the series.

Suffolk
May 1976

Acknowledgements

I am very much indebted to the people with whom I have discussed Freud and his relationship to sociology. Many friends, colleagues and students have stimulated me to develop my interest in Freud as a sociological thinker, especially those in the School of Social Sciences, Brunel University; the Richmond Fellowship; the Graduate School of Theology, Claremont, California; and the Tavistock Centre, London. More specifically, I was helped to develop this book by the editor of the series, Ronald Fletcher, and by my wife, Jean. None of them are responsible for any errors of interpretation or faulty arguments that there may be in the book. They have, however, provided the necessary background of encouragement for me to pursue Freud's sociology. My thanks are also due to Jogita Billings who typed the final manuscript.

Preface

It may seem surprising to be asked to consider the sociology in the work of Freud, for he is almost always identified as the founder of a technique of psychotherapy for use with individuals. His writings do, however, include many propositions of a sociological nature.

Psychoanalysis consists of three main areas: (a) a method of therapy which is at the same time a means of exploring the unconscious; (b) a theory of personality, its development and constituent parts; and (c) a set of statements, which are really sociological, about society and its major institutions. The three areas are intimately interrelated. This book will be concerned primarily with the sociological ideas. The interrelations between these ideas and the other two areas will be examined when it is necessary for a proper understanding of the sociology.

It has been a characteristic of the way in which universities have developed that many specialist areas of knowledge have emerged concerned with various aspects of nature, and of the social and economic world. However, even in philosophy, especially in England and the United States, the concern with man as a whole, related to his physical and social environment, is relegated to a lowly status. The earlier sociologists were concerned with underpinning their systems of analysis with explicit assumptions about man's psychology and biological nature. More recently, ethologists have begun to examine the interrelations between biology, psychology and sociology, and to incorporate some of the conceptualizations of these disciplines.

Earlier in the twentieth century, writers such as Freud, could write about mankind's happiness, and ask under what conditions, if any, is man likely to be happy? Since the Second World War, the notion of human happiness has hardly ever been mentioned in the thousands of texts published in the newly burgeoning social sciences. Rather has it been the fashion to try and make social science 'technical', that is, a scientifically respectable set of sub-disciplines.

In this situation, it is a positive joy to read Freud's own

works, once the initial difficulties of coping with the emotions which may be stirred up in the process have been handled satisfactorily. For he is writing about the causes of human suffering and happiness, and how people seek to avoid the one and attain the other.

In the attempt to clarify the variables which are to be taken into account by sociologists, there has been a reluctance to have anything to do with the body, and the 'instincts', given the desire to concentrate on purely social variables. The result of this has been a conception of people as *tabulae rasae*, who from birth learn all they need to know during the process of socialization, and who have few conflicts with their society as a result. This model of human action is certainly an advance on models which saw everything as the product of innate drives and instincts and gave little or no weight to cultural factors. The pendulum, however, has swung too far the other way. Now sociologists need to think again about how they might reintroduce innate instinctual drives and their possible conflicts with different cultural patterns and values.

The sociological understanding of modern society has been only slightly affected by the work of Freud, and this state of affairs has been produced by both psychoanalysts and by social scientists themselves. Nevertheless, there have been a few exceptions. Some psychoanalysts, most notably Wilhelm Reich and Erich Fromm, have been concerned with the sociology in Freud's work, and some sociologists, notably Talcott Parsons, have examined Freud's contribution to the sociology of the family and the process of socialization. In the area of social philosophy, Herbert Marcuse's work stands out for its bold attempt to use Freud's ideas at a high level of generality, and its reflection upon the forces making for social change, and social calamity. The use of Freudian ideas by social welfare workers in Britain and the United States has been an important area of application.

Very few have developed Freudian thought into a critique of some of the distinctive processes of modern industrial societies. It is unclear how far Freud himself would have wanted to go in such a critique, and a major task of this book is to examine this issue. There is, of course, no reason to suppose that Freud could have developed all the implications which can be consistently derived from the fundamental themes of his work. However, sociologists have not attempted to develop these implications in any systematic way, and have not really given Freudian theory the attention it deserves. I think the time has come to try to redress the balance, to explore the basic themes in Freud's work and to relate them to some of the basic issues and problem areas in sociology.

Sociologists have not taken Freud's findings about unconscious processes very much into account in their theories and models of social action. They have operated with a view of man which underplays emotion and emphasizes ideas, and which stresses conscious rather than unconscious processes. His model of the conflicts people experience derives from the assumption that there is a difference between the basic drives of people and the values which they have imbibed from their parents and significant others.

This idea of an ever-present potential conflict between the desires of the individual and what he is able to allow himself to do is fundamental. It is a combination of a psychological and a sociological explanation, and is very powerful for understanding many areas of social life.

Freud's thought threatens many assumptions of sociologists in so far as they share the general liberal assumptions of Western, middle-class people of the left or the right. His stress on desires and emotions, on the unconscious rather than on reasoning of the intellect, does cut against what remains of Enlightenment values. There is no easy way of reading Freud, with understanding, which does not involve some initial pain for the reader, and for some this is reason enough to leave him well alone. Power, money or cognitive ideas are all seen by one group of sociologists or another as more important, and worthy of more detailed study, than emotions.

Freud wrote about unconscious processes: processes concerning desires, wishes, anxieties, phantasies and fears of which we are usually unaware. There is, however, no logic in the way these unconscious emotions operate. What appear to be, rationally speaking, contradictory feelings can both be present at the same time, as, for example, love and hate towards parents. This world of emotions can seem strange and unfamiliar at first, especially to anyone educated in a modern scientific approach to the world and man. For others, with a more aesthetic educational background, some of Freud's ideas may seem crude and debunking when applied, for example, to the arts.

Readers should beware of rejecting psychoanalytic ideas which they are tempted to reject, or which they may feel are ridiculous. The need to reject an idea in psychoanalysis *may* be more significant than agreement with it. On the other hand, it is important to avoid becoming an over-dogmatic follower of Freud, which can be the initial response of some. Psychoanalysis, as a body of knowledge and theory, was continually being revised by Freud, and has been since revised by other analysts. Therefore any dogmatic statements of psychoanalysis are likely to be partial, to miss out some dimension or other, and to be far too rigid about the nature of the theory and the method.

In order for a person to understand psychoanalytic thinking, from whatever base they start, change may well be involved. Changes, however, can be painful. So people may well resist ideas to avoid painful changes in their views of life, and, indeed, changes in how they live. But the attempt to come to some judgement about psychoanalytic ideas is clearly necessary for a wide variety of people in modern society, because it has grown up into a fairly powerful system of ideas and practices, especially in Western Europe and North America.

A judgement has also to be made about the ways in which these societies have integrated psychoanalysis into their structures and ways of life, and to determine how far these methods of integration are in keeping with the initial thrust of Freud's work, or how far they distort it.

Some recent sociological writers, such as Peter Berger, Paul Halmos and Maurice North, have analysed how a version of Freud's ideas and practices have been built up around social work and psychotherapy, and have been critical of some aspects of these developments. In this type of sociological analysis of the influence of Freudian ideas, there is little attention paid to Freud's work itself. The time seems right to return to Freud himself.

In this book I shall first of all briefly outline the social and intellectual background of Freud's work, and then his major ideas, which I think have some importance for the sociological understanding of modern societies. Any sharp distinction between the individual and society is impossible to sustain, for Freud's theory is not primarily individualistic in orientation. The reasons for the rejection of Freudian theory and practice among psychologists and clinicians will

be examined. It will be suggested that a different
understanding of science is needed to appreciate the
contribution Freud made to both theory and practice in the
human sciences.

The importance of psychoanalysis for sociology lies in its
attempts to build on the fact that man is a biological
organism. Freud's own understanding of the scientific nature
of psychoanalysis was, however, mistaken, as he operated
with a natural scientific model of social science. This does not
affect the actual contribution he made to social science, and
this contribution will be examined and outlined in the
central chapters of the book. It is hoped that this will fill a
gap in the literature, for there is no outline readily available
of all of Freud's ideas, as he understood them, which have
relevance for sociology. Criticisms of Freud will be dealt
with as they arise in relation to particular parts of his work,
but these will be kept separate from the exposition of his
ideas.

The continuities between Freud and early sociological
thinkers are outlined in order to show that Freud does link
in with major themes in sociological theory, as it is usually
understood. Finally, the relevance of Freud's theory for
modern society will be examined in the light of recent
developments in sociology, and, in particular, in terms of the
use made of his theory by the Frankfurt School. The work of
Erich Fromm and Herbert Marcuse will be compared and
their contribution to understanding modern societies
discussed and assessed. Their work is beginning to be
integrated into social philosophy, sociology and social
psychology, and is one of the major growth-points for
establishing better links between Freud's work and
contemporary sociology.

1 Freud's Basic Ideas

Freud's Background

Sigmund Freud was born in Moravia, a part of the Austro-Hungarian Empire, in May 1856. Three years after his birth, his father, who was a Jewish wool-merchant, decided to move to Vienna in order to see if he could improve his business there. Freud's father had been married once before, and Sigmund was the first child of the second marriage. There were already two grown-up sons from the first marriage; these sons were twenty or more when Sigmund was born.

After being enrolled at the university at the age of seventeen, Freud studied physiology, biology and anatomy. He had had a broad general education at school, and seems to have enjoyed Latin and Greek. Freud read widely in German, French and English literature, and was familiar with some Italian and Spanish literature too. He also read some philosophy at university. It was not until 1881 that he decided to take a medical degree; his work up to that time had been in the physiological laboratory under Brücke, where, for six years, he had studied the central nervous system. In 1885, at the age of twenty-nine, he went to Paris to study with Charcot, who at that time was interested in hysteria and hypnotism. Then, in 1886, he returned to Vienna and set up in private practice as a consultant on nervous diseases. The antisemitism in Vienna made his appointment to a university professorship difficult, but as he had married when he had returned from Paris in 1886 he needed to make a living. His wife, Martha Bernays, came from Hamburg, and Freud had met her when she was living in Vienna. They had become engaged in 1882, but the marriage had been delayed until Freud was able to support her and a family.

During the next ten years, until about 1895, Freud was influenced by Breuer, who was interested in hysteria. Breuer used hypnosis as a way of getting the patient to recall a forgotten trauma which was supposed to have caused the symptom. Freud also corresponded with Wilhelm Fliess, a Berlin physician, between 1887 and 1902. He had outlined to him a 'Project for a Scientific Psychology' in 1895, and it was at about this time that Freud began to become dissatisfied with Breuer's approach.

The proposed psychology was, however, to be based on neurological findings.

The turn of the century marks the real change in Freud's work, which had been developing from 1895 through his self-analysis. The year 1900 saw the publication of *The Interpretation of Dreams*, and this was the first full piece of psychoanalytic work to be published. About five years later, the groups of people working with Freud in Vienna were joined by Bleuler, and his assistant Jung, from the Zürich mental hospital. They all met for the international meeting at Salzburg in 1908, having corresponded from 1906 onwards.[1]

By the year 1914, Freud and Jung, having worked together, through correspondence and in meetings of the Psycho-analytic Association, began to diverge. The letters between Freud and Jung document the relationship between them; the difference in outlook between the two men is clear.[2] Freud was a rationalist, impatient with religion, and Jung someone who thought the non-rational and religious areas of human experience held something of worth for modern man. The one sought to control the unconscious, the other to contemplate it.

Jung seemed to have lost the emphasis on the body, and especially on the sexual instincts, which Freud retained in all his work. Once the human body was lost as a point of reference, and as a measure of value, Jung's psychology became relativistic and over-spiritualized. Jung can appear to link quite well with sociology; indeed, he drew indirectly upon the work of the Durkheim School in developing his understanding of collective symbols.[3] In the end, however, his thought eliminates conflict between the individual and the society, because, as in the sociology derived from Durkheim, there is no source of value other than society itself. On the other hand, in Freud, there is the possibility of a conflict between an instinctual wish-impulse and the values and norms of the society. His theory is therefore more able to explain change, and even to initiate change through the understanding which it gives.

Freud moved from Vienna in 1938, when the Nazis took over, and lived for the last year of his life in London. All of his important work was done in Vienna, in the first four decades of the twentieth century.

The patients who came to Freud for psychoanalysis were, as has often been pointed out, drawn from a restricted group: namely, the upper and bourgeois classes of Central and Eastern

Europe. It is often said that because the sample was so un-representative of humanity as a whole, Freud's generalizations about man are unjustified. Furthermore, evidence from other societies does not always support Freud's theories, for example, that there are always five phases in personal development: the oral, anal, phallic, latent and genital phases.[4] Freud's theory seems from this perspective to need firmer grounding in time and space. While this may be the case with certain specific empirical generalizations, it is not applicable to all the theoretical work. It is quite reasonable for someone to draw on specific groups and try to understand particular pieces of action, to use a wider theoretical framework in which to place these actions and try to understand them in this way. The particular pieces of action which Freud was seeking to understand and explain were important limiting cases which, in the *context of discovery*, made new theory imaginable. In the *context of validation* of the theories, other cases would be needed from different cultures and other time periods, and sometimes Freud did try to fill out his work in this way.[5] Others have done so since, as Malinowski did, for example, among the Trobriand Islanders. This research will be discussed later, in the context of discussing Freud's more technical theoretical formulations.

One basic theoretical idea is the connection Freud saw between the development of the individual, *ontogenesis*, and that of the species, *phylogenesis*. The early phases of human evolution, when *Homo sapiens* began to live in families, are seen as in some ways parallel to the early phases of infant development. The key similarity for Freud lies in the dominance of un-conscious processes both for infants and for early man. It is only later in the development of man's societies, and in the develop-ment of the infant, that cultural controls emerge, or are learned, so that unconscious material is repressed. The un-conscious operates according to the pleasure principle alone—there are no values exercising restraint over instinctual impulses. Culture, both in relation to the species and to the individual, is able to operate according to the reality principle, aiming to adapt the group, or the person, to the natural and social environment more realistically than would otherwise be the case. The gain in realistic security for groups, as for the person, in this replacement of the pleasure principle by the reality principle, is only possible at the expense of instinctual gratification. Freud continually wondered whether or not the process had gone too far in modern societies; whether the gains in security were no longer sufficient to offset the loss of pleasures which they entailed.[6]

This is the central issue which is of concern in Freud's more sociological works. He wrote:

> My interests, after making a lifelong detour through the natural sciences, medicine and psychotherapy, returned to the cultural problems which had fascinated me long before, when I was a youth scarcely old enough for thinking.[7]

It is these large themes of the reasons why mankind has developed societies and cultures in the way it has, and the consequences and costs of such developments in terms of happiness, which are the core of Freud's sociology and social philosophy. They need to be understood in the context of psychoanalysis as both a method of therapy and a body of findings about how human beings act. It is therefore necessary to set out systematically these other themes in Freud's thought, and this will be done in the chapters which follow. We shall then be in a position to return to these themes of human civilization and its discontents, and to see the ways in which others have used Freud's ideas.

As a young man Freud had worked on biology, and the human nervous system in particular. This background influenced all his thinking about man in society, for he never forgot that human beings were biological organisms. Darwinian evolutionary thinking influenced him too, and his work on society is shot through with an evolutionary perspective, from the primal horde, a notion he derived from Darwin, to complex technological societies. The notion of 'instinct', which will be discussed in detail in Chapter 6, influenced his theory deeply. The instincts are known to us as impulses, wishes or desires which seek direct satisfaction, unless they are totally repressed. They operate according to principles of an entirely different kind from those of logical, rational thought processes. They are a major and fundamental component of the system of the unconscious, as distinct from the conscious and preconscious systems.

The Unconscious

It was during the first four decades of the twentieth century that the major contours of psychoanalytic theory were first developed by Freud. Beginning with the introduction of the notion of the unconscious to link together dreams, parapraxes and hypnosis, Freud went on to use the concept to understand a variety of neurotic symptoms. Later still, the concept of the unconscious was given an even wider connotation, and was seen to influence not only abnormal individual behaviour, but also normal behaviour of the individual in social institutions. It is this latter application which has importance for modern sociology, but some understanding of the concept of the unconscious as first developed by Freud is necessary before considering its application to social institutions and society generally.

> The division of the psychical into what is conscious and what is unconscious is the fundamental premise of psychoanalysis; ... psychoanalysis cannot situate the essence of the psychical in consciousness, but is obliged to regard consciousness as a quality of the psychical, which may be present in addition to other qualities or may be absent.[8]

So Freud wrote in *The Ego and the Id*, and the same point is found in other outlines of psychoanalysis written by Freud. He was fully aware that, to many people schooled in Western logic and philosophy, such a premise was difficult to accept. He argued that such a philosophical position could not cope with the phenomena of dreams and especially hypnosis. Some ideas can readily be recalled to consciousness, and these Freud thinks of as in the *preconscious*. Other ideas seem to operate on the mind with great force, but they are not conscious, nor readily recalled to consciousness; they are *unconscious*. These terms are purely descriptive, but they are necessary to cope with observed phenomena, especially in psychopathology.

> The state in which the ideas existed before being made conscious is called by us *repression*, and we assert that the force which instituted the repression and maintains it is perceived as resistance during the work of analysis.[9]

The repressed is, says Freud, the prototype of the unconscious. The preconscious is that part of the unconscious which can readily be brought into consciousness; dynamically speaking, the repressed is the unconscious which will not ordinarily become conscious. Not all that is unconscious is repressed, although all that is repressed is unconscious. Freud introduced the idea that a part of the ego is unconscious too. This idea is necessary to account for the censorship of dream material. Not all the impulses of the repressed find simple expression in dreams, but they are filtered and censored, even during sleep. The *super-ego* is introduced as a concept to cope with this problem, its function being to censor and keep repressed material repressed.

There is also an impersonal layer of material in human beings, the 'it', or *id*. The ego reaches down to it in its 'lower' portions, and the repressed merges with the id. The ego is that part of the id which has through perception been modified by the external world. The ego tries to bring the perception of reality, the external world, to bear on the impulses of the id, which seek pleasure, without regard to the external reality in which the organism is placed.[10]

The idea of the unconscious is not simple, and many critics of the concept have not appreciated its links with the concepts of the ego, super-ego, id, and the repressed. The interrelationships between these concepts involve a shift from the descriptive framework in which thoughts and memories can be described as conscious, preconscious or unconscious—and feelings as either conscious or unconscious, but not preconscious—to a more dynamic framework of the psychic life of human beings. This framework brings in the concepts of ego, super-ego, id, and the repressed, which had always been used in Freud's system before the advent of the ego, super-ego, id, model.

The concepts were developed to conceptualize problems which arose in therapeutic work—problems such as the resistance of patients to being well at all, and not merely to particular interpretations offered to them by Freud in his role as analyst. Such resistance to being well necessitated the idea of unconscious forces of guilt; the patients sought to punish themselves through illness. The idea of a severe super-ego developed out of thought about how such a phenomenon was possible.

The idea of basic sexual instincts, which are present from birth and which may also be unconscious, was retained in all Freud's theories. These are impersonal, instinctual wish-impulses which push the infant towards gratifying them in a variety of physical actions, such as thumb-sucking, screaming, playing with faeces and genitals.[11] The notion of the id, in the later theory, picks up this set of assumptions, and stresses their universality in all humans, and their impersonality. Painful experiences or forbidden wishes belong to the repressed, and they too are unconscious. People are not born with a repressed set of experiences, but they acquire them, although at times Freud seems to suggest that some parts of the repressed material of earlier generations is inherited. If this seems too scandalous an idea, as it is for many people, it can be modified without damage to Freud's other theories, and the cultures of human societies may be seen as transmitting the repressed material of earlier generations to the present one.

There are many memories which are too painful, or too wicked, for the patient to remember without the aid of psycho-analysis, and these are said to be repressed. There has therefore to be an agency of repression, and a means of maintaining repressed experiences in the unconscious state. This agency, the super-ego, borrows energy for repression and its continuation from the instinctual energy of the body. This energy is negative in that it is destructive of happiness and health in many cases. In the later theory of Freud, it is this energy which he sees as derived from the death instincts, which are innate destructive energy forces.[12]

The relations between the unconscious system and the preconscious and conscious systems are important. The conscious and preconscious systems may not be able to influence the unconscious system at all, and it is for this reason that the notion of the unconscious has important implications for sociological understanding of human action. Unconscious primary processes can affect action in ways which are beyond ordinary conscious control, as is seen in many forms of mental illness as well as in other actions of 'normal' people, such as occurs in dreaming. The kernel of the unconscious system is the whole set of instinctual wish-impulses which may be represented to consciousness by dream images. Two such impulses may be contradictory, but will not cancel one another out. They may form a compromise which has an intermediate aim. The primary process has two characteristics, both arising from the motility of cathexis, or the capacity of an instinctual impulse to switch from one object to another in trying to achieve gratification. One of these characteristics is *displacement*, the other is *condensation*.

> By the process of displacement one idea may surrender to another the whole volume of its cathexis; by that of condensation it may appropriate the whole cathexis of several other ideas.[13]

The unconscious system is timeless, as may be seen in many dreams in which time is confused and mixed, sometimes going slowly, at other times quickly, and totally different time periods are found to follow one another. The unconscious system obeys the pleasure principle and seeks pleasurable states of the psyche, but would ignore external reality without the guidance of the conscious and preconscious perceptual system. In some patients Freud thought that the unconscious system was not under sufficient control by the conscious and preconscious systems, and that the patient was therefore a potential danger to himself or others. One major aim of psychoanalytic therapy was to try to bring the unconscious under more conscious control, to introduce the reality principle into the workings of the pleasure principle.

> It is a very remarkable fact that the unconscious of one human being can react upon that of another, without the conscious being implicated at all.[14]

This remark had important implications in the theory of the technique of psychoanalysis, where transference—the way the analyst comes to take on the emotional elements of a parent figure for the analysand—plays a key part in understanding the therapeutic effects of psychoanalysis. It also has important implications for understanding action in groups, and this was developed in Freud in his *Group Psychology and the Analysis of the Ego*. It has important implications for sociology, if it is accepted as in any sense true. Sociologists have concentrated on social reality as the product of conscious and preconscious processes, but have done little to develop a sociology of the unconscious.

A Sociology of the Unconscious

A sociology of the unconscious[15] would not only point out the unintended consequences of social action, where these are grasped and comprehended in terms of conscious intentions which are then misunderstood, or reinterpreted, by other groups within the social relationships, and which result in outcomes which neither the original intender nor the others could have foreseen. Rather, such a sociology would be concerned with understanding the part unconscious emotional processes play in both the creation and maintenance of existing societies, and their role in creating change. Freud himself began to develop a general theory of unconscious emotional processes in human societies.

The main area of concern in such a sociology of the unconscious lies in the analysis of social control. From birth, the baby and infant imbibes moral values and learns to control instinctual wishes so that he or she is not chastised by parents, or other agents of socialization. Religious, educational and political institutions all play a part in the process of socialization and social control. Other institutions, such as the legal institutions, borstals, prisons and mental hospitals, become concerned with resocialization when deviance has occurred, been socially noticed, and action taken against the person. These social institutions are involved when actions of a sexual nature or actions of a violent character have occurred. Human cultures prescribe and proscribe the sexual actions of their members; both the action and the object are socio-culturally controlled. Cultures vary in the degree to which they take sexual deviance as a serious sin or crime, but all control sexuality in some way.[16] Similarly, there are cultural controls on acts of violence against other people, animals or property. They change in the same society over time; for example, when one society is at war with another, some people are actively encouraged to wound and kill other people from the enemy group. Ridicule, imprisonment or even death may be used against those who will not fight the socially defined enemy. In peacetime such processes do not occur to the same extent. These two basic areas of human activity are central to Freud's theory and to its application to human societies, as will be seen throughout the chapters which follow.

The two areas of sexuality and violence are interconnected in Freud's theory. Libidinal energy from sexuality has to be available to be used in creating and maintaining society and cultures. Instinctual repression of both sexuality and of violent aggressive impulses are necessary for any human society to be possible at all, the former helping to counteract the destructive aggressive impulses. In living and working together, people develop mutual antagonisms which have to be counteracted by sublimated sexual energy if life and work are to continue. These ideas will be discussed later in more detail, but here it is important to note the interrelationship which Freud posits between the two sets of instinctual impulses. The relationship has not always been pointed out in discussions of Freud's work, and yet it is an essential one if he is to be properly understood.

Within Freud's own working lifetime discussion of the sociological implications of psychoanalysis from a radical, Marxist, perspective was undertaken by Wilhelm Reich. The first part of the work now known as *The Sexual Revolution* was published by Reich in 1929, and the second part in 1935. The outlines of Freud's later theory were made available in *Group Psychology and the Analysis of the Ego* (1921), the first mention of the death instincts having been made in 1920 in *Beyond the Pleasure Principle*. Freud developed the role of the death instincts in group life more fully in *Civilization and Its Discontents* (1930). Reich was seen as too political in his work and was eventually removed from the International Psychoanalytic movement. He tried to apply psychoanalytic findings to political issues, and in particular to trying to change sexual understanding and morality among young people, both students and young workers. Reich thought that there was no need to posit basic death instincts to explain the anti-social, unconscious feelings that he agreed with Freud were present in people in modern societies in Europe and America. It was because people could not enjoy full genital orgasmic potency that they were hostile to one another and anti-social. If people were socialized without a compulsory and compulsive sex morality, and learned to enjoy genital sexuality, then there would be no hostile behaviour.

> The healthy individual has no compulsive morality because he has no impulses which call for moral inhibition. What antisocial impulses may be left are easily controlled, provided the basic genital needs are satisfied.[17]

So Reich wrote in the first part of *The Sexual Revolution*. He argued that Freud was dealing only with one type of human society, namely, the patriarchal authoritarian type. In matriarchal societies there was no sexual misery for the youth, and often no anal phase in between the oral and phallic phases.[18] Reich's use of ethnographic evidence is suspect, but in general terms it could be admitted that there could in Freudian theory be differences of the type which Reich pointed out, even if his evidence may not have been carefully formulated. A key claim of Freud's would remain: namely, that the more technologically advanced societies were those with the patriarchal authoritarian structure, with its associated sexual morality, and that this was no accident of chance, but a correlation that should, and could, be explained by psycho-analytic theory. Reich tended to ignore the interconnection, but it was an important one for Freud's sociology. On his view, modern technological societies could not simply change their sexual morality and sexual socialization without there being consequences in other parts of the society. These consequences will be discussed in later chapters, but it is necessary to see where they fit into the overall theory at the outset, especially given the recent interest which has been shown in Reich's theories.[19]

Reich thought that there were logical consequences of psychoanalytic findings, which led to a need for change in the moral teachings and practice of educators in schools, the home, and in churches. Psychoanalysis showed that repression was a social process. Members of any society were all socialized into a similar set of values and attitudes towards sexuality, with differences for each individual, depending on the particular circumstances in their family. The parents represented the wider community's values to the child, and other social institutions—such as religion, medicine and education—also affected the infant's development. Reich claimed that Freud was not willing to draw the obvious conclusions from psychoanalysis, namely, that changes were needed in these institutions if the sexual repression was to be overcome. If this was political, then so be it, thought Reich. Other analysts criticized him for being both too political and unscientific—science being assumed to be apolitical in principle. In orthodox psychoanalysis, after the repressions of pre-genital and genital sexuality had been pointed out to the analysand, the choice was then either to sublimate these impulses or to reject them rationally. Reich thought that a third possibility was to live out the genital impulses with a partner, and that this was the healthiest outcome, for then people functioned well in work and social life as well as being physically healthier.

Freud, as early as 1908, had written in his paper 'Civilized Sexual Morality and Modern Nervousness':

> Experience shows that the majority of those who compose our society are constitutionally unfit for abstinence. Those who would have fallen ill even under moderate sexual restrictions succumb to illness all the earlier and more severely under the demands of our present civilized sexual morality; for we know no better security against the menace to normal sexual life caused by defective predisposition and disturbances in development than sexual satisfaction itself.[20]

There is little in this paper with which Reich need have disagreed. The differences between Reich and Freud are concerned not so much with the desirability of sexual activity in youth so as to avoid later sexual disturbances, and therefore the need for change in the morality of that period, as with the consequences which could be hoped for as a result. Freud, in his later theory, was less hopeful and optimistic about the results in society as a whole of such changes in sexual morality. Certainly life would be happier for many more people, for there would be less neurosis, not least among women, if such a change could occur. Freud thought, however, that it was another illusion to think that this would solve all modern societies' problems and sources of discontent. There were other problems which would remain because they were to a large extent independent of the problems caused by too restrictive a sexual morality.

It may well be the case that Freud lost some of his earlier desire to see psychoanalysis help to achieve sexual reform. Reich was, however, forty-one years younger than Freud. This factor could help to explain the difficulties in their relationship, and Reich's more reformist, indeed revolutionary, zeal towards society and sexuality. Some such explanation seems called for, given the fact that in many ways the two theories of Reich and Freud did not disagree fundamentally on the one area of the need for sexual reform. Reich, born in 1897, was thirty-two years old when the first part of *The Sexual Revolution* was published in 1929; Freud was already sixty-four years old when the notion of the death instincts first appeared in *Beyond the Pleasure Principle* in 1920. For someone in their early thirties, the sexual theme is still dominant; for someone in their sixties, death is usually a more salient concern!

Freud's theory highlights the way in which social institutions, such as the family, religion, education, law, and political institutions, repress instinctual impulses in people. This enables a community of humans to cooperate in working together to protect themselves against the worst effects of nature, and to obtain greater security than would otherwise be possible. The loss concerns pleasurable experience, which derives from the immediate release of a direct instinctual impulse. Human societies use up the instinctual energy for other purposes than those of immediate individual gratification. As human civilization grows and develops, it does not lead to an increase in human happiness, as utilitarianism would lead us to expect. Instead there seems to be an increasing amount of discontent among people, especially the more highly educated sections of society.

This latter theme is present in the other founding fathers of sociology—Marx, Weber and Durkheim—although they give different analyses of the causes of this unease and lack of real contentment in urban industrial capitalism. The early Marx's notions of alienation, the alienation of man from nature, and of man from man, has parallels in Freud's thought too. Weber's vision of increasing rationalization and bureaucratization, under both capitalist and industrial socialist régimes, also led him to think that the advance in civilization would not lead to greater happiness for everyone. The values of justice and equality would lead to the setting up of bureaucracies which would empty the world of sacred meanings. Freud thought that such a process was occurring and would continue, and that people would have to learn to live without sacred meaning and infantile religiosity. Man would come of age.

Durkheim shared this concern with the failure of modern civilization to produce the happiness promised by the philosophies which had emerged as the feudal period ended. His sociology was also concerned with the development of understanding of the conditions under which men could be happy. Durkheim's view differed from Freud's, however, in that he saw little possibility of happiness for people outside a normative societal structure.

Happiness is to be found, on this view, in achieving goals within a normative framework. Unhappiness stems from confusion about which goals and ends to pursue, and from the lack of a clear set of norms which guide, or control, the pursuit of the goals. Durkheim does not discuss the content of such goals and norms very much, the important thing for him being that there is a clear set of values to pursue. For Freud, there could be unhappiness in such highly structured societies if the values and norms did not allow the expression of instinctual energy, even though some limitation of both sexuality and destructive aggressivity is necessary in any group. Freud preferred to help an individual work out a set of goals and norms for himself, within the psychoanalytic setting, rather than propose a return to a tightly structured civilization. Such a tightly structured normative system, in middle-class Vienna at the turn of the century, had produced his first patients, and his theory was designed to understand the ways in which this normative structure had caused the unhappiness of these people. There could be no Durkheimian solution to such ills, for Freud's model of man-in-society included the idea of instinctual gratification and repression, and it is this dimension which is lacking in Durkheim's thought. There are, however, points of contact in these two writers' theories, as will be shown later.

The concern of Freud's theory was with the confusions and contradictions, the happiness and the misery, in modern society. In these concerns he was within the tradition of the founding fathers of sociology, not outside it. His theory of man-in-society puts stress on the nature of man, whereas some of the sociologists put more stress on the society's structure than on man.[21] All of them were concerned with the interaction between man, the biological organism, and his societies, Freud most of all. They were not afraid to be concerned about the misery and unhappiness of men and women in society, and to ask whether and how positive happiness could be attained. In this sense there is always a connection between value-standpoints and sociology, for it is when the focus on unhappiness, and its reduction, is lost that social scientists lose their way and become trapped in pseudo-scientific thinking.

Freud's psychoanalytic theory has been understood as being primarily about the individual, both by many of those most sympathetic to his work and by many who are hostile to it. One of the major purposes of this book is to show that there is much in psychoanalytic theory and practice which is social, and that to conceive of the theory as being only about individuals is to misunderstand and misinterpret it.

Freud came very close to seeing the individual of modern Western society as being an abstraction from group psychology. The first epic poet of a human group is the first individual.

> The myth, then, is the step by which the individual emerges from group psychology.[22]

By inventing a myth, the epic poet frees himself from the group. This strange argument has far-reaching implications for understanding Freud's theory as being a social one. The individual is a creation, not a given. The nature of this creative process is, however, obscure. Both the group and the person himself are necessary for the process; the epic poet is actively creative and not passively responding to group pressures. He breaks out of the group's culture and psychology by creating a myth.

It would be a complete misunderstanding to discuss this argument as though it were dependent on empirical facts about whether or not myths were the product of one person. Clearly myths are dependent on a language and a symbolic system which is shared, and which is therefore social. The importance of the notion of the 'epic poet' is the stress which it puts on an active, creative person who expresses his dreams in verbal form. The 'epic poet' is a construct, not an empirical description of epic poets. The concept's importance in theoretical terms is that the epic poet catches himself dreaming, and tries to communicate his dream to the rest of the group, through a mythic poem, or a ritual drama.

Dreaming has a key role in psychoanalytic theory. A dream is everybody's contact with the unconscious. Its symbolism may or may not be universal for all mankind, or for all within one culture, but enough dream material is common for others to be interested and gripped by a person who recounts his dreams. The creative process does not lie in the act of dreaming, but in the communication of a dream. This secondary elaboration of the original dream will use poetic language and ritual performance to communicate to others the original dream. The epic poet, the shaman, the artist, the priest, whatever name he is given, is the creator of the mythic and ritual symbolism of human civilization.

From the outset we can see that Freud's theory, while being sociological in its understanding of individualism as social product, has the advantage over Durkheim's sociologism in being able to account for creativity and for change in human societies. At this point Freud is closer to Max Weber's theory, where the charismatic figure plays a similar role in creating change.[23] But Weber did not elaborate the process of creativity to the same extent as Freud.

Another fundamental misunderstanding of Freud's theory, made again by both those sympathetic and those hostile to his work, has been over the part played by abnormal psychology in the theory of psychoanalysis. Freud has been understood as asserting that:

(a) the people he saw as patients were all neurotics, or psychotics, and were, that is, all 'abnormal' to some degree or other;
(b) that the people he did not see were 'normal'; and
(c) that primitive peoples, and our ancestors, were like the neurotics, the 'abnormals', he saw as patients, and unlike the 'normals'.

Anthropologists, following Evans-Pritchard's lead, have reacted against this way of seeing primitive, or non-literate, peoples, and maintained that they do not act as they do for the same reasons that neurotics act in Western society.[24] Similarly, sociologists have challenged the findings of criminologists and psychiatrists as being based on the people who are seen by psychiatrists only, not on those who are never seen in the prison, the clinic or the hospital. Freud's work has been said to be unusable for this reason—that is, that it, too, was based on a biased sample.

Freud's theory is much more complex than many analysts, therapists and critics allow. The first part of assertion (a) above Freud would have held to be the case. However, it does not follow that his patients were all more 'abnormal' than those people he did not see in the consulting room. It would only be possible to say this if assertion (b) were known to be true, and that all those who never consulted analysts and therapists were 'normal'. Freud certainly did not hold this assertion to be true. His criticisms of religion and its associated morality, with its hostility to rational thinking, make it clear that the respected majority of people in Europe and America were not seen as being 'normal' or 'healthy'. Some of Freud's patients became more rational in their understanding of their problems, and they could therefore be said to be nearer than non-patients to the standard Freud held up as worthy of human beings. Although many of his patients were, statistically speaking, 'abnormal', that is, they differed from the average person in their group, they were nearer to the 'normal' in the evaluative sense, that is, in having some rational understanding of themselves.

Like the more recent phenomenological sociologists, Freud saw that there were competing views of reality, some of which were socially maintained and continually reinforced by social processes, others of which were maintained in small groups, families or by one individual alone.[25] A neurotic in a modern Western society could be trying to maintain a view of reality which would be quite close to a version of reality held, in some culture other than his own, to be 'normal'. Equally, some people are lucky enough to find their neurotic desires and needs catered for in a major religion or political movement which is institutionalized in their society. They therefore appear as less neurotic than they might do otherwise, because they are not treated by others as 'peculiar' or deviant. They are spared the agonies of creating their own private neurosis by joining in an already existing one in their culture (for example the physician in Freud's paper 'A Religious Experience' (1928), who has a conversion experience to Christianity).[26]

The importance of empirical material from anthropological research, and from the analyst's research work in therapeutic encounters, is not the relatively superficial one of seeking to explain the actions of people who act in ways which appear as strange and peculiar to the ordinary members of modern Western societies. Certainly psychoanalytic theory helps understanding of some actions of people in pre-literate societies, or of children and neurotics in Western societies. It is here that psychoanalysis has had its most popular appeal, seeming to explain why some obsessionals continually need to wash their hands, or why some children are desperately afraid of horses or dogs, or why some people are afraid to go out of the house. This is a superficial view of psychoanalytic theory, because it fails to see that the prime objective of Freud is not merely to explain the 'odd' actions of neurotics or primitives, but to use their actions to understand and explain what counts as 'normal' and ordinary action in Western societies. For example, being prepared to kill others for the sake of one's country—fatherland or motherland —or the act of 'falling in love' are both considered to be quite 'normal' acts in modern Western society. Freud shares what can be seen as the main element in the sociological imagination, that is, to see what is regarded as commonplace action in a particular society, at particular points in time, as being itself in need of some explanation.[27] It involves an act of imagination to see one's society and culture through the eyes, as it were, of someone from a different culture, to whom the normal ways of living and acting in Western societies appear odd and to demand explanation.

NOTES AND REFERENCES

1. The standard account of Freud's life and work is that of Ernest Jones, *Sigmund Freud: Life and Works*, 3 vols., London and New York, 1953, 1955, 1957.
2. *The Freud/Jung Letters,* edited by William McGuire, London and New York, 1974.
3. C. G. Jung, *Psychology and Religion*, London and New York, 1938.
4. See, e.g., H. J. Eysenck, *Uses and Abuses of Psychology*, Part III, Harmondsworth, 1953. And E. Erikson, *Childhood and Society*, New York, 1950 (Penguin edition, 1965).
5. For the terms 'context of discovery' and 'context of validation', see R. Rudner, *Philosophy of Social Science*, Englewood Cliffs, N.J., 1966.

6. S. Freud, *Civilization and Its Discontents*, 1930, Standard Edition, Vol. 21; *Totem and Taboo*, 1912, 1913, Standard Edition, Vol. 13.
7. S. Freud, Postscript to *An Autobiographical Study*, London and New York, 1935.
8. S. Freud, *The Ego and the Id*, 1923, Standard Edition, Vol. 19. Quotations from W. W. Norton editions, New York, p. 3.
9. Ibid., p. 4.
10. Ibid., p. 14.
11. See S. Freud, *Three Essays on the Theory of Sexuality*, 1905, Standard Edition, Vol. 7.
12. e.g., *The Ego and the Id*.
13. S. Freud, 'The Unconscious', 1915, in Standard Edition, Vol. 14. Also available in paperback in Phillip Rieff (ed.), *General Psychological Theory*, Vol. VI, Collier Books, New York, p. 134.
14. Ibid., p. 140.
15. This term was used by Wilhelm Reich in *The Sexual Revolution*, (1929), London, 1951 and 1972, p. 18.
16. See J. S. Brown, 'A Comparative Study of Deviations from Sexual Mores', *American Sociological Review*, 17:138, 1952. Table reproduced by A. K. Cohen, *Deviance and Control*, Englewood Cliffs, N.J. 1966, p. 13.
17. Reich, *The Sexual Revolution*, p. 6.
18. Ibid., pp. 10 and 81.
19. One of the titles in the Fontana Modern Masters series is Charles Rycroft, *Reich*, London, 1971. This is not very adequate on the sociological elements in Reich's thought, as Rycroft does not understand Reich's serious attempt to link Marxism and psychoanalysis into one framework. See also P. Robinson, *The Sexual Radicals*, London, 1969. (Called *The Freudian Left* in its U.S. edition.)
20. Available in S. Freud, *Sexuality and the Psychology of Love*, edited by Phillip Rieff, New York, 1963, p. 31.
21. The notion of a theory of 'man-in-society' seems necessary here, the hyphens in the phrase being intended to stress the need for such links between a theory of man's nature to be linked to a theory of society, and vice versa.
22. S. Freud, *Group Psychology and the Analysis of the Ego*, London and New York, 1921. Reference to Hogarth Press edition, London, 1959, p. 68.
23. See, e.g., Max Weber, *The Sociology of Religion* (1922), London, 1965, Chapters IV and VIII.
24. E. E. Evans-Pritchard, *Theories of Primitive Religion*, London, 1965, Chapter II.
25. e.g., P. L. Berger and T. Luckmann, *The Social Construction of Reality*, New York, 1966 (Penguin University Books edition, 1971).
26. Available in S. Freud, *Character in Culture*, edited by Phillip Reiff, New York, 1963, Chapter XXIII.
27. C. Wright Mills, *The Sociological Imagination*, New York, 1959.

2 Sociology and Psychological Perspectives

'For sociology too, dealing as it does with the behaviour of people in society, cannot be anything but applied psychology. Strictly speaking there are only two sciences: psychology, pure and applied, and natural science.'—Sigmund Freud, *New Introductory Lectures on Psychoanalysis* (1933), Lecture 35.

In the early days of sociology, that is, in the late nineteenth and early twentieth century, there was much less professional specialization of the two disciplines of sociology and psychology. Many of the early writers in the nineteenth century were not concerned with separating the two disciplines, and marking out the one from the other, but with showing their similarities. The idea of psychology devoted to the study of the individual studied in isolation from social groups, and from society in general, was rejected by all the early sociologists, including Marx, Weber, Durkheim, Spencer, Hobhouse, Cooley and Mead.[1] The stress was on the individual as part of a larger social whole.

Furthermore, they were all writing in the aftermath of Darwin, and had learned from him two important things. The first was the importance of man's biological base, that is, that man belongs to a species which has to survive in a material environment, and that he has certain innate drives or instincts which affect his behaviour, although they do not determine it. Sexuality, in the sense of reproductive sex, was seen as a major instinctual factor by writers before Freud. Freud's notion of sexuality was more inclusive than just sexual reproduction, but he was not unique in pointing out that sexuality was an important biological instinct.

Secondly, many of the writers who established sociology took the notion of evolution from Darwinian biology, and tried to see the part played by man's societies and cultures in the light of this. It was emphasized by Comte, Marx and Spencer, for example, that culture and society were major adaptive means for *Homo sapiens* in aiding its survival as a species. It was also noticed that human societies changed, became more complex, and that their institutions increasingly differentiated from one another. In this way there was in human history a cumulative build up of knowledge and success in adaptation to the environment which made human beings very quick to adapt to new problems—much more easily and quickly than if they had depended only on genetic transmission.

Freud shared this evolutionary perspective with these early writers in sociology, and he too attempted to build on biological knowledge about man. There is nothing which cuts him off from the early sociologists in his basic assumptions about the importance of instincts and their interaction with men's cultures.[2] Nor is there a focus upon the individual, for even in the analytic situation the focus is upon the therapeutic relationship and its similarities to those which the patient had previously with one, or both, parents. Finally, Freud shared with early sociologists an interest in the overall development of human societies, from the most primitive group to modern societies and their possible future.

Given these assertions, it is easy to see that one reason for the neglect of Freud by sociologists, especially in Britain and to a lesser extent in the United States, is as much due to the fact that intellectual fashions have changed as to anything intrinsic to Freud's theory. Particularly since the end of the Second World War, sociology has sought to become established as a major discipline in universities, and to achieve this it has tried to emphasize its distinctiveness vis-à-vis psychology. Equally, psychology has been seeking acceptance as a 'real' science, and has not therefore wanted to emphasize the social side of human action, but rather the physiological, behavioural and physically measurable aspects of human behaviour. Social psychology has been left in the doldrums, having an uneasy relationship with psychology orientated to natural science and an equally uneasy relationship with sociology. This has been because social psychology has had few ways of handling the macro-level political, economic and social change which has been of such great interest to sociologists.

A few writers have seen the links which are possible between sociology and Freud's theory, and have therefore managed a bridge between social psychology and sociology. The members of the Frankfurt School, such as Adorno, Horkheimer, Fromm, Marcuse, have attempted this.[3] Wilhelm Reich also made an attempt to relate Freud and Marx. Talcott Parsons tried to link his sociology systematically with aspects of Freud's theory of the development of personality.[4] In spite of all this effort on the part of some sociologists and social philosophers, Freud has remained peripheral to mainstream sociology.

No doubt one reason for this neglect has been the desire on the part of sociologists to have their discipline accepted in universities as a science, and since many psychologists rejected Freud as being unscientific, this judgement came to be accepted by many sociologists. The arguments against Freud which have weighed most heavily with psychologists are those concerned with his theory's unscientific character. Freud's psychology belongs to the kind which seeks to understand human behaviour rather than to explain it on a scientific basis; that is, it is *verstehende* psychology rather than *erklärende* psychology. The problem is that Freud claims that his findings are as firmly established as the findings of the latter type of psychology, even though he only used the methods of *verstehende* psychology. His theories are based on clinical observations, and not on carefully controlled experimentation or systematic statistical comparison of groups and control groups. Clinical observation is extremely productive of theories and hypotheses, but not of verification of hypotheses.[5]

Therapeutic practice cannot, so it is argued, itself be used to verify the claims of psychoanalytic theories, as is often claimed by analysts. This is because the research which has been done has shown that nearly two out of three neurotic patients recover over time, without any therapy at all.[6] If this is the case, then comparable recovery rates among analytic therapies are hardly remarkable, and may not be caused by the therapeutic technique used with the patients. Furthermore, the conclusions reached through therapeutic work with some patients cannot be generalized to all mankind, or to human beings in very different cultural and social circumstances from those on whom the therapy was carried out.[7]

These criticisms of psychoanalysis, made by scientific psychologists, have some bite to them. It is for this reason that sociologists have often assumed that they must respect the professional psychologists' judgement in these matters, and so have treated Freud from their viewpoint as unscientific and unusable. It has been noticed by others that the type of arguments which count against the Freudian type of *verstehende* psychology would also count against much sociology. Sociologists have either to accept a thoroughly verificationist approach to both Freud and to many of the founders of sociology, or to be inconsistent and accept a judgement made by psychologists about Freud which is based on logical and philosophical assumptions which, if applied to Max Weber or Émile

Durkheim or Marx, would lead to these thinkers being likewise dismissed as unscientific. Sociologists cannot have it both ways: either Freud has to be examined alongside the founders of sociology, or they all have to be dismissed as unscientific thinkers. This latter conclusion would be held by many psychologists and by a few sociologists, and it is a consistent one, given positivist premises.

Most sociologists would wish to maintain that, while their social science does not meet the rigorous criteria of a natural science, in terms of the procedures used for verification of theoretical hypotheses there is some disciplined thinking and testing of ideas going on in sociology which does distinguish it from religious or mystical thinking. Strict logical positivists only have two categories for the logical status of propositions: a proposition is either verifiable or falsifiable, using empirically observable and measurable, variables; or it is a mystical, poetic, emotional insight. There are no other types of proposition except pure mathematics and logic. On such a philosophical basis there is no room for a 'scientific' sociology, as distinct from a revealed social theology, unless it is one based on strict scientific verification.[8] Most sociology is not of this latter type. Nor is it quite like a Papal Encyclical, or a biblical prophecy, for sociology has no basic authority of revealed truth to which it can appeal. Whenever Marx or Freud or any other thinker is used in such a way as an authority of revealed truth, then the community of sociologists opens up discussion on the basic aspects of the theory. It becomes open to rational criticism, and to historical and other empirical checks, in ways which do not happen within the closed system of a community of fellow-believers.

There is a danger of closed-belief systems emerging in the social sciences, but this can apply to the way in which a thinker is excluded from debates about human society as well as to the strict adherence to one thinker, or type of thinker, alone, as a safe source of authority. Freud has sometimes been excluded in this way from sociology, but, as has been shown above, the sociologist cannot simply accept a conclusion from psychology and dismiss Freud for this reason. The reasons that make Weber or Durkheim or Marx discussable within sociology also apply to Freud's work, or a large part of it. It will be shown in Chapter 7 that there are many similarities of concern between Freud and these other major sociologists, and that Freud still has something original to offer sociology.

Psychoanalysis as Part of Social Science

Is Freud's thought, especially in the works most concerned with society, at all scientific? Or has it more in common with the intuitions of art? Freud himself thought that some of this work was nearer to myth than to natural science.[9] Nevertheless there is a problem about the status of many of his theories and propositions if, and when, they claim to be more than speculation.

The nature of this problem is not to do with whether or not they are meaningful, for there is always *some* meaning in aesthetic intuition and metaphysical speculation. It is rather how to demarcate reasonable science from irrational ideologies, such as astrology and racist nationalisms.[10] Astrology is based on many empirical observations about the positions of stars and planets, and about certain vague characteristics of people born at particular times and places. There might even be some positive correlations between these two sets of variables. Astrology, however, does not operate like rational science, for it seeks to confirm its theories, and nothing ever seems to count against them. They are irrefutable, and therefore they lack real explanatory power, for nothing is at stake when they are tested by seeking confirming evidence. People adhere to astrology with a dogmatic frame of mind rather than having a sceptical, critical approach. Does it matter? It does for two sets of reasons. First, error is possible, and someone who based their life on astrology and refused to replace their beliefs with scientific knowledge would probably end up making a number of mistakes. For example, someone setting out on a journey to a malarial zone would be best advised to rely on drugs rather than trusting the stars' message alone as a protection against the disease. Secondly, political and economic affairs are not best conducted on the basis of politicians consulting the stars before making economic or military decisions. Astrology cannot be allowed as a serious contribution to living because it fails empirically in relation to the natural world, and could be foolish, or dangerous, in political and economic affairs.

Is psychoanalysis comparable with astrology in its dogmatic rather than critical attitude, and hence unfalsifiable? It is certainly different in Freud's mind. He was constantly pointing out that theories could be, and had been, revised, changed and discarded as a result of empirical observations. The reason that some have thought that psychoanalysis operates as a closed belief system is, no doubt, a result of the fact that Freud made the point that people usually reject psychoanalytic ideas at first, and the vehemence of their rejection may mask deep repression of material.[11] This appears to be a circular argument, typical of closed-belief systems. But there can be criticism of psychoanalytic theories on a rational basis. The problem is to distinguish this type of rejection of psychoanalytic propositions —the result of the feelings aroused in people by uncomfortable material—from what might be called genuine objections of a kind which are reasoned and scientific.

A more serious objection to Freudian theory is its supposed irrefutability. Just as adherents of astrology, when predicted events fail to appear, find reasons from within the scheme of astrology for the failure, so some apologists for psychoanalysis find reasons why their hypotheses and predictions do not stand the test. Both mistakenly think that it is a virtue for the theory to explain everything. What really matters is an attempt to limit a hypothesis, derived from a theory, and to see how far it can withstand rigorous testing. This is the way science advances. Dogmas, however, survive through being believed in, no matter what happens. Everything is interpreted within the scheme; it does not explain anything, because it can explain everything.

Substantial parts of Freud have stood up to further research —for example, the general presence of infantile sexuality. His work on dreams and symbolism has proved valuable in clinical work. Other components have been found to be false, or unhelpful. For instance, to many researchers there does not seem to be a universal cause of depression: some depressions are due to lost love-objects; some seem to be more constitutionally based.

Some disturbances, especially the neuroses, may in certain people best be cured through a prolonged psychoanalysis. Freud delimited these more than some analysts have done since. The problem occurs with some of his followers, who turn the technique from one of limited use with some people into a total dogmatic world view, ignoring Freud's own strictures against such tendencies.[12] Freud claimed to be committed to science, and he thought a physiologically based psychology was possible, even desirable.

Freud's commitment to science, for all its over-simplification, is a serious one.

> It is simply a fact that truth cannot be tolerant, that it
> admits of no compromises or limitations . . .[13]

Science is not then, in Freud's view, simply tolerant towards
religion, nor towards the untrue aspects of relativism and
Bolshevism. It is in this way a world view, of which psychoanalysis forms an important part.

> Psychoanalysis, in my opinion, is incapable of creating a
> *Weltanschauung* of its own. It does not need one; it is a part of
> science and can adhere to the scientific *Weltanschauung*. This,
> however, scarcely deserves such a grandiloquent title, for it
> is not all-comprehensive, it is too incomplete and makes no
> claims to being self-contained and to the construction of
> systems.[14]

Science, for Freud, involves an open-mindedness, and a
preparedness to discard ideas and theories if they are found
wanting in the light of later research work. He altered his own
theories a number of times; on the nature of anxiety, for
example.[15] He was aware of the speculative nature of much of
his work, and of the need in people to foreclose his work into a
closed system. He might well have written 'Thank God I am
not a Freudian', even though he had a great concern with
preserving psychoanalysis as a coherent method and theoretical
approach to human action.

Science, however, was not for Freud mere empiricism, that
is, a matter of gathering facts. His speculations show his understanding of the need for bold hypotheses and theories. This is a
position which Popper has called *theoreticism* as distinct from
operationalism, with its concern for measuring operationalized
concepts, and distinct from *instrumentalism*, the concern with
using science for predicting impending events. There is a need,
in any science, for theory which offers explanations of an area
of activity bounded in terms of the concepts of the theory itself.
It is easy to explain small and tightly defined areas of activity;
the problems lie in trying to connect the smaller areas together
into wider groups of phenomena, and to explain these within
one theory. The wider the areas covered by the theory, the less
certain is the theory's explanation likely to be and the more
tentatively will it be held by the scientific community.[16]

Theory begins with the critical discussion of myths. Popper
has written:

> A critical attitude needs for its raw material, as it were,
> theories or beliefs which are held more or less dogmatically.

Thus, science must begin with myths, and with the criticism of myths; neither with the collection of observations, nor with the invention of experiments, but with the critical discussion of myths, and of magical techniques and practices.[17]

Although at times Freud seems to hold an empiricist view of science—one based on collecting observations and then finding theories to explain them—he did also use the insights of myths, as with Oedipus. At times he also invents myths himself.[18] Freud even called his instinct theory a mythology:

Instincts are mythical entities, magnificent in their indefiniteness. In our work we cannot for a moment disregard them, yet we are never sure that we are seeing them clearly.[19]

He was very conscious of the speculative status of his death instincts theory in *Beyond the Pleasure Principle*. Some have been worried about the unscientific standing of this later work, but the worries are based on a mistaken view of the way in which science develops, and ignore its need for bold speculations. Towards the end of his life Freud was worried lest 'psychoanalysis as a therapeutic procedure swallow up psychoanalysis as a science'.[20] Freud himself tended to understand his work as part of natural science, that is, as a science governed by the same principles as science of matter, of physical energy. For example, his work on the death instincts in *Beyond the Pleasure Principle* is based on the assumption that he needs to show that all organisms, including mankind, aim to return to a tensionless state of inorganic matter. This proposition is seen by Freud as one which is potentially refutable by further biological research, and which could be completely mistaken.[21] Could biological research really refute the insights Freud formulated about mankind? Surely not, for biological propositions are not about emotion, or the subjective experience of mankind. Indeed, Freud is being reductionist in this account, and is reducing psychological states to their biological sub-stratum in an unnecessary way.[22] The reductionism is produced by his anxiety to be treated as a serious scientist, but he is mistaken in thinking that only biologically observable or biochemically measurable concepts and propositions count as science in the study of human action.

There are still those who argue that only physically measurable concepts count as science in the scientific study of human beings, as in all other scientific studies. Other types of social science are seen, on this view, as being poetic or philosophical visions, but not as science. Such a view is inadequate in that there has come into existence, in the twentieth century, a body of literature in social science which is not poetry, nor is it a traditional style of philosophy. These social sciences of human *action* are a category distinct from sciences of animal and human behaviour. Behaviour is observed and measured from the outside, and propositions about behavioural patterns are readily testable and controllable. Studies of action are concerned with the subjective meaning attached to actions by human beings. This makes the study of human beings different from that of animals and of inanimate objects. The social scientist gains an understanding of the meaning of action through living with the group which he wants to understand. Anthropologists, for example, are able to interpret a culture, at first sight inexplicable to those from a different culture, by living with, talking to and observing people in a community over a period of years.

Sociologists and social anthropologists now have a clearer understanding of the nature of their propositions, seeing them as attempts to provide interpretative accounts of one social group's ways of living to another group, which has a different set of values and assumptions.[23] The groups vary in size, of course, from large cultural areas such as white, middle-class Christian culture, or Indian Hindu culture, to smaller groups such as a tribe, or a gang, or a sub-culture within a larger social arrangement, through to an individual in a family or other small group. This latter type of work, it is claimed here, is not logically as different from the work of sociologists and anthropologists as it is from that of scientists working with animals, plants or inanimate objects. It is like the work carried out by psychoanalysts. Psychiatrists tend to treat their cases more as organisms in need of medical treatment. There is no need to hold that all human beings should always and only be approached using the interpretive action scheme, any more than the reverse claim makes sense if adhered to in all circumstances. The important thing is to be clear about the distinction between the different types of research work involved. Human beings have to be understood, using both types of approach. The overlap area is difficult, and it is therefore better to insist on the rigorous separation of the two methodological approaches than to mix them up in a compromise, or to treat one as logically more worthy of respect than the other. Freud, who was seeking to understand individuals, groups and even a whole culture, confused the two types of methodology. In treating the behavioural approach—the more natural scientific approach— as logically superior, he introduced confusions into his understanding of psychoanalysis.[24]

There is in Freud an explicit commitment to science as a method of gaining knowledge, this being understood to include speculative thought which is then checked against systematic observations of human action and behaviour. There is, however, no final system, no finalized body of 'findings' which never changes, no complete, unchanging set of theoretical propositions which are unrevisable. Sometimes Freud may have appeared not to adhere to this view of science in practice, especially in the way the psychoanalytic movement operated, in some periods, as though it were a new form of sectarian movement. Yet the more open-ended view of science was in principle present in Freud's outlook. It is, indeed, part of what he meant when he claimed to adhere to science as a *Weltanschuung*, as distinct from a religious creed. The greatest difference between this understanding of science and a religion lies in the openness of science to constant revision, by contrast with the unchanging dogmas and sacred authority of religions.

Freud's view of science is not that of a simple empiricist, who assumes that, once something has been discovered in science, it remains true for all times, and that one day science will have discovered nearly all we need to know about the world and ourselves. This assumption leads to the view that science simply replaces religious propositions with a different set of its own which always remain true. For Freud, this would have been to replace one set of dogmatic assertions with another set, held by the believers to be for ever true, and providing a sense of false security for them.[25]

He was aware of the strong emotional needs people had for certainty and for a surrogate parental-authority figure, and he was always wary of the tendency among some to turn psychoanalysis into a religious system, and perhaps himself into a sacred authority. However, when he felt psychoanalysis to be threatened by others, such as Jung and Tausk, he surrounded himself with less questioning people than these. Such action was a betrayal of the intellectual position he held. But this should not, indeed logically cannot, be used in arguments about the system of thought called psychoanalysis. It is only confusing to shift from the intellectual argument to how Freud and others acted. The psychoanalytic movement, partly under Freud's own direction, did develop the characteristics of a sectarian organization rather than those of an open scientific community, but this does not invalidate the arguments for psychoanalysis as potentially a key component of the human sciences. It may be that unless there had been this early sectarian stance by Freud, the body of theory and practice would have become hopelessly confused, so that, from a practical standpoint, Freud's judgement and action was correct.[26]

Psychoanalytic Therapy as Communication

The distinction between natural science and the sciences concerned with human action must be developed further in a way which Freud himself failed to do. Freud held a natural scientific position vis-à-vis psychology, and thought of his own theory in psychoanalysis as capable of being stated in terms of a mechanistic model of energy-flows which could be measured quantitatively. In so far as Freud thought he had done psychology as a natural science, he has been vulnerable to critics within psychology who have applied natural scientific criteria to his work and found it wanting. The activity of psychoanalysis in the therapeutic setting cannot be adequately grasped and stated in mechanistic, quantitative terms. In the statement Freud made about this activity, he sometimes avoided the errors of his own account of the scientific nature of psychoanalysis.

The nature of psychoanalysis as a communicative encounter has been developed and refined by Jurgen Habermas. The therapeutic encounter is one in which two people *communicate* with one another, using a language. The metatheory needed to explicate this activity cannot be one which derives from natural scientific work on a material, object world, in which there is no possibility of linguistic communication with the objects of investigation. Modern philosophy has reached a more satisfactory understanding of the importance of language, language games and grammar, in the sense of the informal logic of language games, than was available to Freud. Psychoanalysis as a therapeutic practice consists of two people trying to construct a life history of the unique development, from birth onwards, of one of the participants, the analysand. The psychoanalyst uses a more general framework of knowledge derived from other analyses, and applies the more general concepts to the individual case so as to make sense of the development of the person. Psychoanalysis is a matter of combating the emotional resistances of the analysand to uncovering repressed material from childhood, and not of simply providing the analysand with more cognitive information, or a new conceptual scheme. As Habermas has written:

> The analyst instructs the patient in reading his own texts, which he himself has mutilated and distorted, and in translating symbols from a mode of expression deformed as a private language into the mode of expression of public communication. This translation reveals the genetically important phases of life history to a memory that was previously blocked, and brings to consciousness the person's own self-formative process.[27]

The act of understanding, to which psychoanalysis leads, is *self-reflection*. This cannot be done by the person alone, because help is needed in overcoming the amnesias and the emotional repressions, and this cannot be achieved by introspection. The transference which develops between the analyst and analysand aids the process by re-creating the early relationships between the individual and their parents, and enables the analyst first of all to see the projections of the analysand in this special setting. The distorted modes of communication which the individual has set up within himself, and between self and the outside world, as a result of fearing to express in public form certain wishes and impulses of an infantile polymorphously perverse character, can be unravelled with the analyst's help.

Habermas's account of the nature of psychoanalysis as a therapeutic encounter, by drawing on communication theory and modern philosophy, as it does, is superior to that of Freud. It rescues psychoanalysis from the confusions it had been led into by seeing itself as a natural science, like physics or chemistry. It also rescues it from the criticisms of positivist psychologists and behaviourists. The more sociological aspects of psychoanalytic theory appear now to be based on firmer foundations, for the theory of the development of the person can be seen to be grounded in the therapeutic encounters of psychoanalysis.

The social institutions of traditionalism, such as religion and ideology, can also be seen as deformed, pathological modes of communication.

> In tradition, the projective contents of wish fantasies expressing defended-against intentions, have been deposited.

They are sublimations representing suspended gratifications, and give 'publicly sanctioned compensation for necessary cultural renunciation'.[28] These institutions are produced for the same purpose as neuroses are by the individual; they are collective solutions for the problem of defence against unsatisfied wishes. Freud had written:

> Knowledge of the neurotic afflictions of individuals has well served the understanding of the major social institutions, for the neuroses ultimately reveal themselves as attempts to solve, on an individual basis, the problems of wish compensation that ought to be solved socially by institutions.[29]

The outstanding achievement of Habermas has been to demonstrate the way in which psychoanalysis has an importance as the science of self-reflection, based, as it is, on the unravelling of distorted forms of communication. It has an additional significance in that it links science and ethics; it unites theory and practice. The therapy produces the theory; the theory is used as part of the communication processes which relieves suffering. The neurotic's suffering is an important component in analysis in that it provides motivational energy to the patient to work at his or her analysis. A premature 'cure' can be potentially problematic for the later development of the analysis, and some degree of suffering is necessary during most of the analysis.[30] The relief of the suffering which does occur in the longer run is the more stable and fundamental as a result of the premature cure being avoided. The patient's interest in being happier links in with the knowledge that he needs to be cured; '. . . the analytic resolution of distorted communication that determines behavioural compulsion and false consciousness is at once both theory and therapy'.[31]

Sociology will need to make use of psychoanalytic theory to the extent that it seeks to be not only accumulating knowledge and developing theory for its own sake, but also acknowledges that by doing this it is changing society's own self-understanding. It is in the area of analysis of ideologies and religions especially that psychoanalysis has a role to play. The distortions of communication which occur in these social institutions are as they are, as a result, in part, of unconscious activity of groups of people over time.

Sociology and Psychoanalysis

The attempt to make sociology as much like a natural science as possible reached its height in the United States in the 1950s and 1960s. During this phase of sociological thought there was a basic rubric, derived from a particular understanding of Durkheim's sociology, that psychological types of explanation were to be strictly avoided. Sociology was to study social systems, psychology studied personality systems, and anthropology was to concentrate on cultural systems. This was the scheme outlined by Talcott Parsons and Edward Shils in *Towards a General Theory of Action* (1951). Although Parsons attempted to integrate Freudian theory of personality development into his schemes, he did so by underestimating the importance of conflict within the individual and between the individual and his culture and society. In an important paper, 'The Over-socialized Conception of Man in Modern Sociology' (1961), Denis Wrong pointed this out in his discussion of Parsons. The latter had developed the view that 'social norms are constitutive rather than merely regulative of human nature before he was influenced by psychoanalytic theory'.[32] Parsons did not substantially alter this view, and as a result lost the stress Freud had placed on conflict.

Denis Wrong also points out that other sociologists, such as Homans and Inkeles, realized that sociology could not manage without a theory of human nature, implicit if not explicit, in its theories. The view of human nature implicit in the sociology of the 1950s and early 1960s was one based on the assumption that man was a role-player constantly seeking social approval and status, and that people therefore conformed to normative expectations to gain approval from peers, superiors or inferiors. This was a step backwards, according to Wrong, for Freud's theory of human nature was more complex and satisfactory than this one. Freud did not hold that instincts directly caused behaviour, uninfluenced by the surrounding cultural values.

> To Freud man is a *social* animal without being entirely a
> *socialized* animal. His very social nature is the source of
> conflicts and antagonisms that create resistance to
> socialization by the norms of the societies which have existed
> in the course of human history.[33]

This point had become confused and lost in the over-socialized conception of man which had developed in modern sociology.

Turning now to the influence of phenomenology, this has affected sociology in ways which are not initially seen as compatible with Freudian theory. The social psychology of

G. H. Mead has been used by Peter Berger and Thomas Luckmann in their *Social Construction of Reality* (1967). Berger sees a discontinuity between the social psychology of Cooley and Mead and that of Freud. Elsewhere he uses sociology to understand the role of psychoanalysis in American society rather than building psychoanalysis into the theory of sociology.[34] This exercise is valuable in helping to show how a distorted version of Freud's ideas has been widely diffused within many institutional spheres of American life, from social work agencies to industrial management training, religious institutions, and to the private sphere of marriage and family life.

There is an 'elective affinity' between the social structure of American society and 'psychologism'—that is, the popularized version of psychoanalytic theory which Berger thinks predominates as a general socio-cultural configuration. The main elements of this configuration are: that there is an unconscious which affects actions in ways the conscious self cannot understand without interpretative aids; that sexuality is a key area of human conduct, and childhood a key phase of human biography; that culture can be understood as a scene of interaction between unconscious motor forces and consciously established norms.[35]

Berger goes on to suggest ways in which this 'psychologism' fits the experience of people in modern society and affects their self-understanding. In this way, such a configuration becomes a self-fulfilling prophecy, because people come to form their self-understanding on the basis of 'psychologism' and the theory seems to be confirmed in people's experience as a result of this process. The elements in modern society which have an elective affinity with 'psychologism' are industrialism and bureaucracy, which have created a gulf between, on the one hand, the world of work and public affairs, and on the other the private sphere of the family and sexual relationships. For most people, identity derives from the private sphere, not from work and public affairs. The family, however, is not sufficiently able to sustain the private identities of people in modern cities or suburbs, and other institutional agencies are needed to support, create, sustain and modify identity. Identity crises are often most acute when family and marriage identity collapses. Psychologism, through its influence in marriage guidance and churches, and also through its effects in the world of work—in personnel management, for example—is able to link the two spheres in a way religion used to be able to do but cannot do any longer.

Identity maintenance needs additional institutional support, especially when the family fails.

The ideology of psychologism also fits in with the need for motivating people for productive work, and at the same time makes possible and legitimates a fascination with mystery and magic.

> Psychologism thus brings about a strange reversal of the disenchantment and demythologization of modern consciousness.[36]

The true self is to be found in the depths of the individual psyche, and there is an aura of the numinous about this process of depth analysis when conducted in the psychotherapeutic situation.

In this analysis Berger deliberately leaves out any consideration of the truth of the theory of psychoanalysis, arguing that a sociological approach brackets off judgements of the practical or scientific usefulness of psychotherapy. This methodological assumption stems from his basic phenomenological approach to sociology, and has some advantages for the sociology of knowledge and beliefs. One of these advantages is that the analysis can highlight the ways in which a theory, or ideology, is distorted by the process of its adaptation to a society and its problems. This gain is only possible, however, if the sociologist operates with the assumption that not all theories are equal with regard to their truth or falsity. Yet Berger writes that:

> Ideas do not succeed in history by virtue of their truth but by virtue of their relationship to specific social processes.[37]

This is to make a useful methodological standpoint within sociology into a dogmatic philosophy of history, and it leads to intellectual confusion, ethical relativism and nihilism by allowing no role to rational scientific work.[38] The error in the phenomenological approach of Berger is that it does not allow him to see that one of the social processes which affects the success of some theories, in terms of their historical effects, is precisely the process of rational discussion and truth-testing which occurs in science. Numerous attempts have been made to stifle theories which some power-holders have found to be unpalatable but which have, over time, become more generally acceptable. The case of Galileo is perhaps the ideal-typical example. Berger's irrationalist pessimism about the fate of ideas in history is neither fully justified by history nor required by logic. In the last analysis, it is illogical because it is self-contradictory. There can be no understanding of what a distorted system of ideas would be like unless there is the possibility of a non-distorted system. Berger's methodology only works because there is the implicit assumption of a non-distorted theory as a possibility with which distorted forms can be compared.

In the case of psychoanalytic theory, there needs to be an understanding, first, of an undistorted version of the theory as stated by Freud, and then various changes in the theory can be seen as either having been made to attain greater rational consistency, or to incorporate new 'findings' which refute some of the previous assumptions, or to have been made as a result of social pressures on theory-makers eager to find a role for their theories in the society. Berger gives a good analysis of this latter process, even though he does not understand it in this way. Other writers have done similar analyses, for example, Maurice North's *The Secular Priests*, Paul Halmos's *The Faith of the Counsellors* and Phillip Rieff's *The Triumph of the Therapeutic*.[39] A reasoned discussion of the theory of psychoanalysis and its possible relevance to sociological theory is a major omission in sociological literature. The only exceptions are Talcott Parsons, and, in a philosophical more than in a sociological vein, Herbert Marcuse, and Phillip Rieff.[40]

There is no mention in Berger's account of the elements of psychoanalytic theory, as developed by Freud, which are not included in the ideology of 'psychologism', presumably because they have no elective affinity with the social structure of modern society. The notion of the 'death instincts' and human destructiveness is missing in Berger's account of psychologism. Erich Fromm has, however, pointed out the ways in which this theory has some fit with modern American assumptions that war is basic to mankind, and that if there is another war, it will not be as a result of American or Russian policies, but a further manifestation of unchangeable biological drives of destructiveness.[41] This is an important point to make, and it can again aid in understanding a distortion which has occurred in the notion of 'death instincts' in psychoanalytic theory. It does not count as an argument in a rational or scientific discussion about Freudian theory, however, any more than Berger's analysis of other sections of the theory does. The main aim of the present book is to discuss the theory of psychoanalysis as such; not to sociologize about it, but to see if it has a contribution to make to sociology itself.

NOTES AND REFERENCES

1. See R. Fletcher, *The Making of Sociology*, 2 vols., London, 1971.
2. See J. Goody, 'Evolution and Communication: the Domestication of the Savage Mind', in *British Journal of Sociology*, Vol. XXIV, 1973, pp. 1–12. This paper does not mention Freud, but does establish the importance of evolutionary concerns in early sociology.
3. See M. Jay, *The Dialectical Imagination*, London, 1973.
4. T. Parsons, *Social Structure and Personality*, New York, 1964.
5. A good summary of these arguments is to be found in H. J. Eysenck, *Uses and Abuses of Psychology*, Harmondsworth, 1953.
6. Ibid., Chapter 10. See also H. Miller, 'Psychoanalysis: A Clinical Perspective', in J. Miller (ed.), *Freud, the Man, His World, His Influence*, London, 1972.
7. See, e.g., J. Goody, 'A Comparative Approach to Incest and Adultery', in *British Journal of Sociology*, Vol. 7, 1956, pp. 286–305. Reprinted in J. Goody, *Comparative Studies in Kinship*, London, 1969, pp. 13–38.
8. See A. J. Ayer, *Language, Truth and Logic*, London, 1936 and 1946, for an outline of the verificationist position of logical positivism. See also, K. Popper, *Logic of Scientific Discovery*, London, 1957.
9. See S. Freud, *Beyond the Pleasure Principle* (1920), Standard Edition, Vol. 18. References to Bantam Books edition, New York, 1959, pp. 47, 100, 103.
10. The discussion here draws on K. Popper, *Conjectures and Refutations*, London, 1963, pp. 40–41.
11. S. Freud, 'The Resistances to Psychoanalysis' (1925), available in P. Rieff (ed.), *Character and Culture*, New York, 1963, p. 261.
12. S. Freud, *New Introductory Lectures on Psychoanalysis*, 1933, Standard Edition, Vol. 22, Lecture 35. References to Penguin edition, Harmondsworth, 1973.
13. Ibid., p. 195.
14. Ibid., p. 219.
15. Ibid., Lecture 32, p. 117.
16. Popper, *Conjectures and Refutations*, pp. 62–3.
17. Ibid., p. 50.
18. This is discussed fully in Chapter 3 of this book.
19. Freud, *New Introductory Lectures on Psychoanalysis*, Lecture 32, edition cit., p. 127.
20. P. Roazen, *Freud, Political and Social Thought*, London, 1969, p. 282.
21. Freud, *Beyond the Pleasure Principle*.
22. See R. Fletcher, *Instinct in Man*, London, 1958, pp. 239–53.
23. See, e.g., A. MacIntyre, *The Unconscious*, London, 1958. D. Emmet and A. MacIntyre (eds.), *Sociological Theory and Philosophical Analysis*, London, 1970. A Giddens (ed.), *Positivism and Sociology*, London, 1974.
24. See A. MacIntyre, *The Unconscious*, London, 1958, and P. Rieff, *Freud, the Mind of the Moralist*, New York, 1959; London, 1960.
25. See S. Freud, *Leonardo da Vinci and a Memory of his Childhood* (1910), New York, 1916; London, 1922. Reference to W. W. Norton edition, New York, 1965, pp. 72–3.
26. See P. Roazen, *Brother Animal, the Story of Freud and Tausk*, New York, 1969. (Penguin edition, Harmondsworth, 1973.)

27. J. Habermas, *Knowledge and Human Interests* (1968), London, 1972, p. 228.
28. Ibid., p. 276.
29. S. Freud, 'The Claims of Psychoanalysis to Scientific Interest'.
30. S. Freud, 'Lines of Advance in Psychoanalytic Therapy' (1919). Available as 'Turning in the Ways of Psychoanalytic Therapy', in P. Rieff (ed.), *Therapy and Theory*, New York, 1963, Paper XIV, p. 185.
31. Habermas, *Knowledge and Human Interests*, p. 287.
32. Available in N. J. Smelser and W. T. Smelser, *Personality and Social Systems*, New York and London, 1963, pp. 68–79 (quotation, p. 72). (This paper originally appeared in *American Sociological Review*, Vol. 26, 1961, pp. 183–93.)
33. Ibid., pp. 78–9.
34. P. Berger, 'Towards a Sociological Understanding of Psychoanalysis', in *Social Research*, Vol. 32, 1965, pp. 26–41.
35. Ibid., p. 35.
36. Ibid., p. 41.
37. Ibid., p. 32.
38. See H. Marcuse, 'On Science and Phenomenology', in A. Giddens (ed.), *Positivism and Sociology*, London, 1974, Chapter 10.
39. P. Rieff, *The Triumph of the Therapeutic—the Uses of Faith after Freud*, London, 1966. P. Halmos, *The Faith of the Counsellors*, London, 1965. P. Halmos, *The Personal Service Society*, Cardiff, 1966. M. North, *The Secular Priests, Psychotherapists in Contemporary Society*, London, 1972. See also C. Lévi-Strauss, *Structural Anthropology*, New York, 1963, Chapters IX and X, for a comparison of shamanism and psycho-analysis. The comparison is done on the basis of Lévi-Strauss's assumptions about the priority of the intellect over affectivity. (See Chapter 4 of the present book for critique of this position.)
40. T. Parsons, *Social Structure and Personality*, New York, 1964. H. Marcuse, *Eros and Civilization*, New York, 1955; London, 1969. P. Rieff, *Freud, the Mind of the Moralist*, New York, 1959; London, 1960. This last book was an analysis of Freud as a moral philosopher rather than as a social scientist, as that term was understood by positivist social scientists.
41. E. Fromm, *The Anatomy of Human Destructiveness* (1973), New York, 1974. See esp. the appendix for discussion of Freud's theory of death instincts.

3 Society and Character

To many people the name of Freud suggests one thing—sex. At the beginning of the twentieth century Freud wrote about sexuality in children, which was, at that time, an original contribution to the understanding of human beings and the problems many of them developed in later adult life. Much of what Freud said has still not really been assimilated into the ways in which doctors and nurses, teachers, magistrates and judges, clergy and bishops speak and act. There is a pseudo-sophistication in our understanding of sexuality and its relation to human actions, for we have not grasped how very difficult it is to cope with all its manifestations.

The main reasons for this are due to the fact that what Freud meant by 'sexuality' is much wider in its connotations than genital intercourse between a male and a female, and also partly due to his assertion that there is no basic sociability, no herd instinct, in men. The main implication of this latter assertion is that energy from sexuality has to be used for 'binding together' people in social groups of all kinds—families, friends, work-teams, towns, nations and international organizations.[1] There is no simple kind of sexual liberation possible which will eradicate the neuroses caused by sexual repression without, at the same time, producing social changes, only some of which may be controllable in rational ways.

As we have seen, Wilhelm Reich was the first to develop these implications, in terms of practical, political action, by pursuing sexual liberation in order to attain economic and political changes without producing a new form of authoritarianism. The problem is that Reich only took half of Freud's theory, and ignored the role of the death instincts which were developed in the later theory of psychoanalysis.[2]

Given this assertion about the sexual nature of social ties, it is incumbent upon sociologists to examine the arguments, the conceptualizations and the observations which led Freud to this position. In the past, sociologists have been content to dismiss such claims as unworthy of serious consideration for a variety of reasons, some of which have already been examined. Freud has been seen as an inheritor of the Hobbesian problem of order. He begins by assuming that men do not naturally co-operate in society, and then seeks an explanation of how society is possible, given the natural state of 'war of all against all'.[3] Undoubtedly there is in Freud's theory an image of this Hobbesian state of nature where life is nasty, brutish and short. However, the theory developed by Freud cannot be dismissed because it assumes an innate mutual hostility among people. The assertion could be true. Freud also assumes that there is a push towards co-operation and sociability which derives from sexuality.

Infant Sexuality

'Sexuality', as the term is used by Freud, has two aspects: first, a variety of possible *objects* for sexual acts; and secondly, a variety of *aims* of sexual acts. There is nothing 'natural' about heterosexual intercourse, for not all human beings engage in this activity as a major form of sexuality. Many humans have taken 'objects', that is, in this case, people, of the same sex, and although they may have some experience of heterosexual intercourse, they may prefer and may frequently perform homosexual acts. Psychoanalytic theory operated from early on in its development with the assumption that there was an interplay between the degree of bisexuality given in the constitution of individuals, and the socialization experiences the child underwent in its family circumstances. Everyone is assumed to be potentially capable of having sexual relations with a person of either sex, although there could be exceptions at either end of the spectrum, that is, there are some people who are constitutionally unable to be anything other than heterosexual, and some who are unable to be anything other than homosexual.[4]

Some people prefer to take young children as their sexual objects, of either sex. They wish to indulge in sex play of the type in which children, under the age of five or six, engage. Other people prefer to take animals as sexual objects (keeping pets may be a sublimated form of this). Children do not make the same rigid distinction between humans and animals that adults learn to make. In their unconscious, an animal may be a symbolic figure for one or other of the parents. Adults who prefer sex with animals may be returning to the stage when there was little distinction between humans and animals, and use an animal as a substitute for sexual relations with a parent. In their unconscious, they have achieved their wish to have sexual relations with the parent of the opposite sex, or even with the parent of the same sex.[5]

The aims of sexual activity may focus on any of the erotogenic zones, that is, those parts of the skin, or those organs of the body, the stimulation of which produces sensual pleasure. An infant uses the mouth as the first organ from which pleasure can be derived, through sucking at the breast and imbibing the warm milk. In adults, the use of the mouth and lips in kissing is the frequently permitted act of oral gratification, although eating and drinking retain a weaker gratification for the oral sexual impulses. The use of the mouth to caress and suck the genitals of either sex is more likely to produce disgust in some people, and is treated by many who indulge in oral sex as a 'problem', an activity they have learned to see as a deviation from normal sexual activity. Therapy will aim to reduce the guilt of such people by helping them to decide whether they will continue to practise oral sex, and, if so, to lessen the conflict within them by helping them accept the activity as pleasurable and human and not highly deviant. Other patients who have the same unconscious impulses to engage in oral sex—for example, an adult male or female who is married and dreams he or she is sucking a man's penis and imbibing the semen—may deny the impulses. The repressed impulse may appear as a psychosomatic disturbance, with symptoms in the mouth or the digestive system.[6]

Infant sexuality moves into the anal phase next, and some adult sexual aims derive from this phase where interest centres on the erotogenic possibilities of the anus. Young children can derive sensual pleasure from retention of faeces, and the subsequent letting go can produce pleasurable sensations in the bowel. Infants can also be observed to enjoy playing with their faeces, something which adults do if they regress to the anal phase when in a confined cell, in prison or hospital. Children are usually stopped by parents from playing with their faeces, and they become interested instead in mud pies, or in building sandcastles or playing with clay and plasticine. Adults may have as one of their sexual aims, or as an exclusive one, the act of anal intercourse. Males can take either an active or passive part in this activity, and can be the active partner with a variety of objects, male or female. Repression of these impulses may produce symptoms in the bowel region.[7]

In Western society, adults may play with money as an acceptable substitute for the unconscious desire to play with faeces. Faeces are used by young children as a 'gift', and sometimes their stools are wrapped up in parcels which they give to a significant person. Old people, in old people's homes, sometimes regress to this stage, and they also can be observed to play with faeces and to wrap them up and present them as a gift. Societies in which people saw gold as precious would give gold as a gift to a loved person, and in our culture money is a substitute for gold, which is, in turn, a symbolic substitution for the first gift—faeces. Faeces can also symbolize babies in the mind of infants, and in the unconscious of adults. One theory children produce about the origin of babies is that they come out of the bowel.

Adult women can attain the aim of possessing a penis through giving birth—a child is a substitute for a penis, also confused with faeces. This might explain the attraction of money-making activities to many men in capitalist and other types of economies, and the comparative absence of women in such areas. (This is not an explanation which is meant to compete with structural explanations relating the phenomenon to the suppression of women, but one which adds another dimension. Such a phenomenon could be *over-determined*, that is, have more than *one* cause.) Freud developed these interconnections in one paper, 'Character and Anal Erotism' (1908), and more fully in another, 'On the Transformation of Instincts with Special Reference to Anal Erotism' (1917). In this later paper he writes:

> To begin with, it would appear that in the products of the unconscious—spontaneous ideas, phantasies, symptoms—the conceptions *faeces* (money, gift), *child* and *penis* are seldom distinguished and are easily interchangeable.[8]

Exhibitionism and voyeurism are closely related sexual aims; the one is likely to become the other. Children make some of their first sexual researches by observing the genitals of other children, especially when they are urinating or defecating. They may also develop a pride in exhibiting their genitals, the penis in the case of boys, and the anus in the case of girls.

Fetishism also derives from the early polymorphous perversity of infant sexuality. Not only can various parts of the body be erogoneous zones, but other objects can become symbolic substitutes for the genitals, such as a shoe.[9]

The sexual aims of sadism and masochism raised difficult problems in the early stages of the development of psycho-

crule,

analytic theory. The element of cruelty in sadism—and in masochism, where the ego is taken as the object of the sadistic impulses—is difficult to account for.

> Cruelty in general comes easily to the childish nature, since the obstacle that brings the instinct for mastery to a halt at another person's pain—namely a capacity for pity—is developed relatively late. The fundamental psychological analysis of this instinct has, as we know, not been satisfactorily achieved. It may be assumed that the impulse of cruelty arises from the instinct for mastery and appears at a period of sexual life at which the genitals have not yet taken over their later role.[10]

Children who witness sexual intercourse in the first few years of their lives see it as a sort of ill-treatment, an assault by the man on the woman; 'they view it that is in a sadistic sense'.[11] The period of preoccupation with the anus and its products is linked with sadistic impulses in the child. It is at this stage that parents begin to exercise authority over the child in terms of where and when he or she may defecate and urinate. The child may retain his stools partly for the erotic pleasure of later letting go, but also as an *act of defiance* against the parents. This is something which remained obscure and undeveloped in psychoanalytic theory until the later developments in the instinct theory were introduced by Freud. These cruel and sadistic impulses were thought, at this point in the theory, to derive from the active, male element of dominating another in the act of sexual intercourse. This view was changed later.[12]

In the *Three Essays on the Theory of Sexuality* (1905) there was almost nothing on the phase which followed the anal, and which became known as the phallic stage. In this third stage both girls and boys are primarily concerned with the penis—as a result of their early observations, girls notice that they do not have one, and boys notice this fact too. There are probably still some children who are never allowed to see the genitals of the opposite sex as small children, but Freud found, even among upper-class children, that there were few who did not manage a way to see the genitals of the opposite sex before they were five or six years old.

In a supplement to the three essays, *The Infantile Genital Organization of the Libido* (1923), Freud introduced the idea of the phallic stage. The polarity of the phallic stage is not male–female, as it is in the later genital stage, at puberty. Rather do children, especially boys, think that there are two possibilities: possession of a penis or a castrated condition, the penis having been cut off.

It should not be presumed, however, that the child instantly and readily makes a generalization of its perception that many women possess no penis; in the way of this there lies the assumption that the absence of the penis is due to a castration performed as a punishment. On the contrary, the child imagines that only unworthy female persons have thus sacrificed their genital organ, such persons as have probably been guilty of the same forbidden impulses as he himself. Women who are regarded with respect, such as the mother, retain the penis long after this date.[13]

Only later do children learn that women give birth to babies but do not possess a penis. Boys may come to envy the womb, just as girls first envy the male penis.[14]

The Oedipus Complex

In the *Three Essays on the Theory of Sexuality* (1905) there is no explicit discussion of the Oedipus complex, though later footnotes added to the work do mention it. Freud had thought about the myth of Oedipus, and the relationships between parents and children, in 1897 in a letter to Fleiss, and there are explicit formulations of the idea in the *Five Lectures on Psycho-analysis*, given in 1909 in the United States. In the fourth of these lectures Freud, having already dealt with the importance of infant sexuality in relation to the body, turns to the emotional relationship between those who care for the baby and the child himself. One of the parents usually becomes especially important. The father tends to be more affectionate in his relationship with his daughter, and the mother is more affectionate towards her son. The feelings aroused by these relationships are not just affectionate ones, but also hostile and negative towards the parent who is not so affectionate.

The complex which is thus formed is doomed to early repression; but it continues to exercise a great and lasting influence from the unconscious. It is to be suspected that, together with its extensions, it constitutes the *nuclear complex* of every neurosis, and we may expect to find it actively at work in other regions of mental life. The myth of King Oedipus, who killed his father and took his mother to wife, reveals, with little modification, the infantile wish, which is later opposed and repudiated by the barrier against incest.

Shakespeare's *Hamlet* is equally rooted in the soil of the incest-complex, but under a better disguise.[15]

Not until a paper published in 1910 does Freud settle on the term 'Oedipus complex'. In that paper, entitled 'A Special Case of Object Choice Made by Men',[16] the material which is discussed concerns the problems of psychical impotence among men who have strong sexual impulses, and who are physically healthy, but who find that they are unable to have an orgasm when trying to make love to certain women. During analysis it appears that they often become involved with women who are attached to another man, and that they are unconsciously seeking to re-create the early family situation. The other man, the injured third party, is the father in unconscious terms, and the woman is the mother. The man is unconsciously seeking to take his mother as sexual object, but during the course of his upbringing he has learned to repress his wishes to make love to his mother, or to his sister. It is not therefore surprising that he becomes unable to make love satisfactorily to the women he chooses since they are surrogates for his mother. In the unconscious of the men concerned, a part aims to give his mother a son, like himself, as an expression of his gratitude to her for bearing him into the world.

In a later paper, 'The Most Prevalent Form of Degradation in Erotic Life' (1912),[17] reference is again made to forbidden wishes of the son to make love to his mother or sister, and the effects of this on later sexual inadequacies with women (inadequate, that is, to the men themselves). Some men become unable to make love to their wives, towards whom they feel affection but not sensual love. They learned to feel affection, but not to express sensual love, towards women they esteemed highly, in the first instance, in the relationship with their mother. Consequently, they feel sensual desire only for women with whom they have few affectionate ties, and who are not highly esteemed by them, nor by others in their social circle. There are also sexual impulses which they cannot incorporate in relationships with their wives, because they and their wives think it would be too animal-like and demeaning to perform them. They can perform them, perhaps, with a mistress.

Frigidity in women has similar causes. It arises where, in the socialization of girls, sexual feelings and actions are almost totally forbidden. The repression can be total in adult women, hence their frigidity. The situation might be improved if young girls were allowed to develop sexual feelings and activities when they reached puberty. Boys do indulge in some sexual activities, such as masturbation alone and with other boys, and perhaps intercourse with prostitutes or lower-class girls. (Freud is writing in the first decade of the twentieth century, about men and women in middle- and upper-middle-class Austria who would have been brought up in the latter part of the nineteenth century.)

Freud is reluctant to say that there would not be unforeseen consequences if the restrictions on young people's sexual activities were altered, for human beings seem to devise conventional restrictions upon sexual life in all cultures. In part, this is because there is extra pleasure to be derived from what is, at times, forbidden. Might there not be another reason? There seems to be 'something in the nature of the sexual instinct itself [which] is unfavourable to the achievement of absolute gratification'.[18] First, there is the fact that the object chosen in sexual activity is a surrogate object; the real desire being for the parent, or sibling, usually of the opposite sex. There is always a sense in which sexual activity is one step removed from fully gratifying the real wish for the mother or the father. The prohibition on incest is, however, needed, for the young person must leave the family, develop independently of it, and build up other social groups and new cultural objects. Secondly, not all the sexual impulses can be gratified, and the more educated ('civilized' in Freud's term) often find it more difficult to gratify as many impulses as other people do. Coprophilia and sadism are two such erotic impulses which many humans can never gratify in real activity with another person.

> The erotic instincts are hard to mould; training of them achieves now too much, now too little. What culture tries to make out of them seems attainable only at the cost of a sensible loss of pleasure; the persistence of the impulses that are not enrolled in adult sexual activity makes itself felt in an absence of satisfaction.[19]

There is, then, a fundamental problem here for mankind. Man's cultural development can arise only at the cost of a persisting lack of satisfaction of those sexual impulses which are seen as improper by men and women—the higher the degree of civilization and education, the greater the number of unsatisfied impulses. This major problem will be discussed again in relation to *Civilization and Its Discontents* in Chapter 6 (page 115).

'The Passing of the Oedipus Complex' (1924)[20] discusses how both boys and girls emerge from the Oedipus complex, and repress the complex into their unconscious or extinguish its effects altogether. The Oedipus complex coincides with the phallic phase, which occurs at about the age of three, in which both boys and girls are interested in the penis. In the case of girls, Freud thinks the clitoris is treated as a penis by the girl. During the course of their upbringing, boys are disciplined by parents or child-minders when they play with their penis. They may be threatened with having it cut off, or having their hand cut off. This threat is to no avail, the boy finds real pleasure in manipulating his penis. When, however, he observes the female genitals, of his sister or playmate, the threat of castration suddenly appears real. The girl comes to see that she has less than the boy, and has been castrated already. The boy now gives up his Oedipal wishes because he would rather keep his penis, and he takes the castration threat seriously, having seen a castrated person. The girl envies the penis of boys, and blames her mother for not giving her one. She transfers her affections, hitherto directed to her mother who has cared for her so far in life, on to her father. Her wish is now to have a baby from him, the baby becoming the substitute for the penis. She has thereby taken the first step towards adult sexuality in developing a wish for a baby.

There have been numerous criticisms of Freud's theory of the Oedipus complex, and of his implied view of female sexuality. It has been said that the theory of the Oedipus complex is culturally ethnocentric, and that in other cultures, with different family systems, there is no Oedipus complex. In cultures where the two-parent family is not the major centre for the rearing of children that it is in Western, middle-class cultures, the Oedipus complex does not develop, for the intensity of the relationships is much less strong between parents and children than in Western society. Margaret Mead, for instance, makes this point in her study of Samoan culture.[21] Malinowski, however, found that among the matrilineal Trobriand Islanders, where the mother's brother, not the biological father, exercises authority over the child, the child feels hostility towards the maternal uncle, not the 'father'. In this different culture it can be said that the basic dynamics of the Oedipal situation appear, albeit modified by the different structural and cultural arrangements.[22]

Much of the anthropological work on the methods of child-rearing, and the type of socialization that children experience in the various cultures humanity has developed, fails to take account of one important interconnection Freud saw between infant sexuality and the need of civilization to use the energy of sexuality for its purposes. There is a connection between the modern family and advanced industrial societies, and between extended kinship networks and agricultural societies, or societies which are still in the process of becoming urban and industrial. A full 'test' (assuming that such a notion of 'testing' is meaningful in this context) of Freudian theory would have to bring in the hypothesis about the causal links between the nuclear family, the Oedipus complex, the methods of handling infant sexuality in middle-class, Western culture, and the personality types which are needed in advanced industrial society.[23] The most important of these personality traits is, in general terms, the capacity to repress, sublimate and defer sexual pleasures. Freud thought that the need for a long period of education for young men and women in the 'civilized' sections of modern societies was linked with the development of neurotic illness because of the deferment of sexual gratification necessary while education took place. Although modern America and Western Europe, as well as Russia and Eastern Europe, are different in some respects from the type of society with which Freud was familiar before and after the First World War, there is still great value in Freud's conceptualizations for understanding some problems in these societies.

A further point in relation to the accusation of the ethno-centricity of Freud's assumptions about gender roles has been made by some people in the Women's Movement, such as Kate Millet and Ann Oakley.[24] It is said that Freud wrote in a male-dominated society, and that his theory about sexuality, and about female sexuality in particular, reflects this in the male bias in his work. Such points miss the remarks Freud makes about the need for females to have more freedom to express and explore their sexuality, both as children and as young adults. More importantly, they fail to take account of the complications that all generalizations about sex and gender roles have given humanity's constitutional bisexuality. For Freud there is no difference between boys and girls in their sexuality in the oral, anal and phallic stages of development. The differences set in with the different ways in which boys and girls *may typically* (not 'must always') resolve the Oedipus complex. The points made by Freud in the theory of psycho-analysis are tentative, especially in relation to female sexuality and to the sequences involved in psycho-sexual development.[25] Given the basic similarity of human sexuality at birth, and the bisexual nature of human beings, Freud sought to account for the way in which men and women are produced in a particular society—namely, middle-class Europe and America in the early twentieth century. He assumed a complex interplay between the type of socialization process people experienced and the basic 'constitution' of individuals. The most important of these constitutional factors, but not the only one, was the difference between the genitals of boys and girls, and the capacity, only visible later in adult life, of females to give birth to children.

There are two types of proposition in Freud's theory which are not always as clearly distinguished as they might have been in his writing. These are, first, propositions about the way in which modern 'men' and 'women' are produced in one particular culture at a given historical time. And secondly, propositions about human sexuality in general, and its relation-ship to the development of human civilizations. They are often intertwined in Freud's work, which explains why he has so often been wrongly accused of a simple type of ethnocentrism, and of sexism. Logically, the distinction between the two aspects of the theory can and should be made.

The Development of the Super-ego

Nothing better illustrates the impossibility of separating off the individual personality from the wider social groups of which he or she is or has been a member, than the analysis of the develop-ment of conscience, that is, in Freud's terminology, the super-ego. Equally, it is impossible to analyse social systems as consisting of norms and values and power relationships without examining the way in which they actually impinge on people. The attempt to do so leads to abstraction in which societies, or systems, seem to behave without any reference to actual people. Talcott Parsons has been one of the sociologists to realize this, contrary to what is often supposed, as will be shown later in this chapter. He attempted to link his social-systems analysis to Freud's analysis of the super-ego as the point of overlap between social, cultural and personality systems.

First, it is important to look at the way in which Freud

developed the idea of the super-ego, and the part it played in his theory. He had first mentioned the concept of ego ideal in his paper 'On Narcissism' (1914),[26] and the notion of ego ideal is later said to be identical with that of super-ego in *The Ego and the Id* (1923.)[27] The work with patients who had the delusion of being watched, and who spoke of the watcher as another person in terms like the following: 'He is waiting for me to go now', or 'He thinks I should do such and such', had first led Freud to suggest that a part of a person's ego can keep watch over another part. Others seemed to derive pleasure from looking at their own bodies and caressing themselves, and from auto-erotic actions, and these people had led Freud to develop his concept of narcissism. Everyone had a potential for narcissism because the baby starts off in a world of its own, in a state of primary narcissism. As a compensation, and as a substitute for the lost narcissism of childhood, 'normal' people develop an ego ideal, a conception, more emotional than intellectual, of how they would like to be.

> That which he projects ahead of him as his ideal is merely his substitute for the lost narcissism of his childhood—the time when he was his own ideal.[28]

The ego ideal of young children is based on those closest to them, usually the parents, and later on other educators and youth workers who have some resemblance to the parents. Boys will usually want to be like their fathers when they grow up, girls to be like their mothers. Conscience is a function of the ego ideal, and is critical of failure to live up to the ego ideal.

> The institution of conscience was at bottom an embodiment first of parental criticism and subsequently that of society . . .[29]

In the later work, *The Ego and the Id*, the instinct theory of psychoanalysis had changed from the two instincts—sexual instincts and ego instincts—which were used in the paper 'On Narcissism'. Freud had always held that the first instinct theory could be changed, and indeed it was. The reasons for this change will need to be examined later, in Chapter 6, but for the moment it should be noted that a change in the instinct theory underpinning this later analysis had been made. This is important for understanding the way in which it will be argued that Talcott Parsons has misunderstood Freud.

The ego ideal, or super-ego, results from two important factors, one biological, the other historical. The biological factor is the length of time that the human child is dependent and helpless and in need of attention from parents. The historical factor is the Oedipus complex. This latter is historical, it would seem, in two senses: one in terms of the history of the individual, and the other in terms of the history of human cultural development, although this last point is not clear in Freud.[30] The ego ideal emerges from the child's attempt to repress the Oedipus complex:

> The child's parents, and especially his father, were perceived as the obstacle to a realization of his Oedipus wishes; so his infantile ego fortified itself for the carrying out of the repression by erecting this same obstacle within itself. It borrowed strength to do this, so to speak, from the father . . .[31]

Both boys and girls make identifications with their fathers and mothers, and the relative strength of these will depend on the degree of bisexuality in the individual: the more masculine the girl, the stronger the identification with her father is likely to be; the more feminine the boy's constitutional make-up, the stronger the identification with his mother is likely to be and the weaker his identification with father. The process of growth out of the Oedipus complex is therefore very complicated, and differs from one individual to another, depending on the balance of male and female factors in the biological constitution of the person's body.

The super-ego is a part of the phylogenetic 'archaic heritage' of the species, as well as being the result of the individual's own development. Religion and morality become important in understanding the ego ideal of groups of people, and of the individuals who are members of these classes, ethnic groups and nations. Social feelings arise, too, through identifications with other members of a group who all internalize the same ego ideal. These issues will be examined in detail in the relevant chapters which follow. It is sufficient to point out here that the 'archaic heritage' of mankind enters Freud's discussion of the super-ego, for he seemed to think that there was an element of this phylogenetic archaic heritage in the id. The experiences of former generations are *inherited* in the id, they are not all learned through the cultural transmission processes with which social scientists are familiar—through education and religious teachings, for example.[32]

It has been thought that Freud was assuming that there can

be inheritance of acquired characteristics, an idea shown to be fallacious in modern biology. However, there is some reason for thinking that Freud may have had something else in mind, namely, the symbols which occur in dream life, some of which are widespread among different cultures and epochs. It is possible to tidy up Freud's theory and see the 'archaic heritage' as transmitted by cultural institutions, such as religious and legal codes, as Freud himself did at times. On the other hand, one can keep an open mind about the *content* of the id at birth, and include in it some basic symbolic material. This is difficult to conceive, and it may be wrong, but some such hypothesis seemed called for to Freud's mind at the end of his life's work in psychoanalysis. It was not an alternative to cultural transmission, but in addition to it. It applies to the symbolic language of dream life, which seems to be almost universal among *Homo sapiens* and which has a life of its own.[33]

In *The Ego and the Id*, the notion of death instincts is used alongside that of the sexual instincts, or Eros, and some of the energy of the death instincts can be used by the super-ego against the ego. This can be seen in melancholia, where the person feels worthless as the super-ego mercilessly criticizes the ego.

> Following our view of sadism, we should say that the destructive component had entrenched itself in the super-ego and turned against the ego. What is now holding sway in the super-ego is, as it were, a pure culture of the death instincts, and in fact it often enough succeeds in driving the ego into death, if the latter does not fend off its tyrant in time by the change round into mania.[34]

Talcott Parsons's Use of Psychoanalysis

During the 1950s, Talcott Parsons made a series of attempts to integrate psychoanalytic theory into his social-action theory. This involved him in showing how Freud's theory needed modification so that it could be integrated into the Parsonian social and culture systems theory. The Freudian concept of 'super-ego' was of central importance in this integration, for here was a direct link with sociology. The process of internalization of values was of major importance to Parsonian theory, for it provided a link between the culture shared by members of a society and the individual's motivation for action.

The common culture which Parsons postulated has three

types of symbolism: (a) evaluative symbols which express moral standards; (b) cognitive symbols which give an account of what there is in the natural and social world; and (c) cathectic symbols, which define appropriate feelings about objects. Freud's theory of the super-ego concentrates on the ways in which the evaluative symbols are internalized by members of the society, and as such is capable of being integrated into action theory. The other types of symbols are equally internalized by society's members, and as this is not part of Freud's theory, Parsons suggests modifications to it to incorporate these types of symbols also.

There are three modifications suggested by Parsons:

> The first point is that it is not only the super-ego which is internalized—that is, taken over by identification from cathected social objects—but that there are involved other important components which presumably must be included in the ego—namely, the system of cognitive categorizations of the object world and the system of expressive symbolism.[35]
>
> Secondly, the ego would be derived from *two* sources—the external world as an environment, as in Freud, and the common culture, which is also acquired from outside. Thirdly, there would need to be modifications to the notion of id-impulses, for these cannot be a direct emotion, unfiltered, as it were, by the expressive symbolism of the common culture.
>
> This may be felt to be a relatively radical conclusion—namely, that emotions, or affect on the normal human adult level, should be regarded as a *symbolically generalized* system, that is never 'id-impulse' as such.[36] [Italics in original.]

This is indeed 'a relatively radical conclusion', for it removes one of the most important gains which could arise from an integration of Freud's theory with sociology as such. If, as Parsons puts it, there can *never* be an id-impulse as such for the individual, since it must always be seen as part of the expressive symbolism of a common culture, then it is not possible to envisage the possibility of someone being in conflict with their society's common culture. But such conflicts between id-impulses and the values, internalized by the individual in his super-ego, do exist, unless the whole notion of 'inner conflicts' is false. These inner conflicts are in part due to the person having 'id-impulses' which he or she has learned to see as wrong, and so has internalized prohibitions against acting on them. These 'id-impulses' may be either for 'perverse' sexual acts which sometimes cannot even be admitted to consciousness as acts which the person desires, or they may be impulses of sadism and destructiveness. To remove the possibility of this type of conflict, which is, at root, a conflict between the id's instinctual impulses and the society's values which have been internalized by the person concerned, is to undermine both the foundations of Freud's work and the theory he built up to explain and conceptualize it. Far from being modifications to Freud, Talcott Parsons's changes to the theory remove the whole purpose of sociologists turning to Freud in order to move away from the over-socialized conception of man.

Again, in a later paper, 'Social Structure and the Development of Personality: Freud's Contribution to the Integration of Psychology and Sociology' (1958)[37] Parsons seeks to establish that the ego, which consists of abandoned object-cathexes, must be cultural. He ignores Freud's other remarks: 'that the ego is that part of the id which has been modified by the direct influence of the external world . . .'.[38] The 'external world' can certainly include the social and cultural systems that Parsons wishes it to, but to eradicate all instinctual impulses in the personality system is to distort Freud beyond recognition. Talcott Parsons accepts that there are some basic biologically-given impulses, such as sucking, crying, smiling or clinging, but he sees these as minimal, even in the oral stage.[39]

It is quite reasonable, and an advance on Freud, to insist, as Parsons does, that the mother–baby relationship is a social situation with sets of expectations between the two being set up. The ways the mother handles the baby will be in part affected by the culture of which she is a member. Still, there are important ways in which the biological organism impinges on the personality system, even later in life, just as Parsons maintains the social and cultural systems impinge on the personality system.

Talcott Parsons concludes this paper:

> Thus it seems to me that the general principles of object-relations through identification, object-cathexis, and internalization must be extended to the whole psychoanalytic theory of personality.[40]

Even the id is to be socialized, as it is 'organized about its experience in object-relationship'.[41] It is for this reason that Parsons can ignore the other aspects of Freud's *The Ego and the Id*, from which he draws so much of his understanding of psychoanalysis, that is, those aspects which deal with the death instincts and the way they impinge on the super-ego. Far from Freud's concept of the super-ego being one which assumes the super-ego to be entirely built up from outside, from social relationships with parents and educators only—as Parsons claims—it, too, contains instinctual elements. This aspect of the super-ego's potential for severity against the ego is completely overlooked by Parsons. This is because, as has been suggested, Parsons eliminates the role of the instincts, the key concept Freud used to link the organism and the personality. Parsons retains some minimal role for erotic needs, but none at all for the death instincts. All signs of conflict are eliminated in the over-smooth workings of the Parsonian social, cultural, personality and organic systems. They all seem to integrate with one another, none makes demands on any other which are not fulfilled. Life has been removed from Parsonian systems theory, and it is ironic that this has occurred because he found no place in his scheme for the death instincts!

NOTES AND REFERENCES

1. S. Freud, *Group Psychology and the Analysis of the Ego* (1921), London, 1955. This work will be examined in detail in Chapter 4.
2. See Chapter 1 of the present book.
3. See T. Parsons, *The Structure of Social Action*, New York, 1937, Chapter 3. See also A. Dawe, 'The Two Sociologies', in *British Journal of Sociology*, Vol. XXI, 1970, pp. 207–18.
4. S. Freud, *Three Essays on the Theory of Sexuality* (1905), Standard Edition, Vol. 7, Essay No. 1. References to Avon Books edition, New York, 1962, pp. 23–5.
5. Ibid., pp. 36–8.
6. Ibid., p. 40.
7. Ibid., pp. 41 and 81.
8. Both these papers are available in P. Rieff (ed.), *Character and Culture*, New York, 1963. (Quotation, p. 204.)
   Freud's translators use the term 'erotism' *not* 'eroticism' in relation to anality. Further developments of Freud's ideas on anality can be found in N. O. Brown, *Life Against Death*, London, 1959, Part Five, 'Studies in Anality'. And also in E. Erikson, *Young Man Luther*, New York, 1958.
9. Freud, *Three Essays on the Theory of Sexuality*, edition cit., p. 45. See also Essay No. 2.
10. Ibid., pp. 89–90. (Section 4 of Essay 2.)
11. Ibid., p. 94.
12. See Chapter 6 of the present book.
13. S. Freud, 'The Infantile Genital Organization of the Libido' (1923). Available in P. Rieff (ed.), *Sexuality and the Psychology of Love*, New York, 1963, pp. 171–5. (Quotation, p. 174.)
14. See B. Bettleheim, *Symbolic Wounds, Puberty Rites and the Envious Male*, New York, 1954.

15. S. Freud, *Five Lectures on Psychoanalysis* (1909). Available in Standard Edition, 1957 translation. References to Penguin edition, Harmondsworth, 1962, pp. 77–8.
16. Available in Rieff (ed.), *Sexuality and the Psychology of Love*, pp. 49–57.
17. Ibid., pp. 58–9.
18. Ibid., p. 68.
19. Ibid., p. 69.
20. Ibid., p. 176–82.
21. M. Mead, *Coming of Age in Samoa*, 1928. Reference to Penguin edition, Harmondsworth, 1963, p. 170.
22. B. Malinowski, *Sex and Repression in Savage Society*, London, 1927. Reference to Routledge and Kegan Paul edition, pp. 80–81.
23. See W. Goode, *World Revolution and Family Patterns*, New York, 1963, 1970. This has useful material in it, but no mention of Freud nor Oedipus complex at all!
24. K. Millett, *Sexual Politics*, New York, 1971. A. Oakley, *Sex, Gender, and Society*, London, 1972, pp. 122–3, 180. For a perspective which draws on Freud, and yet is in the women's movement broad perspective, see J. Mitchell, *Psychoanalysis and Feminism*, London, 1973.
25. Freud wrote: 'I have no doubt that the temporal and causal relations described between Oedipus complex, sexual intimidation (the threat of castration), formation of the super-ego and advent of the latency period are of a typical kind; but I *do not maintain that this type is the only possible one*' (italics mine). (From 'The Passing of the Oedipus Complex' (1924), available in Rieff (ed.), *Sexuality and the Psychology of Love*, pp. 181–2.) And also: 'It may be that the ambivalence displayed in the relations to the parents should be attributed entirely to bisexuality and that it is not, as I have represented above, developed out of identification in consequence of rivalry.' (From *The Ego and the Id* (1923), Standard Edition, Vol. 19. Reference to W. W. Norton edition, New York, 1962, p. 23.)
26. Available in P. Rieff (ed.), *General Psychological Theory*, Collier Books, New York, 1963, pp. 56–82.
27. Freud, *The Ego and the Id*, edition cit., pp. 23–7.
28. S. Freud, 'On Narcissism', available in Rieff (ed.), *General Psychological Theory*, p. 74.
29. Ibid., p. 76.
30. Freud, *The Ego and the Id*, edition cit., p. 25.
31. Ibid., p. 24.
32. Ibid., p. 28.
33. S. Freud, *The Interpretation of Dreams* (1900), Standard Edition, Vols. 4 and 5.
34. Freud, *The Ego and the Id*, edition cit., p. 43.
35. T. Parsons, *Social Structure and Personality*, New York, 1964, Chapter One, 'The Superego and the Theory of Social Systems', p. 30.
36. Ibid., p. 31.
37. Ibid., Chapter Four.
38. Freud, *The Ego and the Id*, edition cit., p. 15.
39. Parsons, *Social Structure and Personality*, p. 83n.
40. Ibid., p. 110.
41. Ibid.

4 The Group and the Primal Horde

The importance of sexuality is stressed again in psychoanalytic theory at the societal level of analysis, as it is in the theory concerned with the development of the person. This emphasis makes Freud's theory unique within sociology. It is also unique in paying attention to other unconscious, emotional components of social life which are often deliberately, or unknowingly, ignored in other types of sociology. This is especially true in relation to hostility in groups and between groups, the conflicts between individuals and their society and the burden of man's past social actions, transmitted through religions, which still affect societies' development.

There are no easily accessible accounts of Freud's major metapsychological or sociological works, and Chapters 4 to 6 will therefore outline and discuss these in some detail. As Freud has been so greatly misunderstood, especially in his more speculative sociological work, this type of exposition seems necessary if his theory is to be given the serious consideration it deserves, and which sociology needs.

The two books to be discussed in this chapter, *Totem and Taboo* (1913) and *Group Psychology and the Analysis of the Ego* (1921), are discussed in reversed chronological order, because the themes of the latter book develop ideas which have already been introduced and discussed in Chapter 3. *Totem and Taboo* then becomes somewhat easier to understand and will be discussed in the second part of the present chapter.

Group Psychology

Freud begins *Group Psychology and the Analysis of the Ego* by showing that there is almost no difference between individual psychology and social or group psychology:

> In the individual's mental life someone else is invariably involved, as a model, as an object, as a helper, as an opponent; and so from the very first individual psychology, in this extended but entirely justifiable sense of the words, is at the same time social psychology as well.[1]

Freud goes on to discuss Le Bon's work *Psychologie des foules* (1895), and deals first with the question of the nature of the mental change which the group forces upon the individual. He leaves the questions of defining what a group is, and of how it acquires the capacity for influencing the mental life of the individual, until later. Le Bon thought that the racial unconscious emerges in a crowd or group, when consequently individual differences vanish. Freud reinterprets the phenomenon of the loss of a sense of moral responsibility that crowds can show in terms of a crowd allowing the individual to be able 'to throw off the repressions of his unconscious instinctual impulses'.[2] The individual appears to throw off conscience and his sense of responsibility, and repressed elements may appear in his words and behaviour. This unconscious repressed material is in addition to the general unconscious 'archaic heritage' Le Bon speaks of, and it can vary in different times and places, although Freud does not give explicit examples of this point, being content with the formal delineation of concepts.[3]

A crowd has no critical faculty, and is wide open to influence; indeed, the notion of 'impossibility' disappears for the individual in such a group situation:

> It respects force . . . What it demands of its heroes is
> strength, or even violence. It wants to be ruled and oppressed
> and to fear its masters. Fundamentally it is entirely
> conservative, and it has a deep aversion to all innovations
> and advances and an unbounded respect for tradition.[4]

This is an expression of 'cruel, brutal and destructive instincts, which lie dormant in individuals as relics of a primitive epoch'.[5] But groups, and crowds, are capable of abnegation, unselfishness and devotion to an ideal; people may have their ethical conduct raised by belonging to a group. Freud takes these points from Le Bon, commenting that contradictory ideas can exist side by side in the unconscious mental life of people, as is seen in children and neurotics.

The group, or crowd, is swayed by words, especially if certain formulae are repeated frequently. Le Bon seemed to have in mind here a church congregation, as in the remarks about people being lifted up ethically in a crowd. This seems distinct from the earlier image of a crowd being roused to the point of demanding blood. Groups demand illusions, not truth, and Freud links this with his observations of neurotics whose mental life has a predominance of phantasy material and who are guided by psychological rather than objective reality. A religion is, however, an illusion of a group, not the private world of an individual neurotic.

Groups and crowds need leaders. They have a thirst for obedience, and will submit to whoever appoints himself leader, although the leader must himself be held in fascination 'by a strong faith (in an idea) in order to awaken the group's faith'.[6] The leader and the ideas have ascribed to them a mysterious and irresistible power which Le Bon called 'prestige', a notion close to, if not identical with, Weber's concept of 'charisma'. Both Le Bon, and Freud following him, seem to be implicitly aware of the need to see that the followers give prestige to the leader and to ideas; that a relationship is involved. They are not, therefore, responsible for an over-individualistic approach to leaders as has sometimes been asserted by critics.

An important fault in Freud's work at this point is the failure to allow for a difference in the content of the ideas which leaders may espouse and develop in a group. Some religious groups have uplifted people's ethical conduct, but at other times they have allowed brutality to others in the name of the religion. There is a need to develop the differences further, rather than just saying that contradictory emotions can exist in the unconscious. Some groups, or crowds, do not behave in the brutal ways outlined in the early part of the analysis, as is admitted by Freud. What then is the difference between the types? Little is said about this. By leaving the analysis at the abstract level, Freud has enabled some psychotherapists to oppose all crowd phenomena in religious and political action, to see it *all* as being pathological. But some movements have, in fact, been more pathological than others. Fascist and nationalist groups have acted like the type of crowd described by Le Bon and Freud, being authoritarian and brutal, as have some religious groups. There are others which have not been like this, but have achieved positive things for their members and for their societies, such as democratic socialist parties.

Freud goes on to use McDougall's analysis of the positive aspects of groups, the *crowd* being distinguished from the *positive group* by the lack of organization found in groups which have been positive in their effects.[7] Groups are capable of great creativity, as in language and folksong, and even in the stimulus and support given to individual writers and thinkers. However, Freud returns to the ways in which 'crowds' affect people by the intensification of emotions and the inhibition of the intellect. He is not impressed by the idea of suggestion as the basis of crowd behaviour, for no explanation is given by simply referring to the suggestibility of people as the reason for crowds being influenced by leaders. It is libido—that is, sexual energy —which holds a group together.

> We will try our fortune, then, with the supposition that love
> relationships . . . also constitute the essence of the group
> mind.[8]

In the case of two examples which Freud takes—an army, and the Catholic Church—there is a leader, the commander, or Christ, who loves the soldiers or the believers equally. They, in turn, love one another, because they are each loved by the same elder brother, or substitute father figure. In a situation of panic, in an army, for example, there is a loss of the libidinal ties which hold the group together, and people behave in ways which take no account of the group: it is each man for himself; orders are ignored. So, for Freud, the extreme situation of a panic shows the way in which the group is held together under more normal circumstances. Panic is not the usual reaction to a dangerous situation for a group of soldiers. They usually help one another more in a dangerous situation. Only when the libidinal ties are weakened do soldiers act in panic, ignoring their comrades.

The history of religions is a history of intolerance and cruelty towards non-believers, and the love extends only to those who are believers and loved by the same supernatural being. Today, with the weakening of religious feelings, the intolerance is not so marked, but another group tie seems to be replacing the religious one: the socialist one. If this is so:

> . . . then there will be the same intolerance towards outsiders
> as in the age of the Wars of Religion; and if differences
> between scientific opinions could ever attain a similar
> significance for groups, the same result would again be
> repeated with this new motivation.[9]

There would, in other words, be hostility and intolerance shown towards those not libidinally bound together in the group. Freud fails to mention explicitly the way in which nationalism may exhibit these characteristics too, even though he was writing just after the end of the First World War.

There are a number of problems with the above analysis, based, as it is, on Freud's assumption that there is a basic element of latent mutual hostility existing between people. How would he explain, for example, the fact that Roman Catholics and Protestants have fought one another, and been mutually hostile to one another, for long periods, as in Ireland in the twentieth century, even though they both have Christ as a figure who loves them? Freud mentions the 'narcissism of minor differences'[10] among national and ethnic groups, for example, and to some extent his analysis would apply to religious groups. Great emotional importance is attached to very small differences in values and action by groups who are in close physical, social and economic contact with one another. Given the analysis as Freud presents it in *Group Psychology*, however, there is no reason why this should occur between members of different sects of the same world religion. The role of the Pope is not discussed by Freud, but it has played a key role in the Roman Catholic and Protestant hostilities. The Pope is the Vicar of Christ on earth, and it may be that on the basis of Freud's analysis there is an important difference between those who are loved by the Pope as well as, and on behalf of, Christ, and those who are not loved by the Pope, and may indeed be actively hostile to him or his representatives. The hierarchy of a church is important in the libidinal ties in churches, for they do not only rest on the love of the abstract figure of Christ, but on living people who are his priests, bishops and ministers in the various groups. Freud seems to give too much weight to the belief in Christ, and too little to the actual people in the church structures and the emotional ties that may build up between the 'secondary leader' and the believers.

Hostility in Groups

The evidence of psychoanalysis shows that almost every intimate emotional relation between two people which lasts for some time—marriage, friendship, the relation between parents and children—contains a sediment of feelings of aversion and hostility, which only escapes perception as a result of repression.[11]

This observation of Freud's has profound implications for the way in which psychoanalytic theory about groups and societies is built up. It is this assumption which many reject, but the rejection is seen by Freud as evidence of repressed hostility. This point, incidentally, when made in a discussion or in a group, makes the upholder of the view that there is no basic antagonism and hostility in human relationships very angry indeed!

So far in Freud's argument we are only concerned with a *descriptive* statement, albeit one with many theoretical overtones, but there is at this point no assertion about the genesis of this hostility, or about the degree to which it is innate, or produced by the way humans are reared, or by the interaction of the two. As an observation it seems sufficiently true, on the basis of simple observation of everyday life, to be worth accepting at this point in the theory, although it is a crucial proposition. There is little systematic evidence of how people in other cultures get on with one another, but it should be noted that within a tribal community there may be such strong libidinal ties among the members that the interrelations among them appear peaceful, and may be so for quite long periods of time. This could even be true without there being any external warfare in which some of the members might engage. However, even if there are some cases of peaceable peoples who rarely feel mutual hostility, they are not easy to find. (Margaret Mead's study of the Arapesh might count as an example.)[12]

> But when a group is formed the whole of this intolerance vanishes, temporarily or permanently, within the group. So long as a group formation persists, or so far as it extends, individuals in the group behave as though they were uniform, tolerate peculiarities of its members, equate themselves with them, and have no feeling of aversion towards them. Such a limitation of narcissism can, according to our theoretical views, only be produced by one factor, a libidinal tie with other people.[13]

This type of object-cathexis, based on sexuality, is not the only kind of emotional tie which is found. *Identifications* are also possible, and these are the earliest form of relationship with another person. For example, the relationship of a small boy to his father—where the boy would like to be like his father when he grows up—is one of identification for psychoanalysis. Boys will choose their mothers as sexual object, and eventually the identification with the father conflicts with the object-choice of the mother. Male homosexuals in a large number of cases, says Freud, do not give up the mother and find another woman as sexual object, but they *identify* with their mother: 'he transforms himself into her and now looks about for objects which can replace his ego for him and on which he can bestow such love and care as he has experienced with his mother'.[14]

The ego introjects the object which is lost or renounced as a substitute for the object. In melancholia, as observed in some patients, Freud sees a similar introjection of the object, where the lost loved object is introjected, and the ego then has two parts. One part turns on the other and sees it as worthless, leading to the self-reproaches and relentless self-criticism of melancholics. In this way the former ego can take revenge on the lost object, which it introjected. The part of the ego which does the criticizing is the conscience, the 'ego ideal', which observes the self, criticizes, censors dreams, and is the chief influence in repression. It is built up as it 'gathers up from the influences of the environment the demands which that environment makes upon the ego and which the ego cannot always rise to . . .'.[15] It is important to notice here that Freud is talking about a part of the ego as being built up from the social and cultural surroundings, but that the whole ego is not built up in this way. This has important implications for the avoidance of the over-socialized conception of man in sociology, and for the retention of a degree of conflict as an ever-present possibility between an individual and the surrounding society.

Sensual love is distinguishable from identification as a means of establishing emotional ties between two people. In sensual love, people's judgement becomes distorted and the loved object (Freud always uses 'loved object', not 'loved person') is highly evaluated, and faults are not seen—the tendency termed 'idealization'. If sexual satisfaction is obtained, there will be some reduction in sexual over-valuation for a time, but where there is no sexual activity, then the over-valuation can increase, and the functions of the ego ideal cease to operate.

> The criticism exercised by that agency is silent; everything that the object does and asks for is right and blameless. Conscience has no application to anything that is done for the sake of the object; . . . The object has been put in the place of the ego ideal.[16]

The ego is thus impoverished in this unrequited love situation, whereas, in identification, the ego is enriched by introjecting the object and its properties.

Hypnosis is akin to being in love in that the same sapping of the subject's initiative takes place, even more so as there is no possibility of sexual satisfaction, which exists as a possibility even in unrequited love relationships. Hypnosis is identical with group formation in that it isolates the relation between the leader and follower, but between two people, not a large number, as in a crowd with a leader. Furthermore, most people under hypnosis do not lose their moral conscience, and their ego ideal retains some critical functions which both the person in love may not retain and which people in crowds may also lose.

A primary group, with a leader, but with little other 'organization' in it, can therefore be said to be 'a number of individuals who have put one and the same object in the place of their ego ideal and have consequently identified themselves with one another in their ego'.[17] A crowd or group of this type has two emotional components: namely, a relationship to a leader similar to the emotional structure of unrequited love, where the loved object replaces the ego ideal; and secondly, identification with other members of the group, where part of the object is introjected, which leads to the strong emotional ties among the members of the group. All these statements are best treated as being theoretical models, which are built up by Freud on the basis of the types of emotional relationship which he had observed during his work with patients and conceptualized in a terminology of his own.

Identification among the members of a crowd, or group, leads to demands for all to be equal; given the numbers involved, it is not possible for particular individuals to be the favourite, so a reaction-formation grows up, expressed as a group demand for social justice and equality.

> If one cannot be the favourite oneself, at all events nobody else shall be the favourite.[18]

Freud considers the example of girls who crowd around a singer, or pianist, who could easily be jealous of one another. Instead, because of the numbers involved, they renounce the aim of their love, and act as a united group. They do not then pull one another's hair out, but,

> would probably be glad to have a share of *his* flowing locks . . . Originally rivals, they have succeeded in identifying themselves with one another by means of a love for the same object.[19]

The demand for equality and social justice—that everyone must be the same—derives from what was originally envy.

> Social justice means that we deny ourselves many things so that others may have to do without them as well, or, what is the same thing, may not be able to ask for them.[20]

Such equalization, which must extend to all members of the group, does not extend to the one 'object' who is the leader. The members are all equal, but all want to be ruled by one person, who is superior to them all. The leader is to love them all equally and in the same way.

The Horde

Man is not, as some have argued (Trotter, for example, in 1916), a herd animal with a herd instinct. A baby which cries when left alone is not satisfied when any other member of the species comes along to comfort it, but may be more upset by seeing a strange person. The crying will cease when the mother, or mother surrogate, comes back and comforts it again. A member of a species which had a herd instinct, Freud thought, would be comforted by any other member coming along to offer comfort, and would not need the attentions of a special individual, the baby's *own* mother. Furthermore, groups of humans with little 'organization' seem to produce a leader, a common love object to love and be loved by. Man, concludes Freud, is 'rather a horde animal, an individual creature in a horde led by a chief'.[21] The biology may not be very convincing in this argument, but it is nevertheless a useful distinction to make, given Freud's purpose of understanding the emotional structure of human groups.

A group reactivates very early parts of humanity's 'archaic heritage', the primal horde—that is, a relatively small group of people ruled over by one powerful despotic male, originally the father. Freud had first introduced this hypothesis in *Totem and Taboo* as a development of an idea of Darwin's. It has important implications in this context of group psychology, for Freud thinks it helps to make sense of the emotional activity in groups. It is introduced as a hypothesis which can bring coherence and understanding into this area—a piece of speculation which has continued to worry empiricists ever since it was first developed since it does not seem to be based on facts. The 'facts' on which it is based are those of the unconscious emotional life of groups, and as such it can be entertained as an important contribution to the understanding of such feelings and actions in human groups.

Groups easily regress to primitive mental activity of a kind ascribed to the primal horde:

> ... the dwindling of the conscious individual personality,
> the focusing of thoughts and feelings in a common direction, the
> predominance of the affective side of the mind and of
> unconscious psychical life, the tendency to the immediate
> carrying out of intentions as they emerge...[22]

The psychology of groups is first asserted to be the oldest form of human psychology, but then individual psychology, of the leader, chief or father, is also added as the oldest individual psychology.[23] Freud tends to confuse here the notion of 'oldest' with that of 'logical priority'. In Freud's model, the equalitarian group, the band of brothers, can only feel equal and united in their common relationship to the dominant chief, or father; that is, to the individual leader. Neither the group nor the individual can be 'older' than the other, for they are conceptualized as involved in a social relationship, the leader with the group. This whole situation is, for Freud, a necessary construct for his group psychology, and it is in this sense *logically prior* to any other construct, or hypothesis, developed in psychoanalytic theory about groups. It is an archaic situation, and lives on in the unconscious of people today, and may emerge in a random group situation, and is in any case present unconsciously and affects the action of people in groups.

The primal father of the horde is masterful, self-confident, independent and absolutely narcissistic; other people are loved only in so far as they serve his needs. At first he was not immortal, but became so later by deification. So, when he died, the younger son, the mother's favourite, had to become the leader. There must therefore be a way for a member of the group to become an individual, the leader. This can be done in only one way, Freud asserts:

> ... the primal father had prevented his sons from satisfying
> their directly sexual impulsions; he forced them into abstinence
> and consequently into emotional ties with him and with one
> another which could arise out of those of their impulsions
> that were inhibited in their sexual aim ... Whoever
> became his successor was also given the possibility of
> sexual satisfaction, and was by that means offered a way out
> of the conditions of group psychology.[24]

In this analysis Freud thinks he has shown how even organized groups like a church or an army are held together. It is not, as they claim in their own idealistic illusions, because the leader loves them all equally, but because they are all persecuted equally by the primal father, the leader, and they all fear him equally. The leader is the dreaded primal father towards whom a passive masochistic stand is taken, for that is the only possible one that can be taken. The leader appears to have a special aura, or power (*mana*), around him which is compared to the power of the hypnotist over the subject, or the power of the analyst in the transference situation in analysis. *Seeing* the primal figure is dangerous; tribesmen avoid the sight of their chief, and God cannot and must not be seen by mortals. The hypnotist uses the act of staring into someone's eyes as his chief technique. The ego ideal is replaced in hypnosis by the primal father, in the primal horde and all groups in which these emotions are used for keeping it together over time.

The replacement of the ego ideal by the leader is facilitated if the separation of the ego and the ego ideal is not very far advanced among the members of the group. Where the ego ideal is more highly separated, the process of identification with others in the group will be necessary for the leader to come to replace their ego ideal. Societies have periodic festivals where the usual prohibitions on activities are allowed to be infringed, and the gaiety of these occasions Freud compares, by implication, with the mania experienced by some individuals when their ego coincides with their ego ideal. In a festival, where the usual rules do not apply, there is a feeling of release, for the ego can more easily coincide with the ego ideal, for a short time at least. More usually there is a sense of guilt, and a sense of inferiority, experienced by those with a clear separation of ego and ego ideal, and who, therefore, feel tension between the two.[25]

Implicitly in this analysis Freud suggests that the group, that is, the primal horde situation, is attractive to people because the tension with the ego ideal is lost when the leader can be put in the place of the ego ideal. For those people whose ego ideal has ruled them with especial strictness, the group situation can appear particularly attractive. There can be oscillations of mood in some people, from mania, where the ego easily coincides with ego ideal and tensions cease, to melancholia, where the ego ideal is very strict and condemnatory towards ego, or part of ego—an introjected, lost loved object, for example. So the group, the primal horde, may be attractive to both those with little tension from their ego ideal, and for those people with a great deal, such as the more 'cultured' among the middle classes in modern societies. Perhaps this is a way of saying that no one is immune from the feelings of attraction towards being merged in a group, or in a commune, a nation, a religious community, a political movement.

For Freud, this lure of the group is a regression away from the tensions of living in civilized society, with its high development of ego ideal, or conscience, among its members. There is no point in developing the demands of civilization to the point where the majority of people find the tensions too great to bear and react, through regression, to the primal horde. For it was in the primal horde that the first murder was performed, and this has haunted mankind ever since. These implications of the theory of the primal horde will be developed later in this chapter, after a consideration of Freud's analysis of taboo in *Totem and Taboo*.

Taboo

Social anthropologists have had great difficulty in giving a clear definition of taboo, because it involves both an element of the sacred, the holy, and of the uncanny, the forbidden, and the dangerous.[26] Taboos are prohibitions which may apply to almost anything, whether it be a place, a person, an object, a state of the body, a piece of clothing, a plant, or an action of some kind. Taboo is distinguished from what the Polynesians call *noa*, that is, the common, or the generally accessible. It, too, can apply to all types of things, and includes all that is not taboo.

Freud compares taboos with the obsessional prohibitions that some neurotics had been observed to set up for themselves, and sometimes for those around them, such as the frequent need to wash their own hands before performing a task. These start with the prohibitions given to young children forbidding them to touch their genitals. Children develop emotional ambivalence about these prohibitions, stemming from their wish to touch and play with their genitals. This wish is merely repressed, not abolished, by the desire to please the parents by obeying their prohibition. Taboos have this emotional ambivalence about them too, for they originally forbid an action, or an interest in something, for which there is a strong unconscious desire. So taboos may exist which prohibit social intercourse between a man and a young girl having her first menstruation, or between females and a young male who has just reached puberty, because there is strong unconscious, or even conscious, desire to have sexual relations with the girls or boys (incest).[27]

Taboos which are broken cause the person who breaks them to become taboo themselves. People respond to the taboo breaker in terms of feeling, 'Why should he, or she, be allowed to do what is forbidden to others?' Such a taboo breaker is dangerous to the rest of the members of the society because they have strong unconscious desires to do the same thing. The act is too attractive, and they are tempted to transgress. Taboo is contagious; it can move from the prohibited act to a person, and by extension the taboo can be displaced on to material objects which become transmitters of taboo. An example of the latter occurs in modern society when objects in a house may have to be removed because they remind the people in the house of a daughter who has had an illegitimate child.

Freud applies his notion of taboo, as being based on emotional ambivalence, to three areas:

First, he applies it to the rites of purification which a warrior has to perform among, for example, the American Indian peoples of Natchez and the Pima, which involve the killer in being taboo for days, weeks or even months after the killing. He is socially isolated during this time.

Secondly, he applies it to rulers, who have to be guarded, and guarded *against*. The Nubas of East Africa fear to enter the house of their king, but may do so by baring their left shoulder, and having the king touch it. The act of the king touching them in this way protects them from the otherwise dangerous consequences of being in contact with the power of the king. (The kings of England, up to and including Charles II, would touch ill people, and heal them through the 'king's evil'.) There have been so many taboos surrounding some kings that it has been difficult, if not impossible, to find anyone to be successor, for the taboos lead to total social isolation of the ruler. (This is reported to have occurred among the people of Niue Island in the South Pacific, and in Sierre Leone.)[28] These taboos are interpreted by Freud in the same way as neurotic prohibitions and obsessive acts, that is, they appear to be performed out of deference and respect, or even positive love and care, but unconsciously they are produced by motives of hostility. They are obsessive, and seem too much, or too many, for the purpose in hand. For example, the Mikado in Japan could not lose any hair or nails for he was so holy, nor could he move unduly as this would mean there would be a flood, or invasion, or some other calamity in his empire. Much court ceremonial, which appears protective of the monarch, masks unconscious feelings of hostility towards the king, which seems to mirror the hostility felt towards the father by children.[29]

Thirdly, Freud examines taboos upon the dead which are common in the South Pacific, in Africa and among Amerindian peoples. For example, dead bodies are not to be touched, and if anyone has touched a dead body they must not themselves touch food. This is not so much for reasons of hygiene, it should be added, but rather from fear of the pollution that can come from the demons of the dead, who are usually thought to harbour hostile feelings towards the living. The dead are treated as enemies, says Freud. (This is now known to be an over-generalization, for in some African societies the dead are related to as though they were still living and treated as members of the kinship group.)[30] Freud argues that people harbour hostile impulses towards their relatives, and that these are normally unconscious. After death there are two sets of emotions to be handled, one concerning the mourning resulting from the loss of a loved one, and the other arising from the unconscious hostility felt towards the dead person, and therefore the unconscious pleasure about the death. 'Primitive' people project these hostile feelings on to the spirits of the dead. Taboos against touching, and against speaking the name of a dead person, are set up to protect them from the hostility of the dead as they see it. These are 'really' expressions of their unconscious hostility to the dead person, hostility which cannot be expressed, especially after the death.

> The survivor thus denies that he has ever harboured any hostile feelings against the dead loved one; the soul of the dead harbours them instead and seeks to put them into action during the whole period of mourning ... The taboo upon the dead arises, like the others, from the contrast between conscious pain and unconscious satisfaction over the death that has occurred.[31]

This may be so for some cultures where the taboos of the kind mentioned by Freud exist, but it cannot account for all the taboos and rites surrounding the dead in cultures where the dead are seen as more friendly. However, Freud's point does sensitize us to look, in all cultures, for the ways in which unconscious hostility towards the dead is handled.

There is an important methodological point worth discussing here, for Freud points out that it is not possible simply to take what people themselves say are the reasons for the taboos they practise, for if the reasons are unconscious, they will not be able to do this. In work with neurotics, and patients unable to recover from the death of a loved one, Freud found it useful to conceptualize matters in the following way. Early on in an analysis, a patient may not be able to verbalize their real feelings, or to admit they had hostile feelings towards the dead person, and that a part of themselves is pleased with the death. Later they may be able to admit these feelings and to begin to emerge from disabling melancholia and grief, and to make contact with other people and to begin to enjoy life again.

There are always two sets of reasons that can be given for psychical events, one that is phrased in terms of the culture's *Weltanschuung*, and the other which the psychoanalytic observer can bring in terms of the unconscious feelings underlying the system.[32] In psychoanalytic therapy, Freud would work towards an avowal from the patient that the interpretation he offered about unconscious feelings was the right one, even though, at first, such an interpretation might be resisted or rejected by the analysand. Over time, the analyst may alter his initial interpretations. Such a procedure is much more difficult when applied to a whole system of taboos in the way Freud does in *Totem and Taboo*. There is no evidence, for instance, that anyone in the tribes ever came to accept the interpretations offered. So there is little check on them, except by referring to clinical case material for prohibitions or actions analogous to those in the tribe. This is, in fact, what Freud does. There needs to be some procedure, however, which is akin to the analysand coming to accept the analysts' interpretations in the analytic setting for the hypotheses to be said to have been tested. It is difficult to see what such a procedure might be. Freud's work should make sociologists wary of always accepting people's own accounts at face value, in the way simple phenomenological approaches do, for then there is no role for theory, and more importantly, no way out of epistemological and ethical relativism.[33]

Freud ends his paper on 'Taboo' with some comments on the differences between a neurosis and a social institution such as taboo. Neurotics may appear to be concerned for others, but this is based on unconscious hostility towards someone, so that their concern that someone may die, or fall very ill unless some particular action of their own is done or not done, really masks an unconscious wish for their death: '. . . the original wish that the loved person may die is replaced by a fear that he may die'.[34]

Neurosis is socially isolating, and there is no social concern for others based on something other than the desire for a sexual object. Although there are similarities between the neuroses and the institutions of art, religion and philosophy, neuroses are distortions of these institutions. They are purely private means devised by the neurotic to achieve what is achieved in society by collective effort. This is because the energy for neuroses comes from the sexual instincts which are seeking private gratifications, rather than the combination of erotic and egoistic elements found in the social impulses.

> The asocial nature of neuroses has its genetic origin in their most fundamental purpose, which is to take flight from an unsatisfying reality into a more pleasurable world of phantasy ... To turn away from reality is at the same time to withdraw from the community of man.[35]

Animism and the Omnipotence of Thoughts

Primitives, in their use of magic, overestimate the power of wishes and thought processes generally, in a way similar to that of neurotics in modern society. For example, one of Freud's patients, who invented the term 'omnipotence of thought', which Freud uses in his third paper in *Totem and Taboo*, used to think that if he thought of someone he would then always meet them, or if asked how someone was, he would hear that they had died.[36]

In the early phases of civilization's development, the first phase of 'animism', people project their inner emotions and impulses outwards and thereby populate a universe with various spirits and supernatural powers. Freud's view here is Comtean; he thinks in terms of three stages for the progress of civilization, beginning with the animistic phase, to which modern obsessional or paranoid neurotics regress, going through an intermediate phase of religion, which is different from the first because people give the powers and omnipotence to gods, and not to themselves as they do in the magical phase of animism. The animistic phase would correspond with narcissism in the development of the child, the religious with object-choice of the parents. In the third phase, the scientific, men acknowledge their smallness and the necessities of nature, but some feelings of omnipotence remain, in the belief in the power of the human mind to conquer nature. This corresponds to the stage of maturity in the individual's development where he or she 'has renounced the pleasure principle, adjusted himself to reality and turned to the external world for the object of his desires'.[37]

There is a different tone at the end of this paper, where Freud writes that our attitude to primitives is like that we ought to take towards children, '. . . which we adults no longer understand and whose fullness and delicacy of feeling we have in consequence so greatly underestimated'.[38] This is not therefore the work of an out-and-out Comtean positivist, but of a man who had some sensitivity to the nuances of primitive world-views, as he did for the problems of children and of his patients.

Totemism

In the late nineteenth and early twentieth centuries, sociologists and anthropologists, including Émile Durkheim, were interested in the reports of travellers and missionaries who had been to parts of Australasia. They had been particularly interested in what was termed 'totemism', that is, the adoption of an animal, bird, reptile, insect or fish as a special emblem for a clan.[39] Members of the same totem clan, among the Australian Arunta, for example, had to marry outside the clan. The totem animal could not be killed nor harmed, except when special ritual killings were allowed and the totem animal might also be eaten. There may be other occasions when some members of the clan dress up as the totem animal, in ritual dancing, for example. The totem is often said to be an ancestor of the clan. (People in Sri Lanka, for instance, talk of a story about the lion who fathered their first ancestors on the island of Sri Lanka, or Ceylon.) Freud discussed anthropological theories of totemism, and offered his own reflections on it, based on psychoanalytic work with children and his observation of children. Children often feel they are close to animals, and relate to them very well, feeling like them, especially in their bodily functions. Often children develop animal phobias, even when they have always had good relations with a particular species of animal.

In the case of little Hans, with his phobia towards horses, there were ambivalent feelings present, of both interest and positive attitudes towards horses and a hatred for them. This phobia was linked with the displacement of fear of his father, as well as love for his father, on to horses.[40] Ferenczi had reported on little Arpad, who had a great interest and identification with chickens. At one time he was always making noises like a chicken. He was both fascinated by chickens and everything to do with them, but he also had a great dislike of them. Freud uses these two specific examples to suggest that psycho-analysis has shown that, in these cases, the animals or birds are being treated as substitutes for a parent, and the ambivalent feelings towards the animal reflect the feelings of the child towards the father—love and fear. He suggests that the totem animal is the father, which many peoples show when they talk of the totem animal as their ancestor. This explains why the totem animal may not normally be killed, and why the totemic clan is exagamous. Father may not be killed, although the wish to do so exists; the boy may not marry his mother even though the desire to do so is there. Hence the strong pro-hibitions.[41] The two acts which Oedipus committed, killing his father and having sexual intercourse with his mother, are forbidden in human societies because there is a strong desire to perform them both.

Totemism is the earliest form of religion, according to Freud, and he quotes Robertson Smith's *The Religion of the Semites* in which the sacrifice of an animal at the altar is said to be the most fundamental element in religion. A sacrifice may be made of anything which can be eaten or drunk; it is then consumed by all present as an actual act of fellowship between the people and their god. There is usually a period of mourning after the sacrifice of the animal or bird, and then a feast after the eating of the meal. The ambivalence which is being expressed on such occasions is caused by the fact that, emotion-ally, the animal is a surrogate for the father, loved and feared, hated and killed. The original band of brothers in the primal horde were excluded from sexual intercourse with any women by their father, and they formed a group, based on homosexual feelings, to perform the act that no one of them could do as a sole individual, namely, to kill their father. After the killing they ate the flesh of their father. Totemism originated after this to cope with the guilt the brothers felt, for the totem animal will protect them like a father, and they will love it, and not kill it under normal circumstances. The killing is repeated on ritual occasions, perhaps at first because the protection the totem gives them is not enough, or because they need to band together again to re-enact the crime which binds them all together, although they use a surrogate for the crime, not the actual father again.[42] All later forms of religion have to handle this problem, and do so even though they use different means.

The guilt about the act of parricide remains, and from the first act civilization, in the sense of social organization, art, moral restrictions and religion, began to develop.

> Society was now based on complicity in the common crime; religion was based on the sense of guilt and the remorse attaching to it; while morality was based partly on the exigencies of this society and partly on the penance demanded by the sense of guilt.[43]

These are propositions about the historical life of mankind, not at this point about the individual's re-enactment of the parricide in his own unconscious. Freud's thought is, at this point, at the very general level of the human species' evolutionary development, and it has been left undeveloped by analysts who have been preoccupied with individuals, even though there is only the hope of some alleviation of their troubles, given Freud's own analysis of civilization.

The application of the theory to some aspects of Christianity is outlined by Freud, without any claim to analyse all the aspects of that religion. The term 'god' can have other meanings outside those of interest to psychoanalysis, and psychoanalysis cannot itself comment on these. Religion is concerned with the feelings of *longing for the father*. Psychoanalysis finds, in work with individuals, that their notion of God, and their relations with God, parallels their notion of, and relations with, their father. In the analysis of the Wolf-man, for example, the relations of one patient to religion, and to his father, are traced in great detail. Here it is only possible to give a general flavour of this case-history:

> His love for his father, which had been manifest in his earliest period, was therefore the source of his energy in struggling against God and of his acuteness in criticizing religion. But on the other hand this hostility to the new God was not an original reaction either; it had its prototype in a hostile impulse against his father, which had come into existence under the influence of the anxiety-dream [concerning wolves and mentioned earlier in the analysis], and it was at bottom only a revival of that impulse.[44]

To return to Freud's analysis of sacrifice. The father is represented twice in religious sacrifices: as the god to whom the sacrifice is offered in order to offer satisfaction to the father; and as sacrificial victim, whether animal or human, as a commemoration, or re-enactment, of the original murder of the father. In Christianity, the problems in the emotional life of humanity are handled by one of the company of brothers offering himself as a sacrificial victim to the father, to redeem the brothers for the murder of the father—the original sin which haunts the brothers. With this sacrifice the son attains what had been an aim of the original murder of the father, namely, the status and power of the father, by becoming God himself. The atonement with the father was the more complete because 'the sacrifice was accompanied by a total renunciation of the women on whose account the rebellion against the father was started'.[45] The son:

> became God, beside, or more correctly, in place of, the father. A son-religion displaced the father-religion. As a sign of this substitution the ancient totem meal was revived in the form of communion, in which the company of brothers consumed the flesh and blood of the son—no longer the father—obtained sanctity thereby and identified themselves with him.[46]

Yet this communion is 'a fresh elimination of the father, a repetition of the guilty deed'.[47]

Did our ancestors actually kill the father? Or were they, like modern neurotics, mistaking a thought, or a wish, for a deed? They *wished* to kill and devour the father and then imagined that they had done so and felt guilty—is this what happened? Freud thought that there is a difference between neurotics and primitives, which is, that primitives proceed very often from thought to deed. Sometimes the deed is a substitute for thought, and so it is likely that there was a primal crime; they did actually kill the father and devour him. The parricide probably occurred in different parts of the globe, where groups were at the first stage in the evolution of *Homo sapiens*. It is probable that the killing was done, although Freud is not insistent on the point, *if* the horror of the actual deed has been faced emotionally and the resistance to the idea that it was a deed is not based on emotional resistances. Furthermore, thought and deed are not distinguished as sharply by primitives or children as they are by modern adults, and therefore the impact on primitives of the *wish* to kill and devour father(s) was as great, psychically, as the *deed* would be to modern people. There is point, therefore, in writing today that it was a deed, in order for the full impact to be experienced by us. Freud seems to be willing to put it this way, and then to want to insist again that it was an actual deed,

otherwise the impact is immediately lost once we allow ourselves to think that it did not happen. We give a sigh of relief—
father was not killed after all.

How do we know that there was an original crime of parricide? The emotional problems contained in 'customs, cere-
monies and dogmas left behind by the original relation to the
father may have made it possible for later generations to take
over their heritage of emotion'.[48]

Psychoanalysis, through its work with neurotics in modern
society, has found that the Oedipal conflicts are of the most
profound importance for later life, and the child's handling of
these earliest sexual feelings and actions towards both parents
has lasting significance on later relationships. These same
conflicts are found when psychoanalysis examines the rituals,
dogmas and morals found in myths and various religions,
including Christianity. Here they are conflicts which are
collective in character, not just within the individual. They
concern religion, morals, art and social organization, especially
political authority, in human society. Religious rituals and the
arts have been, and still are, concerned with handling this
unresolved problem handed down to the present by the
institutions which preserve the archaic heritage of mankind,
especially religions. The generations of this century will, in
their turn, hand on to the next generation the archaic unconscious problems, unless the guilt becomes too strong, the
rebellion so great, the need to kill and be killed so overwhelming
that we hand on nothing at all.

Criticisms

The criticisms of *Totem and Taboo* which have been made by
social anthropologists have often served to clarify issues left
obscure in the original work. The theory only has application
in specific types of social structure, namely, those that are
totemic in structure and matrilineal in descent, like some of the
Australian aboriginal societies Freud used in his work. The
theory is not applicable to all matrilineal societies, for not all
of these societies developed totemic rituals and structures. The
Trobriand Islanders, studied by Malinowski, are matrilineal,
but do not have either a totemic structure or totemic rituals.[49]
On Freud's theory, after the killing of the father, the brothers,
filled with guilt and remorse, set up totemic animals as father
substitutes to allay these feelings. They renounced the women

as sexual objects, even though their desires for the women had been the original motive for killing the father. In matrilineal societies, the father is missing as an important social figure, but there is not always a totemic system operating. No reparation seems to be being made for killing off the father.[50]

Evans-Pritchard's arguments against Freud have been very influential in anthropology and, by extension, within sociology. His main argument is stated succinctly in *Theories of Primitive Religion* as follows:

> Furthermore . . . in an individual's experience the acquisition of rites and beliefs precedes the emotions which are said to accompany them later in adult life. He learns to participate in them before he experiences any emotion at all, so the emotional state, whatever it may be, and if there is one, can hardly be the genesis and explanation of them. A rite is part of the culture the individual is born into, and it imposes itself on him from the outside like the rest of his culture. It is a creation of society, not of individual reasoning or emotion, though it may satisfy both; and it is for this reason that Durkheim tells us that a psychological interpretation of a social fact is invariably a wrong interpretation.[51]

The neurotic cannot be compared with a magician, for example, in a traditional society, for the latter learns his role from the culture into which he is born.

This argument does not really count against Freud, who was well aware of the cultural, institutional character of religious rituals, or of the magician's role. Freud is not saying that the individual feels the emotion which may underlie religious beliefs and practices, and that this is why they are performed. Freud's theory is attempting to explain how religious rituals and beliefs started in human cultures in the first instance. Evans-Pritchard writes that ritual as a part of culture 'is a creation of society'. What does this mean? In part it must mean that past generations of people have created a culture and it has been handed down to the present generation. This point is exactly what Freud was concerned to establish. His concern is with the culture which the past generations had created to be handed down. Why do human cultures contain something which can be called 'religion'? What were the problems these people were trying to handle with their various religious rituals and beliefs? These are difficult questions to answer, and there is little evidence available from the past to help. Freud's speculations provide a beginning for a social scientific understanding of religion's beginnings. They seem to have a reasonably clear meaning, and have the merit of linking diverse bits of information together in a coherent pattern, and it provides *an* explanation for the *content* of Judaism and Christianity especially, and may have some application for understanding and explaining the ritual developments in Hinduism and Buddhism, as will be illustrated in Chapter 5.

Psychoanalytic theory has the further merit of offering explanations about why specific individuals and groups within advanced, differentiated societies develop *a variety of different attitudes* to religion. Some people accept what they are taught by their culture, but some reject it. Still others search for new religious forms, or invent their own in a small group or sect. It is difficult to see how Evans-Pritchard's approach can begin to cope with this sort of variation in responses to a culture's religion.

The view which is developed by Freud that religious responses will reflect changes in unconscious attitudes towards a person's father enables his theory to provide an explanation of the changes in an individual's attitudes towards God. This is not to assert that his explanation is always true, but that it is a theoretical explanation which can be tested empirically, either in therapeutic encounters or, a more difficult task, with interviews using a representative sample. To have provided such an advance on existing theories is no mean achievement. It should be added that Freud explicitly admitted that religious phenomena, both at the individual level and at the societal level, are *overdetermined*, so other factors, such as political and economic changes, could also affect people's attitudes to religion.[52] It is an error, therefore, to oppose Freudian explanations of religion to those of Marx, Engels, Durkheim and Weber. He is complementary to these, and may be more powerful as an explanation in some situations and less so in others.

Evans-Pritchard is suspicious of the parallel drawn by Freud between the evolution of mankind from an animistic phase, through a religious phase, ending in a scientific one, and the growth to maturity of a child, from primary narcissism, through object-relations, primarily parents, to end as a mature, rational, reality-orientated adult. The parallel between primitives and infants is the weakest part of Freud's model, but to suggest that there are parallels between the responses of neurotics in modern societies and some primitive culture's ways of handling their situation is sometimes enlightening. It is a method of approach which is sensitive to the fact that neurotics in modern societies are those who are unable, for a variety of reasons, to get their version of reality accepted generally in the culture. The dominant groups in modern societies, whose definition of reality is accepted, are not necessarily non-neurotic in Freud's sense. Certainly Freud was critical of the religious versions of reality which were generally accepted among the middle classes in the first half of the twentieth century in Europe and America. Particular groups of people are able to set up their versions of reality in any human society, partly because they are politically and economically dominant. Neurotics in modern society are those whose ways of seeing the world are not generally socially validated. In some other cultures, there may have been socially validated ways of defining reality and of acting which would enable them to be less socially isolated, and therefore less neurotic because less privatized.

Freud's model of the collective evolution of some parts of humanity from archaic responses, found in religions, to more rational and reality-based responses, found in science and technology, may be little more than a description of what has happened, but it enables him to avoid the position of cultural relativism and its logical extension—nihilism. Furthermore, it provides the beginnings of a theory which discriminates between responses which offer short-term emotional comfort for people and changes in technology and economy which produce real gains in human happiness and lessen suffering in this life.

There are attractions to some anthropologists in thinking in a completely different way from Freud about totemism. The work of Lévi-Strauss is the most recent sustained attempt to do so. His structuralist theory puts the stress as primary on the classificatory coding in totemism and the intellectual component rather than on the emotional (or the social and emotional, as in Durkheim).

> As affectivity is the most obscure side of man, there has
> been the constant temptation to resort to it, forgetting that
> what is refractory to explanation is *ipso facto* unsuitable for use
> in explanation. A datum is not primary because it is
> incomprehensible: this characteristic indicates solely that an
> explanation, if it exists, must be sought on another level . . .
> It is this . . . which ruins Freud's attempt in *Totem and Taboo*.[53]

This argument might hold if it were the case that affectivity were obscure and incomprehensible. But to whom is affectivity obscure? To an observer from a different culture? Anthropologists usually spend some years learning about the cultures of 'their' people by living with them. Freud's technique of using material obtained from patients to help to understand the emotions of what he called 'primitives' does seem a way into the otherwise obscure area of other cultures' sentiments. The words used to make the feelings communicable to others from different cultures and sub-cultures are not attempts to turn emotions into intellectual propositions and to make them comprehensible in that sense. Affectivity is only incomprehensible if it is expected that emotions can be translated into thoughts with a proposition contained within them. The emotions of others need not remain obscure and incomprehensible to the sociologist or anthropologist. They can be written about in such a way that someone else is able to empathize with them. To write about emotions may mean that at times a piece of writing in social science reads more like a novel, indeed, may sometimes be a novel—Freud called *Moses and Monotheism* a novel, and apologized for some of his case-histories reading like novels rather than scientific treatises.

Apologies are unnecessary, for the technique and language developed by Freud has proved of very great value for anyone who works with 'disturbed' people, children or adults, in residential homes, or in individual therapy. There are few, if any, other such languages available. The social scientist only has to live, and perhaps work, in a mental hospital or therapeutic community to experience the need for making sense of the words and actions of some people in these settings. The language of psychoanalysis does provide a means for communicating about conscious and unconscious emotion in such circumstances. It is true, as sociologists have recently pointed out, that psychoanalysis, or a variant of it, can become a managerial ideology, and may be used by staff in hospitals in order to control and out-manœuvre patients, but this only makes sense as a piece of sociology if there is a possibility that in principle, if not in practice, there could be an uncorrupt ideology or 'science'.[54]

To return to Lévi-Strauss, the point has been made that emotion need not be seen as obscure and incomprehensible, and that Freud's importance is that he made a lasting contribution to explicating how the most obscure actions can be seen to make *emotional* sense. It is, therefore, a mistake to treat emotions as entirely secondary phenomena, and to use structure and intellect as the primary causal factors in sociology and anthropology. As Robin Fox argues in his well-balanced paper 'Totem and Taboo Reconsidered', structural anthropologists,

> have a curious feeling that rules are more stable than emotions. This is patently not so. Rules and customs can be changed overnight—and will be if they fail to meet needs—but motives, especially unconscious motives, are not so readily changeable. It is not, however, a matter of 'reducing' sociological explanations to psychological, but of seeing the relevance of the one for the other.[55]

Totem and Taboo does not just help our understanding of totemism. Freud, like Lévi-Strauss, is interested in how man developed from being among the higher anthropoids to being human. In other words, both are interested in the transition *Homo sapiens* made from Nature to Culture. The key factor for Freud is the prohibition on sexual desire, first set up by the father in the primal horde. The event which followed this restriction on instinctual action was the brothers banding together to kill their father, and the consequent guilt they experienced. 'Articulate thought', in Lévi-Strauss's sense language and intellect, follow on from this basic event of a bio-psychological character.[56]

The problems to which this event gave rise still remain for later generations of human beings, handed down to later generations through myth, rituals, arts, philosophy and, above all, religions. This last is most important, and has been missed on the whole in the anthropologists' discussions about *Totem and Taboo*. (For example, Robin Fox's paper, mentioned above, and the best recent discussion of the problems, ignores other, later, religions and concentrates on totemism.) The assertion about the murder of the father setting problems for the unconscious life of all later generations has been left unexamined in anthropology and sociology. This seems strange, as the complex of problems concerning fathers, God, God's Son, the sacrifice of the Son, and the ambivalence towards women, are fundamental in Christianity. It is still a major world religion, adhered to by millions, and has affected the cultures of Europe, Russia, the United States, Canada, Australia and New Zealand, many societies in Latin America, and in sub-Saharan Africa.

Freud seems to have been right in seeing that, at least in

Christianity and its associated arts, both in works positively related to it and those antagonistic to it, there is to be found the theme of God the Father, and God the Son, who is sacrificed and eaten in Holy Communion. His assertion that the problem remains and is handed down from the first generation of *Homo sapiens* to the present one in the instituticns of religion and art seems to be, *prima facie*, very plausible. It is an assertion that certainly needs bringing into the debate about the Primal Event, and the usefulness of that speculative hypothesis can be seen in relation to the *content* of Christianity, at least.

NOTES AND REFERENCES

1. S. Freud, *Group Psychology and the Analysis of the Ego* (1921). Standard Edition, Vol. 18. References to the revised edition, translated by J. Strachey, London, 1955, p. 1.
2. Ibid., p. 6.
3. Ibid., p. 7.
4. Ibid., p. 11.
5. Ibid.
6. Ibid., p. 13.
7. Ibid., p. 18.
8. Ibid., p. 23.
9. Ibid., p. 31.
10. Ibid., p. 33.
11. Ibid.
12. M. Mead, *Sex and Temperament in Three Primitive Societies*, London, 1935.
13. S. Freud, *Group Psychology and the Analysis of the Ego*, edition cit., p. 34.
14. Ibid., p. 40.
15. Ibid., p. 42.
16. Ibid., p. 45.
17. Ibid., p. 48.
18. Ibid., p. 52.
19. Ibid.
20. Ibid., p. 53.
21. Ibid.
22. Ibid., p. 54.
23. Ibid., p. 55.
24. Ibid., p. 56. (See also Postscript B.)
25. Ibid., p. 63.
26. See, e.g., F. Steiner, *Taboo*, London, 1956. And M. Douglas, *Purity and Danger*, London, 1966.
27. S. Freud, *Totem and Taboo* (1913), Standard Edition, Vol. 13. Reference to Routledge & Kegan Paul edition, London, 1950 and 1960, Chapter Two, 'Taboo and Emotional Ambivalence'.
28. Ibid., 1960 edition, p. 47.
29. Ibid., p. 45.
30. See, e.g., G. Lienhardt, *Divinity and Experience, the Religion of the Dinka*, London, 1961.
31. Freud, *Totem and Taboo*, edition cit., p. 61.

32. Ibid., pp. 64–5.
33. See the discussion in Chapter 2.
34. Freud, *Totem and Taboo*, edition cit., p. 72.
35. Ibid., p. 74. At this stage in the development of his theory, Freud thought that 'sexual needs are not capable of uniting man...' (p. 74) in the way the self-preservative instincts are. This view is changed in *Group Psychology* (1921), as was shown above in the present chapter. See also Freud's paper 'Obsessive Acts and Religious Practices' (1907), available in P. Rieff (ed., *Character and Culture*, New York, 1963.
36. Freud, *Totem and Taboo*, edition cit., p. 86.
37. Ibid., p. 90.
38. Ibid., p. 99.
39. See, e.g., E. Durkheim, *The Elementary Forms of the Religious Life* (1912).
40. See S. Freud, 'Analysis of a Phobia in a Five-Year-Old Boy' (1909).
41. Freud, *Totem and Taboo*, edition cit., pp. 127–33.
42. Ibid., pp. 144–5.
43. Ibid., p. 146.
44. S. Freud, 'From the History of an Infantile Neurosis' (1918), available in M. Gardiner, *The Wolf-Man and Sigmund Freud*, London, 1972. Reference to Penguin edition, Harmondsworth, 1973, p. 229. (Copyright, Basic Books Inc., 1971.)
45. Freud, *Totem and Taboo*, edition cit., p. 154.
46. Ibid.
47. Ibid., p. 155.
48. Ibid., p. 159.
49. B. Malinowski, *Sex and Repression in Savage Society*, London, 1927.
50. See R. Fox, 'Totem and Taboo Reconsidered', in E. Leach (ed.), *The Structural Study of Myth and Totemism*, London, 1967, pp. 171–2.
51. E. E. Evans-Pritchard, *Theories of Primitive Religion*, London, 1965, p. 46.
52. See Freud, *Totem and Taboo*, edition cit., p. 100, Chapter IV.
53. C. Lévi-Strauss, *Totemism* (1962), New York, 1963. Reference to Penguin edition, Harmondsworth, 1969, p. 140.
54. See, e.g., R. Rapoport, *Community as Doctor*, London, 1960. And E. Goffman, *Asylums*, New York, 1961.
55. R. Fox, 'Totem and Taboo Reconsidered', in op. cit., p. 176.
56. See C. Lévi-Strauss, *The Savage Mind* (1962), London, 1966.

5 The Archaic Heritage

> There is not one of the erroneous and superstitious beliefs of mankind that are supposed to have been superseded but has left vestiges at the present day in the lower strata of civilized peoples or even in the highest strata of cultivated society. All that has once lived clings tenaciously to life. Sometimes one feels inclined to doubt whether the dragons of primeval ages are really extinct—Sigmund Freud, 'Analysis Terminable and Interminable' (1937), in P. Rieff (ed.), *Therapy and Technique*.

One of the most important of Freud's contributions to the understanding of modern societies lies in his notion of the archaic heritage as an active element in social life. The archaic heritage consists of religion, tradition and morality, most of which operates unconsciously in people, and yet affects their connections with society. Earlier sociologists paid considerable attention to the religious, moral and collective sentiments of societies, but recently this has not been brought into models of society as fully as it once was. This may reflect the fact that society has changed since the early days of sociology, and religion and its associated values, emotions and beliefs is no longer as important as it used to be. It may, equally, reflect a blind spot in sociology.

Freud's theory provides a conceptualization of the unconscious emotions which used to operate in religions. If religion is less significant than it used to be in modern societies, it may be that the emotional issues are resolved too, or that they have found other modes of expression, in the arts and entertainments, and in political movements. This chapter will consider two major works of Freud, *The Future of an Illusion* (1927) and *Moses and Monotheism* (1939), both of which are concerned with the archaic heritage in society.

The Future of an Illusion

> Every individual is virtually an enemy of civilization . . .[1]

This surprising, indeed shocking, proposition is at the heart of Freud's view of human society and its historical development in the past and in the future. It goes against most Western liberal ideas, and also against what many Marxist intellectuals have thought about man. Freud cannot be said to have been unaware of the variability of human nature in different societies which have other economic arrangements and different cultural aims from those of Europe and America.

Unlike many people since the end of the Second World War, Freud, writing in the late 1920s, remained impressed with the progress made in the use of technology in improving man's life, although not unaware of the potential it had for destruction. This development of technique in sewerage, transport, electricity, etc., was, he thought, among the most important achievements of civilization.

Civilization's other important component, in addition to the technical means for controlling nature, is the corpus of regulations which exist for adjusting the relations between men. Most important among these are those which concern 'the distribution of the available wealth'.[2] Much of the hostility towards civilization felt by people in the suppressed classes is understandable.

> If, however, a culture has not got beyond a point at which satisfaction of one portion of its participants depends upon the suppression of another, and perhaps, larger portion—and this is the case in all present-day cultures—it is understandable that the suppressed people should develop an intense hostility towards a culture whose existence they make possible by their work, but in whose wealth they have too small a share.[3]

Freud accepted that a more equal distribution of wealth would do more to lessen such conflict, and help further the development of civilization for mankind as a whole, than any other reform. It is not, however, the only source of problems, nor of the hostility towards civilization experienced by many people, if not everyone.

Civilization has to be built upon coercion and instinctual renunciations. Some of these renunciations are universal, and still operate in modern peoples. The prohibitions on incest, cannibalism and the lust for killing are examples of such basic renunciations that all civilizations have had since the primal horde phase. Coercion is not needed today for most people in these areas, for the evolution of mankind has led to the internalization of these prohibitions; the super-ego, which develops in most children in modern societies, controls these. In other areas, especially work, most people do not want to renounce enough of their instinctual satisfactions necessary to produce the wealth. Ordinary people have been coerced by minorities to perform the necessary tasks. Modern societies use money as a means of cajoling people to do work they would not otherwise want to do. In 'underdeveloped' societies, the socialist, capitalist or communist élites have to find means to coerce or cajole people into working in order to build up wealth in their previously exploited economies. Freud thought that the masses were lazy, and did not want to impose the instinctual renunciations necessary for civilization on themselves.

> It is only through the influence of individuals who can set
> an example, and whom the masses recognize as their leaders,
> that they can be induced to perform the work and undergo
> the renunciations on which the existence of civilization
> depends.[4]

This appears reactionary because Freud states it in such general, ahistorical terms.

Civilizations offer compensations to some for the renunciations needed to maintain the technical achievements, and the wealth. In class societies, the élites have found compensation in art. Art offers 'substitutive satisfactions for the oldest and still most deeply felt cultural renunciations, and for that reason it serves as nothing else does to reconcile a man to the sacrifices he has made on behalf of civilization'.[5] The masses are often emotionally attached to their masters, and this lessens their hostility to the social order. They derive narcissistic satisfaction from their cultural ideals when they compare themselves with others; '. . . the right to despise the people outside it (their culture) compensates them for the wrongs they suffer within their own unit'.[6] Such satisfactions have enabled civilizations to persist over time, and they have not, therefore, been overthrown by the suppressed masses.

The most important element in the 'psychic inventory' of a civilization is, however, religion. This is of key theoretical importance in many of Freud's writings, both in the more sociological works and in many case-histories. It is necessary to understand the simple distinction between being a non-believer, and even in some respects opposed to religion's influence, and making a judgement about the theoretical and practical importance of religion in human societies. Social scientists seem to confuse the two, and because they oppose religion and are unbelievers, they do little work on religion in human societies. Conversely, they often assume, as do others, that someone working on religion theoretically and empirically does so from the standpoint of a believer, with the underlying assumption, 'Why else would anyone be interested in such a traditional, out-dated, and unimportant institution?' They are, therefore, saved from examining their own basic assumptions about religion. It is, however, because religion is about the archaic heritage of humanity, and involves relations with parent figures, particularly the father, that one would expect emotional reactions to the subject; either religion is the most important part of life, and immune to scientific investigation for that reason, or it is too trivial to be worth a working scientist's time. From the perspective of psychoanalytic theory, religion has a key importance in human societies.

Freud assumes that nature dominates man and seems to threaten humanity with hostile happenings—earthquakes, floods and storms, illnesses and death itself. Religious ideas offer a way of coping with this situation by suggesting that these events occur perhaps to punish men for wrongdoing, and that the gods who cause these happenings can be placated by worship and sacrifices. It is the feeling of helplessness which gives rise to religious ideas and practices which in turn offer comfort and some protection, partly by giving men confidence. This feeling of helplessness has been experienced before, ontogenetically, during the person's own babyhood and childhood, and phylogenetically, when human society began to evolve. The gods, and later the one God, come to be like parents. First, godesses offer comfort, just as the infant's mother did; then male gods, or God, offer protection against external reality, as a father does for a child.[7] Gods are also dangerous figures, again like father. This is perhaps because the infant's relation with its mother is disturbed when the child begins to perceive its father as another figure in the family. These ambivalent feelings are transferred to the gods.

Religious ideas are not checkable by ordinary experience, asserts Freud. They are even admitted to be absurd by Tertullian—'Credo quia absurdum'—and believed in for that very reason; but this is an argument which does not enable us to distinguish which absurd propositions we are to believe Freud thought. Nor does it impress Freud to be told that religious propositions are 'as if' types of proposition, and that one should live 'as if' it were true that there were gods, or God, for there is nothing to lose this way. This argument can make little appeal to anyone not caught up in the artifices of philosophy.[8] The problem arises: why is religion so widespread in the evolution of humanity, and still continues to be so in the modern world? It does not commend itself on the basis of observable experience in the everyday world, and it cannot be easily and rationally justified. So how can its appeal be explained?

For psychoanalysis, religion is an 'illusion'—a technical term, meaning not an error, but an idea, or belief, based on wishes. Delusions are based on wishes too, but they are in contradiction to reality. An illusion is not necessarily false nor contradictory. For example, a girl may have an illusion that a prince will come and marry her. This could happen; but it is based on a wish. That a Messiah will come and establish a New Age is a belief based on a wish too, and it might just happen. It is either an illusion, or a delusion, depending upon how realistic one thinks the belief to be. The appeal of religions is not based on evidence, for there is very little, nor on reason, for the reasons offered for faith are unconvincing, but on illusions—'fulfilments of the oldest, strongest and most urgent wishes of mankind'.[9] These wishes concern the need for protection through love from a parent; the need for relief from the feeling of helplessness which adults retain from their babyhood; and the desire to see justice fulfilled, which is met by positing another, future, life.

> Thus we call a belief an illusion when a wish-fulfilment is a prominent factor in its motivation, and in doing so we disregard its relation to reality, just as the illusion itself sets no store by verification.[10]

This last point implies that psychoanalysis, as such, is not concerned with the truth or falsity of religious beliefs, and that it rather counteracts the earlier arguments about religious beliefs being neither justified by sense experience nor rational arguments. It seems that Freud did regard most religious beliefs as unjustified by experience and by reason, and that they therefore required an explanation in terms of psychoanalysis. This seems to be the most coherent position to hold. It does allow that some religious beliefs could be defended by more rational arguments and by experience, as some people have tried to do,[11] yet the appeal of religions for most people is emotional rather than rational and intellectual.

In *The Future of an Illusion*, the use of the term 'religion' is one which fits the Jewish–Islamic–Christian complex of religions, which are built upon the notion of a Creator God. Freud's theory is less worked out in relationship to Hinduism, Taoism and Buddhism, especially Theravada Buddhism, which explicitly teaches there is no Creator God. Freud's theory might be applicable to an understanding of the popular 'corruptions' of Buddha's teachings—corrupt, that is, from the point of view of Theravada monks. There are many popular devotions to the Buddha's images, even in Theravada countries, such as Sri Lanka (Ceylon) and Burma, and they are not unlike Roman Catholic devotions to the saints. Specific things are requested—offerings of flowers for passing an examination, or burning oil for relief from illness in the next life, and sometimes in this life, and thanks given for safe journeys, or the safe birth of a baby. There are notions of a Creator in Hinduism, and in many of the indigenous religions in Africa. The example of Theravada Buddhism is the most important because it has explicitly taught that there is no Creator God, yet Buddha has been turned into a father-like figure in popular devotion against the best intentions of the monks.[12] The belief in rebirth, held by all Buddhists as well as Hindus, would seem to be an 'illusion' in Freud's sense. It could be true, but it is difficult to prove it empirically. So the best way to begin to understand such a belief system would be in terms of the emotions and unconscious feelings involved; in this case, the wish to live again in Hinduism, and in Buddhism the desire to return to the womb-like state—Nirvana.

Returning to the argument in *The Future of an Illusion* an imaginary antagonist argues that civilization depends upon people continuing to believe in God, otherwise they will not act in a moral way. Chaos, murder and violence will ensue if people ceased believing in God. In reply, Freud considers the rationalist argument that murder is not engaged in because it makes social life impossible if anyone is allowed to murder anyone else.[13] As he had argued in *Totem and Taboo*, murder occurred in the first human groups, and the prohibition on killing came from the father. The antagonist as a religious believer is right to assert that the moral code comes from a sacred source, which he calls God, but which is really the Primal Father. So should psychoanalysis do anything to undermine people's religious beliefs? Or should it remain a neutral research instrument, and not become a *Weltanschuung* of an anti-religious kind? Freud's reply is that the research method of psychoanalysis has revealed that religion has not helped men to be happy, nor moral, nor cultured and intelligent. Religion is the 'universal obsessional neurosis of humanity' which has been an essential stage for humanity to pass through, in the same way as every child must have a neurotic phase.

> This is because so many instinctual demands which will later be unserviceable cannot be suppressed by that rational operation of the child's intellect but have to be tamed by acts of repression behind which, as a rule, lies the motive of anxiety.[14]

Normally the growing child overcomes these neuroses spontaneously; those which are not overcome can be cleared up later in psychoanalysis. Humanity, before it had acquired a strong enough intellect and developed science and technology, had achieved the instinctual renunciations which make communal life possible by using purely affective forces. The neurosis of humanity arose out of the relation to the father, just as it does for the child. It has the advantage for believers of saving them from having to invent their own personal neurosis, and they gain from the social nature of religion rather than the purely private character of a personal neurosis.[15] However, the evolution of mankind has reached the point where it is better to leave religion behind, for it does comprise 'a system of wishful illusions together with a disavowal of reality, such as we find in an isolated form nowhere else but in amentia, in a state of blissful hallucinatory confusion'.[16]

The task of psychoanalysis is to bring the intellect to bear on religion, and to replace the effects of repressions with the rational operations of the intellect. There is no point in continuing to veil the truth in symbolism, for the truths are so distorted, and systematically disguised, in religions that they are unrecognizable as truths to most people. Just as it is unwise to tell children that the stork brings babies, using the stork as a symbol, because this leads children astray if they take it literally, so, in religion, the symbolic language used interferes with the process of developing rationality in human affairs.[17] The time has come for mankind to begin to live without the neurotic relics contained in religions.

The imaginary antagonist next argues that the argument contains a contradiction—namely, that as men are held to be primarily governed by their emotions in the attachment they have to religion, rationality will be of no avail against it. Nevertheless, we are asked by psychoanalysis to put our faith in reason in place of affects. Freud replies to his own argument, that there is no need for man always to be ruled by emotions. It is true descriptively that such is the situation for most men and women now, but it is not necessarily inevitable. Children show a radiant intelligence which contrasts with the 'feeble intellectual powers of the average adult'.[18] Perhaps it is religious education which is in large part to blame for this, together with the restrictions on sexuality imposed upon children in schools and colleges. This latter is especially severe in its effects on women, but both boys and girls are stunted in their intellectual growth, both by religion forbidding some ideas and teaching some false ones, and by the restrictions on the sexual researches of children. Children should be educated without religion. It is only through education that any change is possible in this area; it cannot be done by force, and at one stroke, as was attempted in the French and Russian Revolutions. The voice of the rational intellect may be soft, but it is in the end insistent and victorious.

The aims of religion's God are the same as the aims of reason—love of mankind and decrease in suffering. Science and reason seem now to offer mankind more hope of happiness and a decrease in suffering than is offered in religions. Freud writes of 'our God, Logos' who will fulfil those of our wishes which nature allows, but he will do it gradually and slowly.[19]

It is interesting, however, that Freud does not mention the Gospel of Saint John, which is also dedicated to *Logos*. It begins:

> In the beginning was the Word, and the Word was with God, and the Word was God. The same was in the beginning with God.

The notion of the 'Word' is a translation for the Greek *Logos*. This does not invalidate Freud's approach, but it does complicate matters more than he suggests. There may prove to be less difference between some modern versions of Christianity and Buddhism and psychoanalysis than appears at first sight. Erich Fromm, in his book *Psychoanalysis and Religion*, comes to this conclusion, and argues that Freud is more akin to the great world religious teachers than is Jung.

> Freud holds that the aim of human development is the achievement of these ideals: knowledge (reason, truth, logos), brotherly love, reduction of suffering, independence and responsibility. These constitute the *ethical core* of all great religions on which Eastern and Western culture are based, the teachings of Confucius and Lao-tse, Buddha, the Prophets and Jesus [my italics].[20]

Jung is less interested in reason, more in the emotional symbolism in religions. How far it is sensible to smooth over the differences between religions, and between them and psycho-analysis, in this way is debatable, for it too much lessens the advances made by Freud in the understanding of religion.

There is a further discussion of religion in *Civilization and Its Discontents*, published three years after *The Future of an Illusion*. The central arguments of this work will be discussed in Chapter 6, but here the points Freud makes about religious feelings will be mentioned briefly. It had been suggested that religions were based on a feeling of something limitless and unbounded, a sense of eternity. This feeling was common even to many people who had no formal religious beliefs. It was unaccounted for in *The Future of an Illusion*, and yet it is more a basic and fundamental source of religion than are illusory and delusory beliefs. Freud attempts to give a psychoanalytic account of the state of the baby before the first object-relations begin, when the ego and the world are not differentiated. '. . . originally the ego includes everything, later it separates off an external world from itself'.[21] This primary ego-feeling of an all-embracing kind may persist in some people, alongside the narrower and more clearly demarcated ego-feeling of maturity. It is probably recontacted in the practices of Yoga and the meditations of mystics, and comes to be given an ideational content of a bond with the universe and a sense of 'limitlessness'. Religion is based on the longing for the father, and the infant's wish for a protector to defend it against feelings of helplessness. This is the main appeal of religion to the vast majority of believers, who may or may not have the 'oceanic' feeling of the more mystically inclined.

Considering the discussion of religion in *The Future of an Illusion* and elsewhere, especially in *Civilization and Its Discontents*, it is clear that Freud thought of religion as being in need of explanation because it was irrational and did not further the happiness of mankind. Although it is true that he understood the distinction between a logical argument about the truth—falsity of religious propositions, and an empirical analysis of who holds which beliefs, in which groups—Freud's explanatory theory is based on a judgement about the rationality or otherwise of religious beliefs and practices. This gives it a bite that is lacking in much sociological research, which remains descriptive and under-theorized, and which sees all meaning systems as logically equal. Ernest Gellner and Alastair

MacIntyre have both argued for the need for a judgement to be made about the degree of internal coherence and rationality in belief systems, before the sociologist can know what type of explanation to apply to the beliefs he is studying.[22] Freud did this, even though his *explicit* view of science led him to think the scientist should not make judgements of this kind. This means that because it was an explanatory one, his theory of religion has retained an interest long after later more empiricist studies have lost scientific interest.

Moses and Monotheism

Moses and Monotheism, the last book which Freud published, appeared after he arrived in London in the summer of 1938, having left Vienna as the Nazis took over. It was an attempt to continue the themes developed over twenty-five years earlier in *Totem and Taboo*. The first two chapters of *Moses and Monotheism* were first published as articles in *Imago* (1937 and 1938), and sought to establish, in purely historical terms, that there had been two figures with the name 'Moses' in Jewish development. One had been an Egyptian, who had tried to keep alive the Egyptian Aten religion when it looked like disappearing in Egypt itself from about the year 1315 B.C. He had chosen the Jews in Egypt as a people to whom he would teach this religion. Freud notes that *mose* is the Egyptian word for child. He also points out that many hero myths exist in which the hero is found in a basket, on water. Usually the hero is then brought up in a lowly family and achieves high rank later. Moses was brought up in a high-ranking Egyptian family and then, later in life, led a lowly people, the Jews.[23]

More importantly, there is the evidence of circumcision. Circumcision was an Egyptian practice which Moses introduced to the Jewish people as a token of holiness.[24] The Egyptian god, Aten, was a universal god of all creation, he alone was god, and there were no myths and no magic or sorcery associated with his religion. No images of him have been discovered, no doubt because the religion forbade making images, although hymns have been found.[25] There was no mention of life after death, which was probably unique in Egyptian religion, for all other forms of religion in Egypt revolved around the cults of life after death. This was the God the Egyptian Moses introduced to the Jews. There was another Moses, a Midianite, who introduced the god Yahweh, a local volcanic god—'a coarse, narrow-

minded, local god, violent and bloodthirsty, he had promised
his followers to give them a land flowing with milk and honey'.[26]
The God of the Egyptian Moses was more joyous, against
magic, and a universal god. He remained in the background in
much of Jewish history, but appeared again in the Prophets'
teachings. The Egyptian Moses was murdered, Freud claims,
and this had profound implications for Jewish religion.[27]

Freud had not dared to publish the third chapter of the book
in Vienna. The Catholic Church seemed to offer some hope of
resistance to the Nazis. He thought the Church would be upset
by his researches on Moses and monotheism, and he wanted to
avoid being prevented from practising psychoanalysis. Once in
London, after it had become clear that the Nazis were in control
in Austria, he published his ideas. The figure of Moses, the key
figure for Freud in Judaism, seemed to preoccupy him in these
last years of his life, and it is only understandable that people
see Freud as still wrestling with his own father in this intellectual
activity. It was Freud who made modern people aware of the
unconscious influence of the father. However, it is important to
distinguish between the unconscious elements in work of the
kind he pursued, and the element of correspondence with
reality, or rationality of thought, which is to be distinguished
from phantasy.

Earlier, in 1914, Freud had published a piece in *Imago* on
'The Moses of Michelangelo'.[28] The surprising thing is that he
published this *anonymously*. Moses seems to have had a fascination for Freud. He must have been working on the paper about
the same time as he was writing the papers of *Totem and Taboo*,
or just afterwards. He took up the links again between Moses
and the killing of the primal father at the end of his life.

Religion can only be understood 'on the pattern of individual
neurotic symptoms'.[29] This is a postulate, basic to the psychoanalytic understanding of religions. They are not caused by
individual neurosis, but it is being asserted that religion is best
understood as if it were a symptom of a neurosis of humanity as
a whole. The parricide committed by human beings occurred
over a period of perhaps thousands of years, and was repeated
innumerable times all over the globe, for it was the primal
horde that marked humanity off from nature, and began the
social, historical and cultural evolution of man.

The first form of a social organization came about with a
renunciation of instinct, a recognition of mutual *obligations*, the

introduction of definite *institutions*, pronounced invioable (holy)
—that is to say, the beginnings of morality and justice. Each
individual renounced his ideal of acquiring his father's
position for himself and of possessing his mother and sisters.
Thus the *taboo on incest* and the injunction to *exogamy* came
about.[30]

The killing and the eating of the father which developed out of
this social organization is part of the repressed, archaic heritage
of mankind. Using the work he had done on the influence of a
trauma, on a child under five years of age, and its effects on the
later genesis of neurosis, Freud analysed religions as consisting
of positive and negative reactions to a trauma which has been
forgotten.

In childhood, traumas have a sexual and aggressive component, the two not being distinguished by young children—
the primal scene, when seen by a child under five, is taken to be
an attack by father on mother. The trauma underlying religion,
which has been for long periods of time forgotten, remaining
latent in the unconscious, was also a mixture of sexuality and
aggression. Just as the trauma in the first five years of life of a
child is forgotten, but appears later in the symptoms of neurotic
illness, so the trauma of parricide has been forgotten, but
makes its appearance in symptoms which in this case are
religious actions and beliefs. One set of reactions to a traumatic
experience are termed 'positive', a non-evaluative term, and
consist of compulsions to repeat an action or thought, and
fixation at an early stage of development. 'Negative' reactions
are avoidances, inhibitions and phobias. The positive reactions
are attempts to re-create the trauma, to re-experience it, or to
set up a relationship analogous to an earlier one. For example, a
man with a strong attachment to his mother may marry and
divorce a number of women in search of the first important
relationship with his mother. In religions, the ritual of sacrifice,
and Holy Communion in the Christian mass, is in part an
attempt to re-enact the original parricide. The negative
reactions have the opposite aim: 'that nothing of the forgotten
traumas shall be remembered and nothing repeated'.[31] They
run in the opposite direction to the positive reactions, although
there is a sense in which they too are fixations to the original
trauma. The trauma is still exerting an influence, but in the
negative reactions it pushes against the trauma being re-
created. Christianity probably masks the original parricide by
avoidance of sacrificing the father, using the son instead.

At this point, an example not discussed by Freud is interesting. In Wagner's opera *Parsifal* the trauma of parricide is there in the background, but is unconscious.[32] The father-king figure, Amfortas, is mortally wounded but cannot die. Nor can Kundry, a woman who saw Christ on his way to Calvary, and who is being used by a magician, Klingsor, to tempt Parsifal to fall into sensuality. At the end of the opera, Parsifal heals Amfortas by touching him with a spear, and Kundry is able, at last, to die. If the notion of negative and positive reactions is applied here, it can be seen that the legends surrounding Parsifal, and this opera in particular, are dealing with the trauma of mankind—parricide. The negative reaction pushes for avoidance of the traumatic experience, and thus Amfortas is healed by the spear. It is Kundry who dies. This is a displacement; it is presented as 'a good thing' that at last she is able to die. The fixation is to parricide, but instead of Amfortas being killed by the spear, which is what, after all, people normally assume is what a spear will be used for, he is healed by it. To see Parsifal kill Amfortas would be too near to the unconscious traumatic memory, so the negative reaction pushes for a displacement. The strong appeal of the opera, and its special status as a near-religious ceremonial rather than secular opera, point to the depth of the unconscious material involved.[33] The intertwining of the Christian Holy Communion, the legend of Parsifal, and the renunciation of the women, suggest that the primal trauma is being handled, but indirectly. This example is as an illustration of how psychoanalytic theory might be applied. It is not empirical evidence of a very 'hard' kind, but it shows the theme at work in an art form to add to the material in the Christian mass and Holy Communion.

The Jewish people seem to be in a continuous latency period in that they have forgotten that they murdered Moses, and, before him, the Primal Father. They produced an attempt to cope with the repressed memory in the form of Christianity, where a son was offered as a sacrifice to the father. But this has been turned against them and they are accused of having murdered Christ, God's only Son, or, indeed, God Himself. They will not admit anything of this, and so suffer under the effects of the traumatic experience.

For Freud, antisemitism cannot be explained fully in terms of the Jews being a minority group who are disliked by the host society because they are different. Other societies have examples of religious ethnic-group hatreds and wars, as in India, between

Muslims and Hindus, which can be explained economically and socially. There is something unique about anti-Jewishness among Christian and Muslim peoples. The unconscious seems involved in a deep way, in part due to their setting themselves up as a Chosen People of God the Father. This continues to arouse jealousy among others. Furthermore, the Germans and others who in Freud's time were antisemitic, but who had not yet, as far as it was known, introduced the Final Solution, had been coerced into Christianity quite recently in their history. Their anti-Jewish feelings and actions were, to Freud, caused by a hatred of Christianity.[34]

Freud's interest in Moses is, at root, an attempt to understand the Jews and the fate they were to undergo in Europe. That fate is connected with the primal parricide, and involves at least those nations influenced by Christianity and Islam, that is, those peoples who share the Old Testament sacred writings with the Jews and claim the same God, the same Father in heaven.

The archaic heritage which Freud postulated was innate in all of humanity, not just the Jews, and is of phylogenetic origin; it is not the same as the ontogenetic conflicts of the individual, although it is analogous to such conflicts in the way its effects are to be grasped and understood.

> The behaviour of neurotic children towards their parents in the Oedipus and castration complex abounds in such reactions, which seem unjustified in the individual case and only become intelligible phylogenetically—by their connection with the experience of earlier generations.[35]

The repressed archaic heritage is unconscious. It is subject to the same mechanisms as other parts of the id. The ego, which itself develops out of the id, excludes certain impressions and processes as a defensive process, which become not just pre-conscious, and therefore capable of being remembered easily, but repressed into the id, where powerful emotional factors keep them forgotten.

The archaic heritage consists of dispositions and of actual subject-matter: 'memory traces of the experience of earlier generations'.[36] This assumption means that peoples can be analysed in ways comparable to those used with individuals, for the gulf between individual and group psychology is bridged by the survival of memory traces: '. . . men have always known (in this special way) that they once possessed a primal father and killed him'.[37] The memory of the parricide was both important enough, and repeated often enough, to enter the archaic heritage. It was re-enacted with the murder of Moses and of Jesus.

> A tradition that was based only on communication could not lead to the compulsive character that attaches to religious phenomena. It would be listened to, judged, and perhaps dismissed, like any other piece of information from outside; it would never attain the privilege of being liberated from the constraint of logical thought. It must have undergone the fate of being repressed, the condition of lingering in the unconscious, before it is able to display such powerful effects on its return, to bring the masses under its spell, as we have seen with astonishment and hitherto without comprehension in the case of religious tradition.[38]

This claim has been too often ignored, or too lightly dismissed, by sociologists and psychoanalysts. The former have not attached much importance to emotions and to the unconscious in their analyses of society and its development, or not at least recently. The latter have been too preoccupied, rightly or wrongly, with the problems of individual analysis to pay much attention to these larger-scale ideas of Freud. Indeed, they have been embarrassed by them, having so internalized the epistemological criteria of positivism, empiricism and pragmatism.

The Jews' special characteristics derive from the religion which was given to them by Moses, which stressed one God who was invisible and would not allow images of Himself to be made for worship. Freud sees this aspect of Judaism as marking an advance away from sensuality, from what can be seen or touched, towards intellectuality, thought processes about unseen things, such as God. This the Jews retained, and the associated renunciation of the instincts of sexuality and aggression. It gave them a feeling of being special. This same feeling occurs in an individual who has renounced some instinctual pleasure as a result of an internal demand of the super-ego, as distinct from an external prohibition. The super-ego is that part of the ego which has internalized the demands of the parents and educators for instinctual renunciation.

> When the ego has brought the super-ego the sacrifice of an instinctual renunciation, it expects to be rewarded by receiving more love from it. The consciousness of deserving this love is felt by it as pride.[39]

The same applies in a similar way to a people, such as, in this case, the Jews. Moses, the great man, the father of the Jewish people, was the authority for whom the renunciations were performed. After the work of Moses was repressed, and he had been killed, the Prophets reasserted the tradition of his religion —the return of the repressed—in the form of demands for a return to a more ethical religion, away from the sensual worship of images. The Prophets represent the will of the father, Moses, and before him the great Primal Father. It is this which gives ethical demands, such as those forbidding incest, their sacred character:

> We confidently expect that an investigation of all other cases of sacred prohibition would lead to the same conclusion as in that of the horror of incest: *that what is sacred was originally nothing other than the prolongation of the will of the primal father* [my italics].[40]

The religion of Moses and the Prophets has never avowed that the father was killed. This repressed element, however, reappears in the work of Saint Paul, who, although a Jew, made Christianity into a universal religion. Christianity reproaches the Jews as follows:

> They will not accept it as true that they murdered God, whereas we admit it and have been cleansed of that guilt.[41]

Christianity tried to make a reconciliation with the father for the crime against him, but it ended by putting the son in place of the father.

> It has not escaped the fate of having to get rid of the father.[42]

The implications of *Moses and Monotheism* are far-reaching, and have been left undeveloped by psychoanalysts. The division between individual and social psychology seems to disappear. As the psychoanalyst, or therapist, delves into the unconscious of his or her patients, he will come up against phylogenetic material, memory traces of the experiences not of the patient, but of earlier generations of humanity. For example, the ways in which a child, boy or girl, relates to the parent of the same sex seems to be produced by something more than what is given in the actual family situation.

In his paper 'Analysis Terminable and Interminable' (1937), which belongs to the same period of Freud's life as *Moses and Monotheism*, Freud writes about the way in which nearly all women patients show signs of wishing to be men, and men seek to avoid taking a passive attitude towards other men, including a male therapist. The common link is what was first called 'the castration complex', but a better term would be *the repudiation of the feminine*, says Freud.[43] Women seem unable to ever quite give up their wish for a penis, and they usually begin analysis with the hope they will acquire one during it. Men find it very difficult to accept cure, or care, from another man. These phenomena are observed too often for them to be the product of the individual's development alone. No answer was offered by Freud about why men and women seem to repudiate the feminine.

The analyst meets something of phylogenetic origin in this type of experience in therapy. Equally, it can be argued that there is something about institutions in human societies, especially in politics, law, morality and religion, which seems unnecessary from a strictly utilitarian point of view. Actions are performed with no obvious point to them; taboos persist and elicit sometimes quite violent reactions if they are broken; the archaic heritage of humanity does not disappear. It is still there, and, periodically, repressed material returns to set problems for man which remain unresolved, left over from the first parricide. Utilitarian notions in the social sciences are not enough for even providing a conceptual framework for grasping what actually happens.

The Final Solution for the Jews is one of the more horrific, irrational acts which modern man has performed. It seems to be being forgotten, perhaps it will be repressed, but its effects will not cease. Man needs to have some understanding of how this, and other atrocities, are possible as one of the major ways for avoiding them in the future. Psychoanalysis provides at least a language for talking about these matters, and contains useful speculative hypotheses.[44]

NOTES AND REFERENCES

1. S. Freud, *The Future of an Illusion* (1927), Standard Edition, Vol. 21. References to Revised Edition, London, 1962, p. 2.
2. Ibid.
3. Ibid., p. 8.
4. Ibid., p. 4.
5. Ibid., p. 10.
6. Ibid., p. 9.
7. Ibid., pp. 18–20.
8. Ibid., pp. 24–5.
9. Ibid., p. 26.

10. Ibid., p. 27.
11. See J. Hick, *Philosophy of Religion*, Englewood Cliffs, N.J., 1963.
12. See M. Weber, *The Religion of India*, New York, 1958, Part Three (on Buddhism). N. Wilson Ross, *Hinduism, Buddhism, Zen*, London, 1968. J. B. Noss, *Man's Religions*, New York, 1963.
13. Freud, *The Future of an Illusion*, edition cit., p. 42.
14. Ibid., pp. 38-9.
15. See S. Freud, 'Obsessive Acts and Religious Practices' (1907), available in P. Rieff (ed.), *Character and Culture*, New York, 1963, pp. 17-26. See also discussion of this in R. J. Bocock, *Ritual in Industrial Society*, London, 1974, pp. 28-9.
16. Freud, *The Future of an Illusion*, edition cit., p. 39.
17. Ibid., p. 40.
18. Ibid., p. 43.
19. Ibid., p. 50.
20. E. Fromm, *Psychoanalysis and Religion*, Yale, 1950. Reference to Bantam edition, New York, 1967, p. 18.
21. S. Freud, *Civilization and its Discontents* (1930), Standard Edition, Vol. 21. References to revised edition, London, 1963, p. 5.
22. E. Gellner, 'Concepts and Society', in *Transactions of the Fifth World Congress of Sociology*, International Sociological Association; reprinted in D. Emmet and A. MacIntyre, *Sociological Theory and Philosophical Analysis*, London, 1970. See also A. MacIntyre, *Against the Self-Images of the Age*, Duckworth, London, 1971, Chapters 3, 20 and 21; and 'Is Understanding Religion Compatible with Believing?', in B. Wilson (ed.), *Rationality*, Oxford, 1970, pp. 62-77.
23. S. Freud, *Moses and Monotheism* (1939), Standard Edition, Vol. 23. Reference to the new translation by A. Richards and the Institute of Psychoanalysis, London, 1964, revised 1974, pp. 8-14.
24. Ibid., p. 26.
25. Ibid., p. 22.
26. Ibid., p. 50.
27. Ibid., pp. 47-8.
28. Available in Rieff (ed.), *Character and Culture*, pp. 80-106.
29. S. Freud, *Moses and Monotheism*, edition cit., p. 58.
30. Ibid., p. 82.
31. Ibid., p. 76.
32. R. Wagner, *Parsifal*, first performed at Bayreuth, 1882.
33. See Bocock, *Ritual in Industrial Society*, pp. 158-9 and 28-9. Also Claude Lévi-Strauss, *The Scope of Anthropology*, translated by S. O. Paul and R. A. Paul, London, 1967. Lévi-Strauss sees the Parsifal myth as the reverse of the Oedipus myth, whereas the interpretation offered here is that it is a disguised form of parricide, and that Freud's conceptualizations can handle this. This is not a very scientific procedure as a test of anything in Freud, but simply a point worth noting.
34. Freud, *Moses and Monotheism*, edition cit., p. 92.
35. Ibid., p. 99.
36. Ibid.
37. Ibid., p. 101.
38. Ibid.

39. Ibid., p. 117.
40. Ibid., p. 121.
41. Ibid., p. 136.
42. Ibid.
43. S. Freud, 'Analysis Terminable and Interminable' (1937), available in P. Rieff (ed.), *Therapy and Technique*, New York, 1963, pp. 233–72. (Quotation from pp. 269–70.)
44. See, e.g., N. Cohn, *Warrant for Genocide*, London, 1967. Freudian theory forms a backdrop for this study, but it is not a strict testing of hypotheses, if that were ever possible in this area.

6 Instincts and Society

The originality and importance of Freud's sociology lies in the fact that he never leaves the human body out of account in the way that so much sociology, both before and since his work, seems to aim to do. So much sociological theory seems to be about a world entirely in the realm of the head, or the mind, and so little about a world of bodily states of feeling and action. The sociology of Freud is built on his analysis of instincts, and has usually been given little serious consideration within sociology precisely because the concept of instinct is thought to be unsociological. In the attempt to become an independent social science, sociology has left biology out of account by trying to purify the discipline and to concentrate on purely sociological variables.

Freud's work is now especially significant for sociology as it goes through a reappraisal of its own development. Sociology has to turn in on itself periodically, and seek a new understanding of its own development, in a way akin to that of philosophy. By so doing we, who read and talk about human society, gain a new depth of understanding of ourselves and our place. In the past, Freud has had very little place in such sociological reappraisals, but he needs to be in alongside the other major thinkers about society. His notion of instinct is fundamental to his theory about social groups, for it is a key link concept between man's biological organism and his social existence. This chapter will, therefore, focus on the idea of instincts as developed by Freud.

The Concept of Instincts

The concept of 'instinct' can be criticized for being logically circular. This is because the behaviour which is to be explained as the result of an instinct being present in an organism is, itself, the main evidence for the existence of the instinct in the first place. Some independent evidence is needed to establish the existence of an instinct apart from the behaviour itself if such circularity is to be avoided. To say that there is an instinct of 'hunger', and that the evidence for its existence is the fact that we feel hungry from time to time, is not to explain anything. In the case of sexual instincts, the position is more complicated, and more significant in the light of the importance attached to it by Freud.

To say that human beings from time to time have sexual intercourse, and that this is because they have sexual instincts, is as circular as the argument about hunger. It can be better seen as a necessary precondition for the continuing existence, not of an *individual*, as is the case with hunger, but of the *species*. The notion that Freud has of the sexual instincts is not primarily about reproduction, however, but the generalized capacity of the human organism to find erotic satisfaction from any part of the body being caressed or stimulated, quite apart from the act of reproduction. These 'organ-pleasures' are derivatives, no doubt, from the basic reproductive needs of the species. They have an independence of their own in the *experience* of human beings.

Can the concept of sexual instinct be rescued from the charge of logical circularity? Perhaps it can be done by saying that there is a basic biological species-need for sexual reproduction which gives rise to inner impulses, felt periodically, for full genital contact and orgasm. The impulses to seek general organ-pleasure which all human beings experience may be derivatives of the species-need for reproduction. This latter is a piece of independent evidence, which is distinct from the actions, such as masturbation or thumb-sucking or the hysterical symptoms of neurotics, which are to be explained by reference to the concept of sexual instincts.

Freud's concept of instinct is discussed by him in his paper 'Instincts and their Vicissitudes' (1915).[1] It is a borderland concept between the mental and the physical, and Freud wants to express this when he speaks of an instinct arising as an impulse *within* the organism, not as a stimulus from without. According to Ronald Fletcher, this is inadequate in the light of modern ethology, for some species, such as geese, exhibit 'escape reactions' when they see birds of prey. This piece of behaviour is a combination of an inner impulse and an outer stimulus, and flight does avail against the impulse, whereas for Freud flight is of no avail against an inner instinctual impulse.[2] This argument misses the point that Freud's notion of instinct is a link concept between the bio-physical and the experiential—geese do not experience in precisely the same sense as human beings do. It is true that human beings share some things in common with other species, such as sexual reproduction, but

they are distinct in some major ways, above all in their capacity)
for symbolic communication, as distinct from a sign system of /
communication used by some other species. Freud is not to be
taken to be providing a theory of instinct for all species, but
trying to puzzle out the complex similarities and differences
between man and animals. In this context his concept of
instinct, especially as applied to the sexual instincts, is useful.

An instinct has four elements. First, its *impetus*, which is the
motor force, the energy behind an instinctual demand.
Secondly, the *aim* of an instinct, which is always satisfaction.
The satisfaction may be deflected or inhibited after a certain
degree of it has been obtained, and then Freud speaks of
'instincts which are inhibited in respect of their aim'.[3] Thirdly,
the *object* is that in or through which an instinct can achieve its
aim. The object can be the subject's own body. Finally, the
source of an instinct 'is that somatic process in an organ or part of
the body from which there results a stimulus represented in
mental life by an instinct'.[4] It is important to see in this last
point a clear distinction between the term 'source of an
instinct', which would be studied by physical scientists, and the
Freudian concept of instinct, which is one belonging more to
mental life, for it gives rise to inner stimuli in the *experience* of a
person.

Freud may not always be clear about the standing of this
concept, and continually shows an inclination to justify his
concepts of the experiential life of man by reference to physical,
biological and chemical notions. This confuses the issue, and is
produced by his misunderstanding of philosophy of social and
natural science, as was shown in Chapter 3. His critics have
therefore been able to attack his biology and think they have
disposed of his phenomenology of the unconscious, and of
human experience.

In *Beyond the Pleasure Principle* (1920) there can be found some
of the worst of Freud's biological arguments. As this is his first
book in which the death instincts are introduced as a distinct
conceptualization, it is a pity that the arguments are so poor.
The worst fault lies in a confusion about the notion of 'instinct'
itself. Freud seeks to use it in this book as if it were a purely
biological concept, and furthermore, one which is found among
all living organisms.

This has also been critized by Ronald Fletcher, in a thorough
analysis, because it is based on a false view of the human
nervous system. Freud assumed that the nervous system's main

task is to abolish stimuli and as far as possible 'maintain itself in an altogether unstimulated condition'. Some movements of organisms, certainly in man, are 'functionally positive movements directed towards stimuli', and 'the nervous system is active before it is reactive'.[5] These assertions are made on the basis of research in modern ethology, and the arguments will not be discussed in any detail as they belong to a different universe of discourse from that of psychoanalysis and sociology.

The important point for the purposes of the argument being developed here is that although Freud may have been mistaken in his biology, the notion of the death instincts retains a usefulness which is missed by critics who reject the notion on the basis of ethological and biological evidence.[6] Although it is the case that many of Freud's speculations were mistaken, something he half, if not fully, expected would happen within biology, it is not possible to ignore the other aspects of the death-instinct theory which have an application within psychoanalysis, and its extension into sociology.

During the First World War, before the publication of *Beyond the Pleasure Principle*, Freud had published a paper, 'Reflections upon War and Death' (1915), in which there are references to the theory of *Totem and Taboo* (1913). The view in this paper is that the sense of disillusionment many people were experiencing during the first year of the war resulted from an over-valuation of man's nature, and an attempt to deny the reality of death for people one loved. The over-valuation of man is an 'illusion', based on the wish that man could be better and live for ever. There are primitive layers, even in modern Europeans who were then fighting the war, which mean that man has a capacity for brutality exceeding that of other animals. Primitive man, wrote Freud,

> liked to kill, and killed as a matter of course. That instinct which is said to restrain other animals from killing and devouring their own species we need not attribute to him. Hence the primitive history of mankind is filled with murder.[7]

At this point in his work, Freud would be much more acceptable to modern thinkers, for he shows that he is not deriving man's destructiveness from a similar instinct in animals. There is something unique about man's capacity to kill, and even to eat, his own species. It is this which ought to have been properly recalled in Freud's later work, and he could then have introduced the term 'death instincts' to *describe* this basic, and in terms of the later theory, *innate* predisposition to kill other human beings. In *Totem and Taboo*, the suggestion was that early groups of men killed the primal father, and in his recapitulation of the argument Freud, in this paper, uses Christianity as evidence that a murder must have been committed if the Son, Christ, had to be a human sacrifice to atone for the sin of men. The original sin of mankind was the murder of the father. As was pointed out earlier, in Chapter 5, this crime has consequences for mankind as a whole, and not just for the individual in relationship to their own father.

> And so, if we are to be judged by the wishes in our unconscious, we are, like primitive man, simply a gang of murderers . . . Psychoanalysis finds little credence among laymen for assertions such as these. They reject them as calumnies which are confuted by conscious experience, and adroitly overlook the faint indications through which the unconscious is apt to betray itself even to consciousness.[8]

It would be better to admit that these murderous wishes and impulses exist than to deny them, and feel guilt-laden as a result of not allowing ourselves to see them for what they are. As a consequence, people would have less fear of death, because the fear of death, especially the fear of the death of loved ones, arises from emotional ambivalence—the love and hatred felt towards parents, friends, husbands or wives, and children. Part of us wishes to see these loved ones dead, and if we refuse to acknowledge this, then we will worry about their possible deaths, and not cope with grief and guilt after they do in fact die.

It is quite remarkable how the denial of death, and the denial of the secret wishes for the death of others, persists even among those who have read Freud and have been analysed. It would be possible to acknowledge that this type of emotional layer exists in human beings, and that it finds expression in the brutality men are capable of inflicting on one another. This layer of unconscious emotion could be seen, however, as produced by the prolonged nature of human socialization, and the special nature of the repression of sexuality that humans impose on their young to build up civilization and culture. The existence of the emotions could be admitted, but their origin in an innate core of impulses could be denied. This view has rarely been developed by Freud's critics.[9] Freud was so impressed by the amount of brutality men have inflicted on one another, and have continued to inflict on one another, that he felt justified in developing what he thought of as a mythology of two conflicting instincts: sexuality and death, Eros and Thanatos.

The reason these are best seen as an innate, given set of instincts is that such a view suggests it is not possible to conceive of how man could be man and not experience these unconscious impulses of hatred and killing which some human beings act out. So even the 'softer' position outlined above, that the unconscious layer of murderous wishes may not be instinctual in origin, has to accept these emotions and actions as a necessary part of the human situation, and an unavoidable aspect of it. There seems to be a degree of excess hostility among members of the same group, and the same society, apart from the hostility towards people from other societies. More hostility exists than can be accounted for on political and economic theories of the Marxist type. Freud thought that communism could not be established over the world as a whole without a great deal of bloodshed, and that even then, although the human potential for brutality and killing may be less, it would not disappear entirely.

This is not, however, a completely pessimistic position. In a letter to Einstein, Freud called himself a pacifist. He thought it was possible to seek to produce more lasting ties of unity among and within societies by educating a rational group of leaders. In spite of the old-fashioned view of leaders implied in this letter, there is, in the last analysis, no other position which can be put forward which does not depend on some group of leaders claiming to be more rational in their understanding of what human societies need in order to develop peacefully. The education of rational leaders would entail the elimination of church censorship upon freedom of thought—a radical point for Freud to make in the context of Austria, and the strong position held by the Roman Catholic Church in education in that country at that time.

Whatever fosters the growth of culture works at the same time against war.[10]

There is therefore some hope that, through the influence of education, the arts, travel and the growth of international cultural contacts, and the lessening of the influence of authoritarian religion, brutality and wars can be lessened, and even eradicated. It is, however, a very difficult task.

In his paper 'Formulations Regarding the Two Principles of

Mental Functioning', Freud argues that individuals begin their mental development with unconscious, primary processes being dominant.[11] These primary processes always seek pleasure and avoid pain, that is, they function according to the *pleasure principle*. This is the oldest type of mental functioning for individuals and for mankind as a whole, and it is one to which neurotics return when they find parts, or the whole, of external reality too painful. In the course of development, the child learns to form conceptions of the external world and to act in ways which produce satisfaction in that world, and not just in the mental world. The development of science and education has done something similar in the development of mankind, and is more successful than religions in providing real gains in the external world, because its image of the external world is more accurate than those which are based on religious notions. *Phantasy* is that part of mental functioning which continues to work according to the pleasure principle, even after the emergence of the reality principle in mental life.

The reality principle does not dethrone the pleasure principle, but rather safeguards it. Momentary pleasures are given up, but only because a more lasting pleasure is promised later. This replacement of the pleasure principle by the reality principle is expressed in mythic form in religious notions of rewards in an afterlife for the instinctual renunciations of this life. Science promises rewards later in this life, and they are more certain than those of religion.

At this stage in the development of Freud's thinking, there are two sets of instincts: the sexual and the ego instincts. Freud always said that his conceptualizations of the instincts were for specific purposes and could be further developed and altered later on, as indeed they were. In the early conceptualization, the ego instincts served to preserve the individual, and the sexual instincts aimed at the preservation, through reproduction, of the species. In this early formulation, the feelings of hatred, leading to the murder of the father, had been acknowledged, as in *Totem and Taboo*. They are seen as a consequence of the demands for instinctual renunciation of sexuality that the father demands of his sons.

There were some stubborn cases in his clinical work, however, which suggested to Freud that something else was at work apart from sexual instincts and ego instincts. Some patients seemed to gain psychological advantages from being ill with their neuroses, and were peculiarly difficult to cure. Very often, if they lost their income or savings, or had a bad marriage, or developed a serious organic disease, they did recover from their neuroses.

There seemed to be an intractability about some aspects of human existence outside the consulting-room too. The early conceptualization of the instinct theory was developed before the First World War. After living through this event, with its profoundly shattering consequences to Europe, Freud becomes more concerned with the idea of there being a basic mutual hostility between human beings. This was not just between nations and ethnic groups, but in families, between friends, and in work groups. The later theory of instincts, which included the death instincts, as well as the sexual instincts which were retained from the first formulation, seemed to solve the theoretical difficulties that arose with the first theory of instincts. It could successfully handle the problems which arose in the therapeutic setting with the masochistic patients, always a key requirement of a theoretical change for Freud's theorizing.

It also met a further requirement which Freud demanded of a new theoretical formulation, namely, that it help to explain the sociological and historical development of humanity. The war was, therefore, as much in need of integration into psycho-analytic theory as were masochistic patients. Later theoretical developments of psychoanalysis have been by analysts who have largely given up this second requirement of a theoretical conceptualization, yet it was a fundamental one for Freud himself.

Beyond the Pleasure Principle (1920) was the first attempt to begin to formulate the notion of the death instincts. At one point in this work Freud wrote:

> The upshot of our inquiry so far has been the drawing of a sharp distinction between the 'ego instincts' and the sexual instincts, and the view that the former exercise pressure towards death and the latter towards a prolongation of life . . . [On] our hypothesis the ego instincts arise from the coming to life of inanimate matter and seek to restore the inanimate state.[12]

This first attempt to include the notion that the aim of some instincts seems to be to return to an earlier stage of development, to inanimate matter, was based on his observations of war neuroses and on the compulsion to repeat earlier emotional relationships in the analytic situation. The dreams of people who had had traumatic experiences in the war, and who had developed neurotic symptoms, often contained material about the situation in which they were traumatized. This was difficult to explain given the postulate, itself based on years of observation, that dreams fulfil wishes. To Freud it was, therefore, a surprising fact that these patients did not dream of being cured of their neurosis, but returned to the original painful situation. A strong impulse must exist within the personality for this kind of repetition to occur, and one of a new kind, for the unconscious worked according to the pleasure principle, and always sought to avoid painful experiences and to reduce tensions of the kind that these dreamers were reproducing for themselves when asleep. The same problem arose with patients who reproduced, unconsciously, early painful relationships they had had with their parents in their relationship with their analysts. Hence the new postulate in psychoanalytic theory: that there must be an underlying biological instinct which expressed itself in mental life as a compulsion to repeat unpleasant experiences. The very concept of instinct, as used by Freud, is just such a bridge concept between organic, biological impulses and the experiences of human beings in their mental life. Therefore there should be little surprise that Freud first links this compulsion to repeat pain on to the non-sexual instincts, for it must have some instinctual base, and this cannot be the life-affirming sexual instincts, for they do seem to operate on the pleasure principle *par excellence*.

This solution was found to be unsatisfactory as soon as it was stated. Only a few pages later Freud withdraws his connection between the ego instincts and the death aims of those instincts which seem to push towards the death of the organism. The ego can itself be an object for libidinal attachments, as it is in narcissism, a stage in the development, or rather the starting-point for development, of every person. The first conceptualization had then to be changed so that it could handle this happening. The concept of narcissism had been developed, in part, through work with patients who seemed to withdraw all their libido into themselves, and had no interest in any things or people in the external world. As part of their attempt to cure themselves they developed their own delusionary worlds, which were in turn often treated by non-analysts as a symptom of a disease instead of being seen as an attempt at self-cure.

In his paper 'On the Mechanism in Paranoia' (1911), Freud had made use of this notion of narcissism to understand paranoia and the constructs of persecutory world systems often developed by paranoids.[13] If the ego can become an object for libidinal attachments in this way, the simple dichotomy between the ego and the sexual instincts is not adequate for all cases. A new dimension is added, and the conflicts are placed between ego instincts and object instincts, both of a sexual, libidinal nature. This is really a *differentiation* within the category of sexual instincts as first conceived, the ego instincts of the first conceptualization being taken into a differentiation within the sexual instincts instead of being opposed to them. It was, again, an unsatisfactory solution, and Freud began to see that these earlier conceptualizations could only be used for a limited number of problems which arose in psychoanalysis, and that a new, more fundamental conceptualization was required.

The arguments in *Beyond the Pleasure Principle* which sought to establish that all organisms aim at death, a return to the state of inanimate matter, were admitted by Freud to be ones which could be overthrown by later biological research. The arguments were admittedly speculative:

> What follows is speculation, often far-fetched speculation, which the reader will consider or dismiss according to his predilection.[14]

Most readers have had a predilection to dismiss the arguments and speculations.[15] Freud came to see, later, that human beings are not predisposed to admit that they are organisms which die and are destructive any more than they had been prepared to admit that young children, under five years of age, were sexual. The arguments that Freud advanced are unnecessary to establish the conceptualization of the death instincts, and their eternal struggle with the sexual instincts, in the unconscious life of humanity. He, like many of his critics and followers, failed to see that the claims for a new scientific conceptualization rest not only on the 'facts' they are concerned to put into some kind of order, but also on the capacity of the new theoretical framework to bring out connections between what, until the new framework is used, appear as unconnected bits and pieces of information. Freud's mistake was to think he was trying to bring order into the information gathered and arranged by biologists, instead of trying to bring order into the information gathered by psychoanalysts. Certainly there could be links between the two universes of discourse of biology and psychoanalysis, but it was premature and unnecessary for

Freud to engage in building up such links before he had established his theory within psychoanalysis. It seemed that at times he wished to bolster up his psychoanalytic theories with appeals to 'hard data' in natural, biological sciences. This was to misconceive the ways in which the theories of natural science can ever link with theory about human action and behaviour. 'Facts' do not just exist, they have to be grasped by the intellect, using a conceptual framework. This makes it extremely difficult to transpose 'facts' from one field, such as biology, to another as complex as psychoanalysis.

As was suggested above, there were, within the internal development of psychoanalysis, new findings which necessitated a new conceptualization which could account for the compulsion to repeat unpleasurable experiences. It might be said that if psychoanalysis had not posited the pleasure principle as the basis for the functioning of the unconscious, there would be no problem about this set of phenomena of 'compulsions to repeat'. The way any scientific field develops, however, is through organizing observations around such general principles, and these are retained unless there is very good reason to abandon them. If Freud could manage to retain the pleasure principle, and also outline theoretically how other principles might operate, using energy from different instinctual sources, then this would be a perfectly reasonable development. This is precisely what Freud did by introducing the '*Nirvana principle*' into the theory of psychoanalysis.

> The dominating tendency of mental life, and perhaps of nervous life in general, is the effort to reduce, to keep constant or to remove internal tension due to stimuli (the 'Nirvana Principle', to borrow a term from Barbara Low)—a tendency which finds expression in the pleasure principle; and our recognition of that fact is one of our strongest reasons for believing in the existence of the death instincts.[16]

This principle can even apply to sexual intercourse, where tensions mount and pleasure derives from the reduction in tensions after orgasm has been reached. At this point in the theory, the Nirvana principle is conceived of as deriving its energy from the death instincts, and the pleasure principle serves these too sometimes, and therefore it loses its former primacy in the unconscious life of man.

Sadism had always been of theoretical interest to Freud, and he suggests in *Beyond the Pleasure Principle* that it derives its energy from the death instincts. It can become linked with the sexual instincts, and turned on to external, loved objects. In masochism the energy is directed on to the ego, not an object, where the ego is itself libidinized as in narcissism. In this way Freud had moved some way to producing a new synthesis of the three dichotomies: ego instincts, and sexual instincts; ego and object choices within one set of instincts only, the sexual instincts; and, finally, the life instincts (sexual) and the death instincts.

The principles of mental functioning, which had been conceptualized as being two in the 1911 paper, 'Formulations Regarding the Two Principles of Mental Functioning', namely, the pleasure and reality principles, had had a third principle, the Nirvana principle, added. In *Beyond the Pleasure Principle* the position is that the pleasure principle may be serving the death instincts, which would imply that the Nirvana principle is basic to mental functioning alongside the reality principle. The pleasure principle would then be seen as one form of the more fundamental Nirvana principle.

This view is changed in *The Economic Problem of Masochism* (1924). Clearly masochism raises special problems for the concept of the pleasure principle because, by definition, the masochist does not seek pleasure and avoid pain in the usual sense. Pleasure and pain cannot be seen as a lowering of tension and a heightening of tension respectively; there can be a pleasurable heightening of tension, as in sexual activity (a new admission compared with the position Freud took in *Beyond the Pleasure Principle*) and a painful lowering of tensions. This increased flexibility in the conceptual framework allows Freud to see the Nirvana principle alone as the principle which seeks the reduction, lowering or elimination of tensions, and the pleasure principle as seeking pleasure and avoiding pain. The reality principle remains concerned with adjusting the organism to external reality.

> In this way we obtain a series, a small but an interesting one: the *Nirvana*-principle expresses the tendency of the death instincts; the *pleasure*-principle represents the claims of the libido and that modification of it, the *reality*-principle, the influence of the outer world.[17]

The death instincts provide what might be termed the 'negative energy' that is used in the compulsion to repeat unpleasant experiences, which is a masochistic use of primal, sadistic impulses which take the ego as object, rather than an external object. The death instincts provide the negative energy which is used in destructive aggression between human beings, either between individuals or between groups and nations. Psychoanalytic theory reached a point where it could not account for all the observations made within the analytic setting, nor for the murdering impulses shown in mankind's historical and cultural development. Some conception of destructive energy, what has been called above 'negative energy' (not a term used by Freud), was needed to counterbalance the positive, life-affirming energy of the sexual instincts. The concept of the 'death instincts' provided psychoanalysis with such a source for this negative energy. Without it, psychoanalytic theory could not account for all that it had been observed human beings could do to themselves and to one another. It therefore has a central place in the development of psychoanalytic theory. Theories of personal development, or of the historical and sociological development of humanity, which ignore it or dispense with it, make psychoanalytic theory less advanced than it was when Freud left it at the end of his life.

It is precisely because Herbert Marcuse, for example, has retained the notion of the death instincts that he is to be seen as having advanced psychoanalytic sociology and social philosophy.[18] Similarly, the work of Melanie Klein can be seen to have built upon Freud by retaining the death instincts in the area of the theory of personality development and psychoanalytic therapy.[19] It is an unfortunate fact that Klein has almost no sociological theory, and that Marcuse has no therapeutic theory. Erich Fromm, who has continued to work on both lines of development together, as psychoanalysis should, has equally unfortunately dropped the death instincts, and at times the sexual instincts, out of his work.[20] Chapter 7 will examine the work of Erich Fromm briefly, and that of Herbert Marcuse in more detail. The work of Melanie Klein is omitted because it relates to the technicalities of psychoanalytic therapy, which is not of central concern here, where it does not impinge on sociology. Before this, however, a major work of Freud's must be examined, for it is central to his social philosophy and psychoanalytic sociology.

Civilization and Its Discontents

Why is it so hard for men to be happy? This is the central

question of *Civilization and Its Discontents* (1930).[21] There are three main sources of unhappiness: the human body and its illnesses; external nature and its independent power; and the inadequacy of the way human relations are experienced in the state, the family and society generally. A number of ways of seeking happiness are possible, and discussed by Freud, first of all in common-sense terms. Some people seek to be independent of others, and live as hermits, or as close to that condition as possible. Others pursue erotic relationships and sexual pleasures, as long as they are able to do so. Some others seek satisfactions in science and in associated professional work. For others, the arts and beauty are their prime source of pleasure and happiness. Intoxicants and drugs are used by some to escape physical or psychological pain. Yoga provides others with techniques for reducing desires and instinctual impulses, and happiness is therefore a little easier to attain. Nevertheless, happiness is difficult to find, and it seems man is unable to remain happy even when he finds a way of living that seems to suit his psychic constitution—a combination of biological givens, and the consequences of the individual's resolution of his conflicts during his personal development.[22]

Religion is not particularly helpful, because it restricts choice by imposing on everybody one path to happiness and protection from suffering. It devalues this life, offers a delusional picture of the world, and thereby intimidates the independent use of intelligence. Religion keeps people in an infantile state, but by drawing them into a mass delusion, it succeeds in sparing many people an individual neurosis.[23]

Technology and applied science have done much more to alleviate the worst effects of nature by providing help against, for instance, floods, storms, diseases, droughts, infertile soils and long distances. Even so, people living in the highly technological societies do not feel fully content, and imagine that they might be better off with a return to primitive technical conditions. The 1920s in Europe, at least, had seen some of the same romanticism about leaving technically advanced civilization as occurred again in the 1960s and 1970s. However, although technology and agriculture may not be sufficient conditions for human happiness, they are certainly a necessary prerequisite, Freud argued. Here he is surely right; only the educated and affluent people in Western societies are attracted by the idea of returning to primitive conditions. Freud considers that there may be something intractable in humanity as we know it, a part of our basic psychic constitution which remains uneasy, discontented, even hostile to civilization, and that this finds expression in such romantic ideals as the return to nature.[24]

One of the greatest sources of human happiness is sexual love, and some people try to pursue this source of satisfaction above all else. It is, however, a way of living which many wise men have advised against, because if the loved person should not return the love, or be absent for some time, or worst of all, should die, then there is no misery worse than that of someone who has lost their sexually loved partner.[25] Many religious ethics teach that people should not love sexually, but cultivate feelings of affection for all mankind. This is the most satisfactory form of sublimation, of aim-inhibited love, where the energy is derived from sexuality, the instinct's aim being deflected away from genital aims on to others such as doing good works, creating beautiful things or building up close friendships.

There is a tension between human beings' sexual drives and civilization, because the latter needs people who will sublimate sexuality into activities which help to build up and preserve civilization. Most work requires that energy be diverted away from direct sexual satisfactions, and used to produce the gains of technical civilization. One source of hostility towards civilization, felt by probably everyone at some points in their lives, and by some most of the time, arises from the restrictions which moral codes place on sexual activities, confining it, in West European cultures, to heterosexual relations with one partner over the whole of a lifetime. This is held up as the norm, even though only 'weak' characters follow these restrictions fully throughout their lives! The sexual bond pulls people away from the wider community, but civilization aims at uniting more and more people into wider communities in order to gain from co-operation. Freud refers back to *Totem and Taboo*, and mentions the band of brothers who gained from co-operation among themselves, having left the first family groups, and achieved what each could not do alone, that is, the overpowering of the father.[26] This discovery, that a combination can be stronger than a single individual, or a couple, marked a major step in humanity's development as a species, but carried with it restrictions over sexual activity, because this leads to two people aiming to be independent from everyone else.

We are saying much the same thing when we derive the antithesis between sexuality and civilization from the circumstance that sexual love is a relationship between two individuals in which a third can only be superfluous or disturbing, whereas civilization depends on relationships between a considerable number of individuals.[27]

Civilization, that is, human societies, goes further than just linking family groups together through a set of work tasks that they have in common.

It aims at binding the members of the community together in a libidinal way as well and employs every means to that end.[28]

There must be a further factor which could explain this. Indeed there is, but this factor is disavowed by people. The further factor is:

... that men are not gentle creatures who want to be loved, and who at the most can defend themselves if they are attacked; they are, on the contrary, creatures among whose instinctual endowments is to be reckoned a powerful share of aggressiveness. As a result, their neighbour is for them not only a potential helper or sexual object, but also someone who tempts them to satisfy their aggressiveness on him, to exploit his capacity for work without compensation, to use him sexually without his consent, to seize his possessions, to humiliate him, to cause him pain, to torture and to kill him.[29]

Human beings developed the ethic of 'Love thy neighbour as thyself' within historical times, and it occurs in religions before Christianity.[30] The latter religion pushed it further and added 'Love thine enemies'. These religious ethical teachings are surrounded by sacrality, and they have to be reiterated in this way over and over again because nothing runs so counter to man than to love his neighbour, including his enemies.

Given this view of there being a primary mutual hostility among human beings, Freud is able to explain why civilization restricts sexual activity. As much aim-inhibited libidinal energy as possible is needed to keep people bound together in communities and work situations, and to counteract their violent desires towards one another. This is a powerful explanation because it succeeds in linking the fact of there being a restriction on sexuality in religions which preach brotherly love to all mankind, especially Christianity, Islam and Buddhism. Puritanical movements have time and time again, in Europe and America, linked a rigorous sexual code of practice with pacifism and an ethic of non-violence. Since Freud wrote, some groups, such as the Quakers, have altered their sexual code towards a more liberal position, but there are still restrictions.[31]

Freud also considered the view of communists, that it is the institution of private property which has corrupted man's nature, but that man is basically co-operative and good: people could be naturally well-disposed towards their neighbours if only private property was abolished. While not wishing to comment on the economic arguments for communism in terms of its capacity to create more wealth more equally distributed, an aim Freud thought to be very important for the future, he thought that communism contained an 'illusion' about man's nature. There is a deep wish to believe man is not basically destructive, as well as loving, and to see people as being naturally co-operative with one another.

> Aggressiveness was not created by property. It reigned almost without limit in primitive times when property was still very scanty, and it already shows itself in the nursery almost before property has given up its primal, anal form . . . If we do away with personal rights over material wealth, there still remains prerogative in the field of sexual relationships . . .[32]

It is always possible for humans to live peacefully, in a relatively small community, as long as there is another group to receive the manifestations of their aggressiveness. This occurs among national groups in the phenomenon Freud termed 'the narcissism of minor differences'. It is also found among religious groups who love one another, but are hostile towards those who are not of the same religious group, or sect, as themselves. Communists can be hostile and aggressive towards Western capitalists. Freud thought it was difficult to see how communism could be generalized to the whole world, unless national rivalries could cope with aggression without full-scale wars.[33]

Civilized people have exchanged direct instinctual gratification of sexual and aggressive drives in return for more security and a longer life. Primitive, that is pre-literate, societies of the present period also exhibit restrictions on the instincts, but have less physical security because technology has not developed so far. These societies are not to be confused with the primal type of primitive group, where instincts were not restricted. This latter is a construct in Freud's overall theory, but he seems constantly to confuse his theoretical primitive group and actual primitive societies, which, he acknowledges, do have such controls.

Instinct Theory and the Super-ego

The sexual instincts had always been a part of psychoanalytic theory, and they remain in the later formulations. The early idea of ego instincts, the self-preservative instincts, did change, however, with the introduction of the concept of narcissism, for here the libidinal energy of the sexual instincts is directed to an inner object, the ego. Carl Jung had made the concept of libido, the energy of sexuality, coextensive with instinctual energy in general, as the earlier distinction between it and the ego instincts could not be maintained in the face of the pheno- menon of narcissistic libido. As has been shown, Freud had discussed the phenomenon of a compulsion to repeat—and the conservative character of instinctual behaviour, as found in patients in analysis who repeat in the transference relations the situation they first experienced as young children in relation to their parents—in *Beyond the Pleasure Principle*. In this book he tentatively introduced the idea of *death instincts*, which aim at restoring an earlier state of things. In the case of living organisms, the aim is to achieve a state of inanimate matter again. 'The aim of all life is death.'[34]

Alongside the sexual instincts, the life-enhancing Eros, seeking greater and greater unity among living organisms, there is a destructive force at work too—the death instinct. Freud wanted to retain the dualism of his early theory of ego and sexual instincts, and had been critical of Jung for the monistic aspect of the more general notion of libido which he used.[35] The new dualism was found in the opposition between life and death instincts. He had himself felt resistance to the idea that man had an instinct of destruction, of death, as well as a set of sexual instincts. Over the ten years between *Beyond the Pleasure Principle* and *Civilization and Its Discontents*, the idea of a basic destructive set of instincts grew in his mind. For example, the two instincts can combine together in varying ways, and this enabled psychoanalysis to gain a greater theoretical under- standing of sadism, where the destructive aggression is pro- jected on to another object, and masochism, where the destructive aggression is turned against an inner object. There was also destructiveness of a non-erotic type which had to find a place in the theory, but had not done so for a surprisingly long time, and was still resisted by some analysts. Where destructive aggression is not linked with eroticism, it provides a narcissistic satisfaction for ego.

> ... we cannot fail to recognize that the satisfaction of the
> instinct is accompanied by an extraordinarily high degree of
> narcissistic enjoyment, owing to its presenting the ego with a
> fulfilment of the latter's old wishes for omnipotence.[36]

Mankind undergoes a special process, namely becoming
'civilized', which is the work of Eros, and aims at uniting men
into larger and larger unities, until all mankind becomes one
great entity, libidinally bound together. This is opposed by the
death instincts, whose main derivative, in social terms, is
destructiveness. There are few, if any, clues about why human
beings are undergoing this process, for other animals do not.[37]

How does human society, civilization, handle destructive
aggressiveness, which Freud postulates as a given, innate
instinct? Clearly it can find outlets in destructive activity of
various kinds, some of which are socially sanctioned, as in work
involving destructive action, or in a war, or even in policing the
society. More important from the point of view of the historical
development of mankind is the introjection, the internalizing,
of aggressiveness, for then society itself does not suffer destruction. The aggression which could have been enacted upon
other people is, instead, turned by one part of ego against
another part by the super-ego against the rest of the ego.

> The tension between the harsh super-ego and the ego that is
> subjected to it, is called by us the sense of guilt; it expresses
> itself as a need for punishment. Civilization, therefore, obtains
> mastery over the individual's dangerous desire for aggression
> by weakening and disarming it and by setting up an agency
> within him to watch over it, like a garrison in a conquered
> city.[38]

The process of building up the super-ego starts with the
relationship between the child and an external authority,
usually a parent—often the father—or a nanny; later on it may
be teachers, and religious figures. The external authority
demands some instinctual renunciation of the child, and
threatens it with the loss of love, and sometimes also with
physical chastisement. The severity of the child's own super-ego,
which is the introjected, internalized, external authority figure,
will depend in part on the severity of the parent towards the
child. However, this cannot be the whole source of super-ego's
severity, for children from lenient parents are found to have
very harsh super-egos. The child who is subject to lenient
parents cannot express any aggression towards them because

they are so good to him or her. So the aggression that would otherwise be used against the parents is turned around, and the super-ego, the conscience, becomes more aggressive towards the ego as a reversal of the aggression felt by the child towards the external authority.

In the straightforward situation of a child subject to parental authority, renunciation of instinct was performed so as not to lose the love of the parent. No sense of guilt then remained.

> But with fear of the super-ego the case is different. Here, instinctual renunciation is not enough, for the wish persists and cannot be concealed from the super-ego. Thus, in spite of the renunciation that has been made, a sense of guilt comes about . . . A threatened external unhappiness—loss of love and punishment on the part of the external authority—has been exchanged for a permanent internal unhappiness, for the tension of the sense of guilt.[39]

To reiterate a point made above, the severity of the super-ego depends not just on the aggression of the parent towards the child, but on the child's feelings of aggression towards the parents. If these cannot be expressed, and there is renunciation of the aggressive, destructive, instinctual energy by the child, then the aggression is internalized and used by the super-ego against the ego, and produces more guilt feelings.

At this point it is worth noting how simple distinctions between social psychology and a purely individualistic, intra-psychic, psychology cannot be maintained. The attempt to understand the intrapsychic processes of a person inevitably comes up against the micro-sociology of the family relationships in which the person was involved. These reflect, in their turn, the economic and political circumstances of the family, and these, in their turn, are part of the macro-sociological and biological processes of the historical development of the human species. Although such moves, from the intrapsychic via the socio-historical institutions to the most general reflections about human development and evolution, are regarded by many academics, in this period of Western history, as intellectually suspect, they are the mark of Freud's originality and intellectual daring. They may turn out to be among the most important statements made in this period of humanity's development, because they further our self-understanding not, primarily, as individuals in a privatized world, but as a social group which makes up part of the species *Homo sapiens*.

In the last sections of *Civilization and Its Discontents*, Freud develops the similarities and distinctions between the onto-genetic process of the child's development of a conscience, a super-ego, and the phylogenetic process in the species. Some commentators have tried to make a distinction between the value of some of Freud's work and other sections. This is often done in terms of showing a preference for the individual-in-the-family elements of social psychology in Freud, and ignoring the grander design of the later theory. Others make a different distinction:

> Freud's studies of totemism and the origins of the social group (*Totem and Taboo; Moses and Monotheism*), despite much that is interesting, can be dismissed as speculative evolutionary theorizing at its most extreme. But *Civilization and Its Discontents* and *The Future of an Illusion* both raise problems of great importance in the relationship between personality and culture.[40]

Such a distinction is really impossible to sustain, especially given the constant references made by Freud to *Totem and Taboo* in the two works said to be of greater importance.

A major difference between the phylogenetic and the ontogenetic development of conscience lies in the fact that the aggressiveness felt towards the primal father led to the actual killing of the father by the band of brothers, and not to instinctual renunciation of destructive aggression. In the light of the theory concerned with the ontogenetic development of guilt in man, there should not have been any guilt after the carrying out of the deed of parricide. It cannot have been remorse of the sort which follows the disobedience of the conscience, if the deed is meant to explain the existence of the conscience, the capacity to feel guilty, for this would be illogical.

> This remorse was the result of the primordial ambivalence of feeling towards the father. His sons hated him, but they loved him, too. After their hatred had been satisfied by their act of aggression, their love came to the fore in their remorse for the deed. It set up the super-ego by identification with the father; it gave the agency the father's power, as though as a punishment for the deed of aggression they had carried out against him, and it created the restrictions which were intended to prevent a repetition of the deed. And since the inclination to aggressiveness against the father was repeated in the following generations, the sense of guilt, too, persisted, and it was reinforced once more by every piece of aggressiveness

that was suppressed and carried over to the super-ego. Now, I think, we can grasp two things perfectly clearly: the part played by love in the origin of conscience and the fatal inevitability of the sense of guilt. Whether one has killed one's father or has abstained from doing so is not really the decisive thing. One is bound to feel guilty in either case, for the sense of guilt is an expression of the conflict due to ambivalence, of the eternal struggle between Eros and the instinct of destruction or death. This conflict is set going as soon as men are faced with the task of living together. So long as the community assumes no other form than that of the family, the conflict is bound to express itself in the Oedipus complex, to establish the conscience and to create the first sense of guilt. When an attempt is made to widen the community, the same conflict is continued in forms which are dependent on the past; and it is strengthened and results in a further intensification of the sense of guilt. Since civilization obeys an internal erotic impulse which causes human beings to unite in a closely-knit group, it can only achieve this aim through an ever-increasing reinforcement of the sense of guilt. What began in relation to the father is completed in relation to the group.[41]

This long quotation contains the key links Freud needed in his grand theory of mankind's development, a grand theory which links with the deepest feelings of every person. It is meant to explain, within the terms of psychoanalytic theory, why human beings both strive for ever greater unity among the species as a whole, through their religions and through political movements, yet find the task difficult if not impossible to fulfil. It does not lead to a greater sense of happiness as promised, but to increasing feelings of tension and guilt. The strain periodically becomes too much, and men renounce the renunciations of the destructive instinct. These insights follow from Freud's living through the First World War, and seeing its effects on Germany, but, of course, they precede Hitler's rise to power and the Second World War, the gas chambers, the dropping of the atomic bomb on two Japanese cities, and the wars in South-East Asia and the Middle East. Reading Freud, with the references to antisemitism, and the strains for mankind in continuing to renounce destructive aggression, one sees that long before anyone else in European culture, he articulated an insight of what was about to befall the world. However, in 1930 he wrote, at the end of *Civilization and Its Discontents*:

And now it is to be expected that the other of the two 'Heavenly Powers', eternal Eros, will make an effort to assert

himself in the struggle with his equally immortal adversary.
But who can foresee with what success and with what result?[42]

It might be said that this was written twenty years too early, for not until 1950 did Eros manage to reassert himself. And who can say for how long this time?

The development of the individual aims at happiness, whereas in the development of civilization the happiness of the individual is pushed into the background. There is, therefore, an additional tension for the individual, which results not from a conflict between the death instincts and Eros, but a contest within libido itself. For on the one hand Eros pushes the individual towards union with others, and to greater and greater unities, while on the other it pursues the happiness of the individual, especially sexual gratification. This latter leads to the loving couple wishing to be independent and without others. Civilization, however, needs the energy of the sex instincts to bind people into larger unities.

An important similarity between the process of individual development, and that of civilization, is that 'the community, too, evolves a super-ego under whose influence cultural development proceeds'.[43]

Personalities influence the community, just as they do in the individual process. Jesus Christ is a good example of such an influential figure. His teachings on the ethics of loving your neighbour as yourself, however, set up demands on people which can be too severe. Just as in individual therapy it is necessary to lower the severity of the super-ego's demands, so it is with the cultural super-ego, in the shape of the Christian religion in this case.

> The commandment is impossible to fulfil; such an enormous inflation of love can only lower its value, not get rid of the difficulty. Civilization pays no attention at all to this; it merely admonishes us that the harder it is to obey the precept the more meritorious it is to do so.[44]

Freud goes on to add an important political point:

> I too think it quite certain that a real change in the relations of human beings to possessions would be of more help in this direction than any ethical commands; but the recognition of this fact among socialists has been obscured and made useless for practical purposes by a fresh idealistic misconception of human nature.[45]

(The direction he is talking about here is towards greater rewards being given to people in this life on earth, and not merely empty promises of rewards in heaven.)

Pursuing the parallel between the individual and civilization's development of a super-ego, could it not be that some civilizations, or particular epochs, or indeed mankind as a whole, have become neurotic? It is difficult but not impossible for this type of judgement to be made. The difficulty is that in judgements about individuals there is some background of 'normality' against which his particular upbringing can be judged. This does not apply in the case of civilizations—we have no such common background against which to judge disorders which affect whole societies.[46]

> The fateful question for the human species seems to me to be whether and to what extent their cultural development will succeed in mastering the disturbance of their communal life by the human instinct of aggression and self-destruction.[47]

NOTES AND REFERENCES

1. S. Freud, 'Instincts and their Vicissitudes', 1915. Available in P. Rieff (ed.), *General Psychological Theory*, New York, 1963, Chapter IV.
2. See R. Fletcher, *Instinct in Man*, London, 1957 and 1968. See Reference to Unwin University Paperbacks edition, London, 1968, p. 174.
3. Freud, 'Instincts and their Vicissitudes', in Rieff (ed.), *General Psychological Theory*, p. 87.
4. Ibid., p. 88.
5. R. Fletcher, *Instinct in Man*, pp. 175–6.
6. See, e.g., D. Holbrook, *Human Hope against the Death Instinct*, London, 1971.
7. S. Freud, 'Reflections upon War and Death' (1915), available in P. Rieff (ed.), *Character and Culture*, New York, 1963, Chapter IX, p. 125.
8. Ibid., pp. 130–31.
9. Wilhelm Reich came close to a position such as the one outlined, rejecting the need to posit any innate destructive, aggressive instincts. See his *The Sexual Revolution* (1929 and 1935), London, 1951.
10. Freud, 'Why War?' (1932), in Rieff (ed.), *Character and Culture*, p. 147.
11. Freud, 'Formulations Regarding the Two Principles of Mental Functioning' (1911), in Rieff (ed.), *General Psychological Theory*, Chapter I.
12. S. Freud, *Beyond the Pleasure Principle* (1920), Standard Edition, Vol. 18. Reference to Bantam Books edition, New York, 1959, p. 78.
13. S. Freud, 'On the Mechanism in Paranoia' (1911). The case of Dr Schreber is briefly discussed in this paper, available in Rieff (ed.), *General Psychological Theory*, Chapter II.
14. Freud, *Beyond the Pleasure Principle*, edition cit., p. 47.
15. See R. Fletcher, *Instinct in Man*, pp. 239–53. This is a useful analysis of Freud's arguments from a biological point of view.

16. Freud, *Beyond the Pleasure Principle*, edition cit., p. 98.
17. S. Freud, 'The Economic Problem of Masochism' (1924), in Rieff (ed.), *General Psychological Theory*, Chapter XI, p. 191.
18. H. Marcuse, *Eros and Civilization*, New York, 1955.
19. See, e.g., H. Segal, *Introduction to the work of Melanie Klein*, London, 1964.
20. Good examples of Erich Fromm's work are: *The Fear of Freedom*, London, 1942; *The Sane Society*, New York, 1955.
21. S. Freud, *Civilization and Its Discontents* (1930), Standard Edition, Vol. 21. Reference to revised edition, London, 1963, p. 13.
22. Ibid., Chapter 2.
23. Ibid., pp. 21–2.
24. Ibid., pp. 23–4.
25. Ibid., p. 19 and 38.
26. Ibid., p. 37.
27. Ibid., p. 45.
28. Ibid.
29. Ibid., p. 48.
30. Ibid., p. 46.
31. See the discussion in Chapter 7 below on Max Weber's work in relation to Freud. See also B. Wilson, *Religious Sects*, London, 1970.
32. Freud, *Civilization and Its Discontents*, edition cit., p. 50.
33. Ibid., pp. 51–2.
34. Freud, *Beyond the Pleasure Principle*, edition cit., p. 70.
35. Ibid., p. 93.
36. Freud, *Civilization and Its Discontents*, edition cit., p. 58.
37. Ibid., pp. 59–60.
38. Ibid., p. 61.
39. Ibid., pp. 64–5.
40. S. Budd, *Sociologists and Religion*, London, 1973, p. 30.
41. Freud, *Civilization and Its Discontents*, edition cit., p. 69.
42. Ibid., p. 82.
43. Ibid., p. 78.
44. Ibid., p. 80.
45. Ibid.
46. Ibid., p. 81.
47. Ibid., p. 82.

7 Freud and Early Sociological Theory

Many sociologists have ignored Freud in the way they conceive of the development of sociology, and have seen him as concerned with a set of issues remote from those which are thought of as central to the other founding fathers. Sociologists interested in religion, however, have usually included Freud in their overviews of the theories of religion, but as this area has suffered from a lack of attention among sociologists generally, the concern with Freud in this specialized area of sociology has not done much to rectify matters, Religion and morality were of central concern to the founding fathers, especially to Weber and Durkheim. Marx and Engels, too, were interested in values, and therefore in the religious generation of values. Concern for meaning, and for religion, has recently reappeared in sociological theory, especially in the work of Peter Berger and Thomas Luckmann.

There are a considerable number of continuities and overlaps between the theories of Freud and Marx, Weber, Durkheim and Mead, and these will be brought out in this chapter. The discussion of these issues has to be brief. The main aim is to suggest that there are more overlaps between Freud and the various theorists to be discussed than are allowed for in the more usual approach of sociologists, which puts the stress on competing schools of thought, rather than on the cumulative body of theory that can be found in sociology. No doubt there has since Talcott Parsons wrote *The Structure of Social Action*[1] been a reaction against the stress which he put on the continuities in sociological theory, in part justified because he missed out Marx, whom he did not see as of central importance for sociology's development. In Europe, this has appeared to be a distorted view, for European sociology seems to live off problems raised initially by Marx.

There is a need to suggest, therefore, the continuities that can be found between sociologists and Freud. Such an attempt assumes that there are also continuities not just between Freud and each of the other thinkers to be considered, but also between each of them. Given the focus of the present book on Freud, major assumptions will have to be made, rather than proven, about the continuities between Marx and Weber, and between Weber and Durkheim, and perhaps between Durkheim and George Herbert Mead.[2] Such assumptions have to be made for the purposes of establishing the relation of Freud to each of these thinkers in turn.

The connection can best be seen by taking each of the major theorists and seeing the ways in which Freud's theory links with them, develops, or contradicts them. The thought of Marx, Weber and Durkheim constitutes the major source of modern sociology, and so they will be the centre of attention first of all. The work of the American social psychologists, Cooley and Mead, is also important for the purpose of seeing Freud within the broad context of sociological concerns.

Marx

There have been a number of attempts made to link Marxian and Freudian theory in this century. (The major attempt, which was made by members of the Frankfurt School, will be discussed in Chapter 8.) Here, the similarity between Marx's concept of man-in-society and that of Freud will be pointed out. They are both writers who took Darwin seriously,[3] and who wanted to develop a view of man based on the facts of his biological evolution and his organic relationship with the material environment. In the nineteenth century, when Marx began to do this, it was a novel enterprise. Looking at man as a material being, seeking to survive in a variety of natural environments, Marx was led to make *work* a central concern of his theory. 'Work' was the term to be given to the relation between man and his natural environment, and it is primary, in the sense that it is through work that mankind survives.

When Marx looked at human societies, he could see that not everyone was involved in primary work with the natural environment, but that very early in the development of man, a surplus of food and wealth occurred which led to the emergence of a separate group of people who did not work on nature. In later, more complex societies, the relative size of the group which does not work directly to produce food, or, more generally, wealth, increases. Classes develop on the basis of different relationships to the means of producing wealth, and distributing it among populations. Those who own the means of production, distribution or exchange are able to live at a further remove from the natural production process than those who own nothing, but have to work in order to survive.[4] This is not the place to discuss the concept of class in Marx, the important thing rather being to notice that the starting-point for Marx is man's relationship to nature, and then the relations between different groups of men in terms of their ownership of land, animals, factories, mines, banks, shops and so forth.

Freud shares this concern with starting with the situation of man as a biological organism seeking to survive in a natural environment. This common concern can be seen to stem from their acceptance of Darwin's biology and its implications for understanding mankind. Furthermore, Freud implicitly accepted the point Marx made about the difference in societies between those who work directly to produce wealth and those who own as being a fundamental one.[5] Both Marx and Freud have a common starting-point in their conception of man as a biological being, relating to nature through work, and developing social, economic and political structures around the different relationships of groups to the work process once there is any degree of surplus wealth being produced.

Whereas Marx made class structure the most central element in his theory, Freud did not. As was shown in the chapters on group psychology and instincts (Chapters 4 and 6), Freud did not think that work in common was enough to explain the way groups held together over time. Human societies seem to go to great lengths to use libidinal energies to keep groups cohesive, and to lessen the effects of the destructive power of the death instincts. Freud's later theory is built up on the interrelationships postulated between the sexual instincts and the death instincts, the one counteracting the other. Work uses energy derived from the sexual instincts, especially in keeping the group together, and from the death instincts, as in the destruction of animals, buildings, plants and trees.[6] In Freud's later theory, the social, economic structure does not take over from the biologically rooted psychic energies of the instincts, as it does in Marx.

Freud's later instinct theory can be seen as complementary to Marx's theory, rather than contradictory to it. A larger degree of economic equality, in terms of property ownership and incomes, would do a great deal to lessen conflicts, in modern capitalist societies, Freud thought. As was seen in an earlier chapter, however, Freud thought that it was a mistake to think there was no other source of human conflict, of hostility, and of violence to other human beings, than that of property relations.[7] Marx, on this view, could be said to have not been rigorous enough in moving away from idealism, for such a theory about humanity as his was based upon a *wish* that mankind has no basic destructiveness within him.

The attempt of Wilhelm Reich to link Marxism and psychoanalysis was based much more on the early theory of Freud, in which the sexual instincts have a key portion and the death instincts no major part. Reich thought that there could only be a humane revolution if it was both an economic, political revolution and a sexual revolution at the same time. Only in this way could authoritarianism be overcome, for sexual repression was necessary to maintain a compliance to authority in the army, state, education and religious organizations. People who were guilt-ridden about their sexual feelings had little emotional energy remaining to be critical of authorities and to be agents of change. Parents, teachers, clergy, youth workers and politicians all tried to keep young people, who were biologically and psychologically ready for sexual relations, away from sexual activities, and they remained thereby conformist, compliant and repressed people. The damage done in childhood, and again in adolescence, by sexually repressive morality, remained with people throughout life. It was this hypothesis, and its ramifications, which Reich took from Freud's work, and he tried to link it practically with Marxism by, for example, giving sexual education to young workers. Theoretically, he sought to link these ideas of Freud with the reasons for the failure of the Russian Revolution to achieve the results he had hoped for, and for the emergence of fascism in Europe, and especially in Germany and Italy.[8]

The sexually repressive moralities of the Communist Party, of fascist parties, and of the Roman Catholic Church particularly, were functional for maintaining totalitarian control over people. The organizational élites of all these parties and religious groups could maintain control over others by creating guilt about sexuality, and by offering authority figures on which these weakened personalities could depend. Reich could see that many working-class Germans admired Hitler, that they wanted a strong authority to rule over them, to take responsibility away from them. So although, as Marx pointed out, the work situation radicalized men and women who worked in industrial factories, institutions like the family, supported by churches, schools and political parties, made them reactionary in their basic emotional structure.[9]

This Reichian hypothesis was a powerful one, for it could begin to offer an explanation for the nationalist sentiments which were so strong among working-class people in Germany, Italy, France and Britain. In the First World War, when many Marxists had expected the workers of Germany to unite with those of France and Britain and overthrow their own bourgeoisies, there had been intense nationalist feelings among working-class people and little evidence of the true international brotherhood of socialism. Reich offered an explanation, derived from a part of Freud's theory, for these sombre events.

Reich succeeded in his attempt to marry Marx and Freud's theories only at the cost of leaving aside Freud's challenge to human self-aggrandizement, which had been formulated in the notion of the death instincts. It has been Herbert Marcuse who has sought to link Marxism with the Freudian theory of Eros and Thanatos, and his work will be examined in Chapter 8. It has to be concluded that, although Reich's theory is very useful for helping to understand and explain totalitarian politics and religion, it is a partial theory in that there are fundamental elements of Freudian theory missing—the independent death instincts.

To return to the more direct comparison of Freud and Marx, there is an important set of issues concerned with their respective analyses of the role of religion in mankind's revolutionary development. They both share the attitude of post-Darwinians to religion, that is, that religious beliefs and practices marked a phase in the development of humanity which is destined to be surpassed by science. Science would for Marx find its expression in political economy, and for Freud in the practice of psychoanalysis. Neither Marx nor Freud saw science as merely academic research, nor as technology, although they both thought that technology had a central importance for the future of man's development. The scientific standpoint could also be applied to human affairs, and not just to nature; or rather, human affairs had to be seen as part of the 'nature' science sought to understand. They both were concerned to link theory and practice for the benefit of man's development. Their conception of science involved applying it to the values which men pursue, and the notion of a value-free science, totally removed from the ends of human action, had no place in either of their theories.

Marx concentrated on the role of religions in societies which were built on the alienation of man from nature and the alienation of man from man. Religions expressed the hopes and the sufferings of people in such an alienated condition. Some religious institutions expressed the hopes of repressed people for deliverance, often to be in another life, not here on earth, but sometimes the change was to be on earth. Other, established religions expressed the political and economic interests of the dominant class group in a society at a particular stage of its development.[10] In a simple sense, there is little difference between Freud and Marx here, for Freud also saw religion as the expression of wishes—wishes for health, life after death, good fortune and compensation for sufferings in this life. Both gave some weight to the more positive aspects of religion in mankind's development. In Marx and Engels there was some attention given to the aspect of religion, found, for example, in Judaism and Christianity, which could lead to a demand for change in political and economic class differences.[11] In Freud, religion was seen as being capable of linking people into wider groups and purposes, and as such was preferable to individual neurosis, which isolated people from common purposes and projects with other people. In spite of these features which they each respectively saw in religions, neither Marx nor Freud placed much hope in them for furthering the future happiness of mankind. The persistence of religion could be expected as long as the conditions which caused it to appeal to people remained in various human societies.

The causes of religion's development in human societies, as well as its persistence in modern societies, were rather different in the two theories. The common element in Marx and Freud's theories is that religion stems from some form or other of alienation of men and women from nature, both outside themselves, within themselves, and from other people. In Marx's later theory, religion has a small part to play; it is economic change, and the associated political changes which will result from the abolition of private property ownership of the major means of production, which is central. All else hinges on these changes in the external economic relations between classes which may, themselves, be brought about by changes in the technological means of producing things. The concern with the alienation of man in his inner life, and in his relations with nature and other people, found in the more philosophical aspects of Marx's thought, are expected to right themselves as a result of taking part in the revolution that establishes world socialism and world communism. Religion will wither away, like the state, when it is no longer needed either by the ruling economic class to preserve its privileges through religious mystification, nor by the oppressed to express their unfulfilled hopes. As Marx put it:

> Thus the criticism of heaven turns into the criticism of the earth, the criticism of religion into the criticism of right, and the criticism of theology into the criticism of politics.[12]

Religion has a more important role in Freud's theory, for it handles the deep-seated guilt humanity feels, unconsciously, about the primal murder. Judaism and Christianity are handling the guilt left over from the killing of the father. Christ is offered as a human sacrifice to try to make amends to the father for the original killing. Jesus becomes himself a new god-figure, and takes over from the father. Freud's theory of religion is about the unconscious content of religions. This content will not simply disappear after a revolution, and man will not be de-alienated, therefore, for the root disturbance in his psychic life will remain.[13]

Alienation cannot be eradicated simply by external changes in technology and economic class relationships. Nor can revolutionary action be entrusted with the task of de-alienating men from nature and from one another. Indeed, Freud's theory of the attraction of crowds as a way of escaping the tension between the super-ego and a person's actual actions, and his analysis of the way the crowd lowers humanity to more primitive levels of functioning, can be applied to much revolutionary action. The result of doing so entails being less optimistic about the capacities of such revolutionary actions to de-alienate men than was Marx. Freud's theory seems to lead to the expectation that revolutions are more likely to set up régimes of terror—as, in fact, they have often, if not always, done—than achieve the real liberation of man from torture, injustice and the violence inflicted on people by others.

The revolutionary crowd is likely to be seeking unconscious satisfactions and not only acting to right economic and political injustice. The revolutionary leader, who is not a part of Marxist ideology as developed by Marx, but an addition made by Lenin, Stalin, Mao, Castro, et al., plays a role in the unconscious emotional life of the revolutionary movement, usually as the ego ideal of the members. He can articulate the wish of the revolutionary band of brothers, to establish justice and equality by repeating the primal murder. The father must be slain. At one and the same time, the guilt for the deed must be assuaged by sacrifice to the father in the form of a willingness to die on the part of the revolutionary.

Max Weber

There are some overlaps between Freud's work and another major figure of sociology, Max Weber. Although they were concerned with different types of problem, Weber with large-scale change in human societies, and Freud with neurosis, there was a common interest in meaning, emotion, tradition and values, and in the biological basis of human life.

The latter point can be dealt with briefly, for Weber did not really develop his thought in this direction. It is interesting to see how he thought it might fit in with his own work, and so it is worth quoting him on this.

> [Biological work and animal psychology] may throw light on the question of the relative role in the early stages of human social differentiation of mechanical and instinctive factors, as compared with that of the factors which are accessible to subjective interpretation generally, and more particularly to the role of consciously rational action. It is necessary for the sociologist to be thoroughly aware of the fact that in the early stages even of human development, the first set of factors is completely predominant. Even in the later stages he must take account of their continual interaction with the others in a role which is often of decisive importance. This is particularly true of all 'traditional' action and many aspects of charisma. In the latter field of phenomena lie the seeds of certain types of psychic 'contagion' and it is thus the bearer of many dynamic tendencies of social processes.[14]

There is an assumption in the above remarks that human societies evolve from early forms, in which instinctual forces are predominant, to later forms, where rational action is more dominant. This perspective is one shared by Freud who, in his work in *Totem and Taboo* and *The Future of an Illusion*, for example, shows how early society still affected modern society through the influence of religions and morality. They both saw the growth of relatively more rational action, as in modern technology, for instance, as a major characteristic feature of modern societies, but the influence of emotions persists, and traditional values and modes of action do not disappear completely in such societies. Freud can also be seen to have developed the area of 'contagion', as Weber called it, in his work on group psychology, and as was shown in the chapter on this section of Freud's work (Chapter 4), there are links with Weber's notion of charisma in his analysis of the influence of the leader over the members of a group. In these ways, then, Freud can be said to be congruent with Weber's conception of sociology, and to have worked on areas of instinctual, affective, traditional and charismatic action, in Weber's terminology.

Turning now to more substantive areas, there are important ways in which Weber's work on the Protestant ethic and the spirit of capitalism can be rounded out by reference to Freud's idea of 'character', and the 'anal character' in particular.[15] A number of writers have commented on this possibility— C. Wright Mills, Erik Erikson, Norman Brown and Erich Fromm, for example.[16] Perhaps the most important point of connection lies in Freud's understanding of the role of asceticism in the process of sublimation of libidinal energy into work, and into professional callings, such as that of the scientist or the businessman. The Calvinist's distrust of the body and its sexuality ensured that there would be energy available to such a character for other activities in which this energy could find expression. In the specific case of anal erotism, the Calvinist's concern for care for detail in money matters, for saving and leading a frugal existence, and for bookkeeping can be seen as sublimated forms of this element of sexuality. The dedication to hard work was important in Weber's analysis of the growth of capitalism and science, entailing active mastery over the world by men, rather than mastery over the self alone in the specialized setting of the monastic life.[17] Freud provides an understanding of the instinctual, psychological and unconscious dynamics of this ethic, and can be seen as deepening the understanding which Weber had reached, quite independently, of the Calvinist character-type and his relationship to emerging modern, rational capitalism.[18]

In an important paper, 'Religious Rejections of the World and Their Directions' (1915),[19] Weber discussed the tension between religions of brotherly love and the economic, political, aesthetic, erotic and intellectual spheres. The discussion refers to historical examples in a way which Freud rarely does, and shows more sensitivity to the variety of ways in which the erotic sphere, for example, can be experienced depending on the way it is institutionalized in a particular society. The knight's love for the 'lady' differs from the ancient Greek love of the boy, and people with preferences for homosexuality, or for loving other men's wives, fare differently in the two societies. Weber's analysis is at other points very like that of Freud. For example:

> The rejection of all naïve surrender to the most intensive ways of experiencing existence, artistic and erotical, is as such only a negative attitude. But it is obvious that such rejection could increase the force with which energies flow into rational achievement, both the ethical as well as the purely intellectual.[20]

This point is the same as Freud's notion of the sublimation of sexual energy into other types of activity such as work. Weber is also explicit in seeing religion and sex as linked psychologically:

> Certain psychological interrelations of both spheres sharpen the tension between religion and sex. The highest eroticism stands psychologically and physiologically in a mutually substitutive relation with certain sublimated forms of heroic piety.[21]

The mystic union with God is such a substitute for sexuality.

> This psychological affinity naturally increases the antagonism of inner meanings between eroticism and religion.[22]

Weber is in his analysis extremely sensitive to the fact that the attractions of eroticism to some people in modern society is precisely the one sphere where irrationality can be experienced, and a connection made with man's animality. This attraction has increased as rational spheres of action have spread within society, including even marriage and modern family life. For others, the irrationality of sex is precisely the reason why it is condemned.

> The brotherly love ethic of salvation religion is in profound tension with the greatest irrational force of life: sexual love.[23]

Weber is at this point again close to the connections which Freud found to exist between the brotherly love ethic of Christianity, for example, and the use of sublimated libidinal energies to achieve this. However, Freud went further than Weber in explaining the reason for this in his assumption of the basic hostility of human beings towards one another. It is this mutual hostility which requires the energy of sexuality to be sublimated into brotherly love if human groups are to be cohesive.[24]

Weber's analysis is an illuminating description of the tension between religion and sex, whereas Freud offers an explanation which goes beyond Weber's analysis. There is, however, a remarkable similarity in their concerns and analyses in the area of religion and sexuality. For both of them, religion has had a crucial part to play in the development of human societies, not least because it provides the most fundamental layer of meaning and values, and associates sentiments with these values. Religion is seen to have this importance because, for both Weber and Freud, it draws its energy from sexuality. Sexuality is a key 'instinct', and provides the fuel for the evolutionary development of human civilization.

Émile Durkheim

There has been considerable misunderstanding of Durkheim's position on the relations between sociology and psychology; he has been thought to have been concerned to maintain that sociology must have nothing to do with psychological levels of explanation. His main concern, however, was to make *social association* the central creative feature of human beings. It was man's sociability which was crucial in the development of conscience, morality, sentiments, and this must come first, before the concept of the individual, in understanding men's actions in society. This area of social conscience, or morality, cannot be understood by using a psycho-physiological approach, but needs a socio-psychological approach.[25] Durkheim is concerned, therefore, to establish that a psychological approach based on physical, individual variables cannot explain the emergence of social conscience, which is for him the central feature of all human society.

His understanding of the role of instinct is interesting:

> Truly, conscience only invades the ground which instinct has
> ceased to occupy, or where instinct cannot be established.
> Conscience does not make instinct recede; it only fills the
> space instinct leaves free. Moreover, if instinct regresses rather
> than extends as general life extends, the greater importance of
> the social factor is the cause of this. Hence, the great difference
> which separates man from animals, that is the greater
> development of his *psychic life*, comes from his greater
> sociability.[26]

There are a number of important similarities between Durkheim and Freud here. First, the common assumption that humans have instincts, but that they also have a characteristic *in addition*, namely sociability, which animals do not have to the same degree. Secondly, Freud's later theory of the super-ego, as well as the work in *Group Psychology*, puts a similar stress on the importance of conscience, which is as much a social product in Freudian theory as in Durkheim's. As was shown above, Freud retains the idea of conflict being possible between instinctual impulses and conscience. This consists of values which the individual internalizes as a result of his participation in various social groups and institutions. Such conflict is not central to Durkheim's theory, but the two theories are similar in the conceptualization of instincts and the way they are overlaid by the development of society, or civilization in Freud's terminology. Thirdly, Durkheim uses the term 'psychic life' to describe the difference that arises between animals and men as a result of the latter's sociability. Freud can be seen to have been concerned with precisely this. It has been argued in the earlier chapters of this book that Freud *understood the social generation of this psychic life, as well as its roots in instinctual impulses.*

The importance that Durkheim gives to 'society' lies in his recognition of the fact that it is when individuals come together in social interaction, especially in great collective events such as revolutions of a political, intellectual, artistic or religious kind, that new ideals are formulated. This is the way societies change. Later on, after the exhaustion of these creative moments, more traditional ritual forms emerge which commemorate these creative moments, and regenerate people's commitment to the ideals, as in political parades and meetings, religious services and theatrical events—and, one might add now, in film and on television and radio.[27]

> When individual minds are not isolated but enter into close relations with and work upon each other, from their synthesis arises a new kind of psychic life. It is clearly distinguished by its peculiar intensity from that led by the solitary individual. Sentiments born and developed in the group have a greater energy than purely individual sentiments.[28]

There are remarkable continuities again with the thought of Freud. Starting out with different concerns, namely, the understanding of neurosis, Freud arrives at a theory not unlike that of Durkheim. For example, the obsessive ritual of the neurotic is isolating, and it is this which makes the condition of the individual neurotic worse. Religious ritual is collective, unites the person with others in common purposes and ideals, and is therefore to this extent health-enhancing.[29] The role of what Freud termed 'civilization', and Durkheim termed 'society', is central in the two theories for understanding the way in which people act, and understanding how societies change and evolve. In this process the role of moral ideals and religious rituals, and in modern societies various political movements such as nationalism and socialism, are central for both Freud and Durkheim. It is perhaps also important to point out that Marx's notion of the role of revolutionary change, and of the key importance of societal movements to generate change, although based on materialistic, economic motivation, does have similarities with Durkheim's. Durkheim writes:

> Society is also of nature and yet dominates it. Not only do all the forces of the universe converge in society, but they also form a new synthesis which surpasses in richness, complexity and power of action all that went to form it. In a word, society is nature arrived at a higher point in its development, concentrating all its energies to surpass, as it were, itself.[30]

It is this general insight which was so exciting also to Marx, and the later generation of sociologists at the turn of the century, for it was a novel discovery. Freud can also be seen as part of this general movement of thought towards concern for the scientific study of social change in order to generate a scientific basis for values to guide the next changes. Although, in Marx, the stress was more on the technical and the economic variables in change, in Weber there are already developments of the crucial role which religions have played in generating basic change, and a search for its alternatives in modern societies. This did not exclude the economic concerns of Marx, but added to them a further dimension. It was only as a result of religious change in the Reformation period that economic motives had been allowed to have an independence and therefore to become agents for change among the capitalists and among the proletariat.

Durkheim and Freud developed our understanding of moral values and religion as generated by society, and the ways in which they act back on society and affect the directions of change. Alternatively, religion and morality may help to contain change, which leads to stability and eventually to sterility.

C. H. Cooley (1864-1929) and G. H. Mead (1863-1931)

There has been a tendency to see Cooley and Mead, the American social psychologists, as being distinct in their thinking from Freud. Berger and Luckmann, for example, make the two theories discontinuous and even contradictory.[31] There are, however, many similarities between the approaches of Freud and Mead. Cooley and Mead both saw man as being born with instinctive energies which were not fixed in the direction they could take, but malleable through the use of human reason. They both assumed that the instincts were subject to alteration by the culture of a human society, and in this they do differ from Freud in the emphasis to be placed on the degree of malleability of man's instinctive endowment. Fundamentally, though, there is a similar view about the way in which people are seen as a complex mixture of instinctive energy, reason and the ideals and values of the social groups in which they have been brought up.

Cooley denied that any hard-and-fast distinction could be made between the individual and society, for,

> the individual has his being only as part of a whole. What does not come by heredity comes by communication and intercourse; and the more closely we look the more apparent it is that separateness is an illusion of the eye and community the inner truth.[32]

Freud came to see the interconnections in this way too, as was shown in our earlier discussion of *Group Psychology and the Analysis of the Ego*.[33] The more psychoanalysis explored the conflicts of people, the more it became clear that it was not a matter of a conflict between the person as an individual and 'society', but a conflict between a wish or desire that the person had, and a value he had internalized. 'Society' is in the most intimate regions of the person's psyche. The confusion arises because the term 'society' is a concept on a more abstract level than that of the concept 'individual'. The two are not therefore comparable concepts. This is the confusion which Cooley, Mead and Freud can all be said to have tried to solve in a remarkably similar way.

The person is formed in primary groups, that is in relatively small, face-to-face unspecialized groups, such as the family and play groups. The relationships in such groups are very intense and intimate, and involve the *whole* person, not just a part, as in secondary relationships. They are relatively permanent groups, such as families and neighbourhood communities, and membership of them is typically involuntary, as people are born into them. It is in such primary groups that human beings are formed, and without them people feel depressed and unhappy if, later in life, they become isolated from such primary relationships. The traditions and values of the primary group are communicated to the new generation in such settings; they are imbibed by children as being the only way of life and they are socialized to accept it as normal. This stress on the key role of the primary group, and later between pupil and teacher, is common to the American social psychologists and Freud, especially in the latter's analysis of the development of the super-ego.

There are some differences between Cooley and Mead's conception of instincts and those of Freud. Mead, for example, thought that there was a gregarious instinct, expressed in the relationships between neighbours, whereas, as was shown in Chapter 4 of the present book, Freud held that the gregarious behaviour of human beings was not a basic instinct, but was derivative from sexuality as well as from the necessity of men to co-operate to achieve things in the environment. One of the gains that humanity made was expressed by Freud in his mythic theory of the band of brothers learning that co-operation made some tasks easier than was possible for the individual, even though the task performed was murder! The nature of sexuality was also conceived differently by Mead, who stressed the social nature of sexual relations, and Freud, who stressed the auto-erotic nature of infant sexuality. In Freud's theory, people have to learn to take other people as sexual objects, and to relate to others; some people do not find this easy, and practise auto-eroticism, or remain celibate.

This different conception of sexuality in Freud leads to a more *organic* notion of sexual instincts in his theory rather than to the more *social* aspect of Cooley and Mead's notion of sexual instincts. This has further consequences in terms of understanding conflict. For Cooley and Mead, there cannot be as fundamental a conflict between the person's organic desires and the values of his society which he has internalized as there can be in Freud's thought. This is because the desire cannot make itself felt outside a culturally derived conception of the desire, so the degree of anticipated conflict on this view is much less than in Freud's theory. In Freud's work with his patients, he found that there can be people who experience desires for sexual activities that they have learned to think of as disgusting and wrong. This is why Freud retained the notion that an instinctual impulse can be exerting pressure, on the individual which at first is unconscious. The person rejects this instinctual desire because of the socialization process to which he has been exposed.[34] Both Cooley and Mead's theory gives an adequate account of how the socialization process works in 'normal' development, and it is, indeed, in most important respects congruent with Freud's theory. Their theory is less adequate in understanding the less successful socialization process which leads to neurosis. This is more widespread, in Freud's view, than many people wish to admit.

Before looking at Mead's development of Cooley, it is important to note that Mead also included the idea of hostile, destructive aggressive instincts in his view of the biological endowment of humans. Societies have to develop institutions for containing these hostile attitudes and expressing conflicts in ways which do not lead to total destruction. So Mead's theory contains conflict, hostility and destructiveness as well as co-operation in society.[35] In this there is an important parallel with Freud, and one which is worth noticing because of the rejection by so many writers of Freud's notion of death instincts, whose major social expression is in hostile, and destructive, acts between groups of people. Mead was working in an independent way within the American tradition of Cooley and Giddings, and he reached conclusions which were not dissimilar in this respect to those of Freud. No doubt the killing and destruction in the First World War had to be integrated into the social psychology of the Americans as it did into the thinking of Europeans, and the similarity of concern with destruction is understandable. The lack of concern about destruction among some later writers is less comprehensible, especially since the Second World War and its aftermath.

Mead's development of the distinction between the 'I' and the 'me' moved social psychology on from where Cooley had left it. Mead thought that there was a part of the self which was conscious and experiencing on-going events, the 'I'; and that there was another part, the 'me', which was the object of consciousness when a person reflected on himself.

In order to become aware of himself as such he must . . . become an object to himself, or enter his own experience as an object, and only by social means—only by taking the attitudes of others towards himself—is he able to become an object to himself.[36]

Ronald Fletcher has suggested that there is a similarity here between Mead and Freud, especially in the latter's distinction between the conscious and the pre-conscious, the store of memories which can be recalled relatively easily.[37] There is also the important similarity between the process Mead is describing and the way the analysand learns to take himself as an object of observation, by learning to do so in the therapeutic relationship with the analyst. Freud's stress on the analytic situation is in part due to this fact that it is a learning process; the individual can become more conscious of himself, not just in terms of the memories in the pre-conscious, but by integrating and reflecting upon unconscious material too.[38]

Fletcher, in his discussion of the parallels between Cooley, Mead and Freud, also points out the importance of the notion of the ego ideal in Freud (sometimes called the super-ego, and identical with it, sometimes a *part* of the super-ego). The harshness of the super-ego is often stressed more than the ego ideal and the way people aspire to achieve their ego ideal; this latter process has much more to do with the moral aspirations of the person and of the group. Freud's analysis of the group includes the notion of the members all having taken the same ego ideal into themselves through introjection, and this process is not dissimilar to the way in which both Cooley and Mead thought of the primary group's part in developing morality.[39] It is only in a primary group that morality can develop and become active, and yet without such moral values no human society is possible.

In conclusion, it has been pointed out in this chapter that there are a number of important ways in which Freud's thought can be seen to link in with the mainstream of sociology and social psychology. The ideas of Marx, Weber, Durkheim, Cooley and Mead have been taken to illustrate this point. Freud certainly had an original contribution to make to sociology and social psychology, in his theory of unconscious desires of both a generalized sexual nature and of a hostile, destructive nature. This does not place him completely outside the areas of concern to sociologists. There are many continuities and similarities between Freud and other sociologists which are only now being perceived. It is time that Freud was brought in from the cold, and his ideas integrated more into general sociological understanding.

NOTES AND REFERENCES

1. T. Parsons, *The Structure of Social Action*, New York, 1937 and 1949. Marx does not have a major set of chapters devoted to his work. Parsons concentrated on Pareto, Durkheim and Weber, with some discussion of Marshall, and very little on Marx.
2. For discussion of the continuities in sociology, including Marx, see the following: A. Giddens, *Capitalism and Modern Social Theory*, Cambridge, 1971. R. Fletcher, *The Making of Sociology*, 2 vols., London, 1971. I. Zeitlin, *Ideology and the Development of Sociological Theory*, Englewood Cliffs, N.J., 1968.
3. See K. Marx, *Capital* (1867), Vol. 1. Quoted by T. Bottomore and M. Rubel, *Karl Marx, Selected Writings in Sociology and Social Philosophy*, London, 1956, 1961. Reference to Penguin edition, Harmondsworth, 1963, pp. 78–9. (Freud used Darwin's ideas in *Totem and Taboo*, Chapter IV, for example.)
4. See Bottomore and Rubel, *Karl Marx*, Part Three, Chapters 4 and 5.
5. See S. Freud, *Civilization and Its Discontents* (1930), Standard Edition, Vol. 21. Reference to revised edition, London, 1963.
6. Ibid., esp. Chapter V.
7. Ibid., p. 80.
8. See W. Reich, *The Sexual Revolution* (1929 and 1935), London, 1951.
9. See W. Reich, *The Mass Psychology of Fascism* (1934), New York, 1946.
10. See K. Marx, *Contribution to the Critique of Hegel's Philosophy of Right* (1844), Introduction.
11. K. Marx and F. Engels, *On Religion* (collected pieces), Moscow and London, 1955.
12. Ibid., p. 42.
13. See the discussion on the primal horde in Chapter 4 above (pp. 64–7), and of instinct theory in Chapter 6 above (pp. 117–19).
14. M. Weber, *Theory of Social and Economic Organization*, New York, 1947, p. 106.
15. M. Weber, *The Protestant Ethic and the Spirit of Capitalism*, London, 1930.
16. H. Gerth and C. Wright Mills, *Character and Social Structure*, New York, 1953. E. Erikson, *Young Man Luther*, New York, 1958. N. O. Brown, *Life Against Death*, London, 1959, Part Five, 'Studies in Anality'. E. Fromm, *Fear of Freedom*, New York, 1941.
17. See H. Gerth and C. Wright Mills, *From Max Weber, Essays in Sociology*, London, 1948, Part Three, Chapters XII and XIII.
18. See S. Freud, *On the Transformation of Instincts with Special Reference to Anal Erotism*, Vienna, 1917.
19. Gerth and Wright Mills, *From Max Weber*, Part Three.
20. Ibid., p. 350.
21. Ibid., p. 348.
22. Ibid.
23. Ibid., p. 343.
24. See the discussion in Chapter 6. (pp. 115–19).
25. And É. Durkheim, *Sociology and Philosophy*, London, 1965, Chapter One.

26. See É. Durkheim, *The Division of Labour in Society*, translated by G. Simpson, New York, 1960, p. 346.

27. See R. Bocock, *Ritual in Industrial Society*, London, 1974.

28. É. Durkheim, *Sociology and Philosophy*, translated by D. F. Pocock, London, 1965, p. 91.

29. See Chapter 5 above (p. 90).

30. É. Durkheim, *Sociology and Philosophy* (trans by D. Pocock), London, 1965, p. 97.

31. P. Berger and T. Luckman, *The Social Construction of Reality*, New York, 1966; London, 1967.

32. C. H. Cooley, *Social Organization*, New York, 1962, p. 9.

33. See Chapter 4 above (p. 56).

34. See, e.g., S. Freud, ' "Civilized" Sexual Morality and Modern Nervousness' (1908), available in P. Rieff (ed.), *Sexuality and the Psychology of Love*, New York, 1963.

35. G. H. Mead, *George Herbert Mead on Social Psychology*, Chicago, 1965, p. 265.

36. Ibid., p. 244.

37. R. Fletcher, *The Making of Sociology*, Vol. II, London, 1971, p. 551.

38. See S. Freud in P. Rieff (ed.), *Therapy and Technique*, New York, 1963.

39. R. Fletcher, *The Making of Sociology*, Vol. II, pp. 556–7.

8 Freud and Recent Sociological Theory: the Frankfurt School

Apart from the work of Talcott Parsons, there have been no major attempts systematically to link Freud's theory with mainstream sociology. The work of the Frankfurt School is now coming into the mainstream of sociological theory, with the breakdown of positivistic schools of sociology. Critical theory is the only alternative base for sociological theory to that of positivism in all its varieties, apart from the phenomenological approaches which have recently emerged and been developed, for example, by Cicourel, Berger and Luckmann.

Talcott Parsons deliberately limited his use of Freudian theory to the area of the development of personality, ignoring the later use of instinct theory in Freud's own sociology. As was shown in Chapter 3, this had serious consequences for Parsons's understanding of Freud, especially in relation to the concept of the super-ego, and of guilt, in the advanced sections of modern societies. The potentiality for conflict between people and certain aspects of their cultures and institutions is lost, and the dynamic for change is masked, by the way Talcott Parsons uses Freud.

The work of phenomenologically influenced sociologists has also been discussed above, in Chapter 2, especially in relation to Berger's sociological understanding of psychoanalysis. This sociologizes about the elective affinity between psychoanalysis and modern society, but does not discuss it as a contribution to theory as such. This is legitimate as an exercise in the sociology of knowledge, but not as a full understanding of the relations between psychoanalysis and sociology.

Phenomenological sociology, and psychology, can collapse into ethical, political and religious relativism. This is what seems to have happened to Laing and Cooper, for example, two psychotherapists influenced by phenomenology, and who at first seemed to have a coherent political, if not sociological, position. Their work has become more and more relativistic as they moved away from 'Western rationality', and from Freud, who was seen as someone over-influenced by this particular form of thought.[1]

The Frankfurt School discussed many of these issues in the

1930s. There has always been a suspicion among them that phenomenology and positivism led to ethical relativism, which begins by appearing scientific, objective, tolerant and sophisticated. It ends in fascism, and its basic belief that *the act* is all. Might becomes right. It is this adherence to applying rational and scientific thinking to human affairs, to ethics and to politics, that had first put this group of thinkers out of court for respectable academics. It is now this which makes them appear to be of great importance again in the human sciences. They sought to link Freud's psychoanalysis with a Marxian sociology, modified by Weber.[2]

Given the importance of this group of writers, this chapter will concentrate on the Frankfurt School, and on the work of Erich Fromm and Herbert Marcuse in particular. The work of Jurgen Habermas, a recent writer in this tradition, has already been discussed in Chapter 2, so will not be discussed again here.

Early Work of the Frankfurt School

Before the Second World War, Erich Fromm had developed some of the links between Marx and Freud and had helped to establish this distinctive and, at the time, novel endeavour of relating Marxism and psychoanalysis. Two of his important papers, first published in 1932 and now available in English in Fromm's *The Crisis of Psychoanalysis* (1970), were attempts to develop an analytical social psychology which sought 'to understand the instinctual apparatus of a group, its libidinous and largely unconscious behaviour in terms of its socio-economic structure'.[3]

At this point in time, the early 1930s, Fromm accepted the key role of libido in Freud's thought, and still operated with Freud's early model of two instincts, sexuality and self-preservation; the death instincts, which Freud began to write about in the 1930s, were never accepted by Fromm.[4] Already, though, Fromm was critical of the universality of the Oedipus complex in the light of anthropological work in other cultures where it was found not to exist. The work of Malinowski[5] was important in this respect, but even more influential in Fromm's later thought was the work of a mid-nineteenth-century writer Bachofen, who had written about matriarchy and mother right.[6] Fromm came to think that Freud's theory was too restricted in that it might apply to patriarchal cultures, but not to matriarchal ones. This interest in matricentric societies tied up with his interest in socialism for modern societies, in that such matricentric societies stressed happiness, security, 'the harmonious unfolding of one's personality', rather than rational calculation, competitiveness and hard work, the values of Protestant, patricentric societies.[7] It also proved to have fundamental consequences for his thinking which increasingly, and especially after the end of the war, set him apart from the other members of the Frankfurt Institute.

Initially, Horkheimer had been quite appreciative of Fromm's work, but later he remained more strictly Freudian than Fromm. Horkheimer agreed with Fromm on the need for an individual psychology to add to the political, economic and macro-sociological analysis of Marxism. He also disliked Freud's notion of death instincts, for Freud missed the historical component in oppression, and thereby absolutized the status quo and became 'resigned to the necessity of a permanent élite to keep the destructive masses down'.[8] However, Horkheimer preferred Freud, with his insistence on the importance of sexuality, to the way Fromm began to spiritualize sexuality into 'loving relationships' as a result of his interest in matricentric cultures.

The other member of the Frankfurt Institute who has affected the way Fromm's work has been understood and received was Adorno, who examined the work of Horney and Fromm in a paper written in 1946.[9] Adorno argued that Freud's theory of instincts was not as mechanistic as the Freudian revisionists suggested, that they over-concentrated on the ego:

> Concretely, the denunciation of Freud's so-called instinctivism amounts to the denial that culture, by enforcing restrictions on libidinal and particularly destructive drives, is instrumental in bringing about repressions, guilt feelings, and need for self-punishment.[10]

Adorno here uses Freud's work on destructive or death drives in a way which Fromm seems to have failed to do because of his early dislike of death instincts as formulated by Freud.

Adorno also brought out the difference between the revisionists' use of a model of 'whole' personality in place of Freud's fragmentary, disjointed personality model.

> The stress on totality as against the unique, fragmentary impulses, always implies the harmonistic belief in what might be called the unity of the personality, [a unity that] is never realized in our society. It is one of the greatest merits of Freud that he has debunked the myth of this unity.[11]

The moralism and stress on love, and the assumption that change can come from attempts to increase loving relationships between whole persons, were seen as naïve by Adorno, who thought that our society was such that 'the reality of love can actually be expressed only by the hatred of the existent, whereas any direct evidence of love serves only at confirming the very same conditions which breed hatred'.[12]

The real bond of bourgeois society was and is the threat of bodily violence, not the competitiveness described and disliked by the revisionists, and by Fromm in particular. These remarks were first made by Adorno in the immediate aftermath of the Second World War. They were taken up a decade later by Herbert Marcuse, the one member of the Frankfurt School who had remained in the United States after the others returned to Germany, and who wrote in English, and hence became better known than the German-language writers like Adorno.

The Fromm–Marcuse Debate

Marcuse's *Eros and Civilization* appeared in 1955 and was sub-titled 'A Philosophical Inquiry into Freud' to distinguish it from purely clinical theory and therapeutic uses of Freud.[13] Marcuse was not a practising analyst, whereas Fromm was, and this, in part, explains their different approaches to Freud. Nevertheless, Fromm has written sociological works which do not in any direct or explicit way link with his therapeutic work, although he would maintain that the ideas he uses are derived from clinical practice.[14] Fromm objects, in his paper *The Crisis of Psychoanalysis*, that Marcuse approaches Freud too philo-sophically, and seems to be removed from the clinical base of Freud's own metapsychology. It is not necessary to be a thera-pist, or even to have been analysed, to understand Freud, but it is important to see the relationship between the clinical basis and the other ideas in Freud. This seems a perfectly reasonable point to stress, but it cannot carry the weight Fromm makes it do.

> For [Marcuse] psychoanalysis is not an empirical method for the uncovering of the unconscious strivings of a person, masked by rationalization . . . Psychoanalysis, for Marcuse, is a set of metaphysical speculations about death, the life instinct, infantile sexuality, etc.[15]

Psychoanalysis is both a method of discovery of unconscious

materials, a therapeutic practice and a theory about man-in-society. They are interrelated areas certainly, but Fromm cannot maintain that psychoanalysis is only a method, and treat the theory and the metapsychology as 'metaphysics'—a term Fromm is using in the above quotation to imply 'nonsense' in the way a strict empiricist would see metaphysics. In other contexts, Fromm is not an empiricist, nor a positivist, for he argues that psychoanalysis is not value-neutral, but implies an ethic and a view of man which can help us make social and political choices, not only personal ones.[16] Psychoanalytic theory does not fit into existing academic departmental categories, and Marcuse's use of the term 'philosophical' is really not very significant; no more so than the departmental boundaries in universities. There is an area of discussion, a universe of discourse developed by Freud, of psychoanalytic theory about man-in-society, which is sociology, social psychology, anthropology and political philosophy as these terms are used in contemporary universities. It cross-cuts them all. There are propositions in Freud's work which can be discussed; 'tested' would seem an absurd notion in this context. There is not just a method, then, as Fromm claims, but an area of discussion which Marcuse somewhat arbitrarily called philosophical, but which might just as well be called either 'metapsychological' or 'sociological'.

The important thing for the Frankfurt School about Freud's work was its potential for critical theory. Both Marcuse and Fromm seem to be agreed on this point. In his paper 'The Crisis of Psychoanalysis' (1970), Fromm was himself critical about the ego psychology school of revisionism, with whom he does not identify himself, though Marcuse seems to ignore this. In discussing Hartmann's work on defining mental health, Fromm wrote:

> Hartmann has . . . removed the most important—and
> radical element in Freud's system: the criticism of middle-class
> mores, and the protest against them in the name of man and
> his development. With his identification of 'human' and 'social'
> health, and the implicit denial of social pathology, he is in
> opposition to Freud who spoke of 'collective neuroses' and of
> the 'pathology of civilized communities'.[17]

This is similar to Marcuse's discussion of Sullivan's views of mental health:

> This 'operational' identification of mental health with
> 'adjustive success' and progress eliminates all the reservations

with which Freud hedged the therapeutic objective of adjustment to an inhuman society [in his *A General Introduction to Psychoanalysis*] and thus commits psychoanalysis to this society far more than Freud ever did.[18]

In this context of discussion about the definitions of mental health which stress adjustment and conformity to society, both Fromm and Marcuse make the same point: that to define mental health and the purpose of therapy as conformity and adjustment without qualification, is to misinterpret Freud and to miss the degree to which his theory was critical of middle-class life, both in his own society and, by implication, in contemporary society. The state of affairs underlying the criticisms of modern civilization made by Freud has not altered quite as much as some assume. The advances of our technical civilization will require instinctual renunciations of sexual and destructive impulses, with the result that there is no overall increase in happiness, but rather more discontentment. This is in line with Freud's comment that '. . . the price we pay for our advance in civilisation is a loss of happiness through the heightening of the same sense of guilt'.[19]

Marcuse and Fromm also agree, at least in principle, on the dangers of overemphasis on the conscious ego by the revisionists, and see the originality of Freud to have been in the stress he put on the id, the irrational impulses in man. Ego psychology creates a picture of men and women as reasonable beings, orientating and adjusting in both a natural and social environment, to pursue particular goals. Since this view is the one that Freud was trying to alter by stressing unconscious processes[20] and conflicts between 'id' impulses and the environment, it seems rather absurd to end up, as revisionists have done, with an analysis based on extending the role of ego, the rational assessor, in place of id, and claim it to be an advance on Freud. It ought to be seen as almost the rejection of Freud; at least this would engender some clarity into the disputes. Fromm wrote:

> Ego psychology constitutes a drastic revision of Freud's system, a revision of its spirit, no—with some exceptions—its concepts. This kind of revision is the regular fate of radical, challenging theories and visions.[21]

And later, in the same paper, Fromm continued:

> The majority remain fixed to outworn and unrealistic categories and contents of thinking; they consider their 'common sense' to be reason.[22]

Here Fromm remains clearly in favour of interpreting Freud's work as critical towards the common sense of twentieth-century people, and not towards taking this common-sense reality on its own terms and adjusting people to it by therapy. It is itself to be understood from a perspective outside of itself, rooted in Freud, and Fromm, like other Frankfurt School thinkers, would add Marx.[23] This gives Freud a critical edge towards the on-going society, and this makes it the more valuable as a system of thought and knowledge about man than it otherwise would be.

Marcuse's critique of revisionism is, in this respect, similar to that of Fromm. Both want to preserve the potential for conflict between man's biological desires and impulses, and the social and natural environment, from ego psychology's loss of psycho-biological givens in terms of which social, economic, political and cultural structures can be analysed, to see the extent to which they fulfil some rather than others of these givens, or satisfy none at all. It is when it comes to providing a detailed analysis of psycho-biological givens that Marcuse is most critical of Fromm, and discusses him alongside other revisionists, such as Sullivan, Horney and Thompson, in his Epilogue to *Eros and Civilization*, titled 'Critique of Neo-Freudian Revisionism' (first published as an article in *Dissent*).

So far it has been argued that Marcuse has underestimated the degree to which Fromm shares the criticisms of neo-Freudian revisionism. However, Marcuse argues that Fromm has shifted from the materialistic and biological needs to more idealistic and moral concerns, and thus loses the basis for critical analysis of on-going societies, which he sees Freud to have provided in the whole corpus of his work.

The central area of change in Fromm is in relationship to the importance of sexuality, libido, and it is here that Marcuse's points against Fromm seem to be strongest. For Fromm again reiterates points he made throughout his post-war work about the less central role of sexual repression in contemporary society, compared with Freud's time, in *The Crisis of Psychoanalysis*. The pathology of contemporary society is in the areas of,

> alienation, anxiety, loneliness, the fear of feeling deeply, lack of activeness, lack of joy. These symptoms have taken over the central role held by sexual repression in Freud's time ...[24]

This does mark a considerable shift away from Freud's work, for he was always insistent on the need to keep sexuality at the forefront of any analysis of precisely the problems which Fromm claims are now new, and characteristic of our society. Freud wrote:

> First and foremost we have found one thing. Psychoanalytic research traces back the symptoms of patients' illnesses with really surprising regularity to impressions from erotic life. It shows us that the pathogenic wishful impulses are in the nature of erotic instinctual components; and it forces us to suppose that among the influences leading to the illness the predominant significance must be assigned to erotic disturbances, and that this is the case with both sexes. I am aware that this assertion of mine will not be willingly believed. Even workers who are ready to follow my psychological studies are inclined to think that I overestimate the part played by sexual factors . . .[25]

It is interesting to note that it is the practitioner of analysis, Fromm, who accuses Marcuse of being too removed from clinical data in his understanding of Freud, and yet it is the philosopher, Marcuse, who retains the importance of sexuality in Freud's work.[26] Marcuse is certainly more correct in his interpretation of Freud, for certainly the spirit of Freud is, rightly or wrongly, towards the stress on the psycho-biological drives of sexuality and destruction.

The changes which have taken place in the area of sexuality since Freud's period, particularly those produced by the widespread use of the contraceptive pill and the more open discussion of some sexual matters, seem to have produced changes towards a less repressive moral system among educated, Western, middle-class people. If one reads Freud's paper 'Civilized Sexual Morality and Modern Nervousness' (1908), where he distinguishes three stages in cultural development, it is possible to see, at least impressionistically, that some change has occurred in the mores. The first stage Freud outlines is one where sexual impulses may be freely exercised in regard to aims which do not lead to procreation, for example, homosexuality; the second stage is where sexual impulses are repressed except those subserving procreation, and the third, the stage of 'civilized' sexual morality, where only legitimate sexual procreation is allowed as a sexual aim. Although the Roman Catholic Church still upholds this third stage of sexual morality in its attitude towards divorce and birth control, other churches are changing their values towards more adaptation to the second stage which would allow divorce and remarriage after divorce, and premarital sexual intercourse, and there are signs of adaptation to the first stage too, in tolerance towards homosexuality, masturbation, premarital erotic stimulation, if not for sexual perversions.[27]

It makes nonsense of Freud's clinical work and his more speculative theoretical works to deny the key role of sexuality and the need for civilization to control its expression through restrictions and renunciations of libidinal gratifications, internalized in all adequately socialized individuals. In Freud's later work, especially *Civilization and Its Discontents* (1930), *Beyond the Pleasure Principle* (1920) and *The Ego and the Id* (1923), the analysis of the role of sexuality is related to that of the destructive drives. The main reason for the necessity for a civilization to control the outlets of sexuality is so that there will be surplus libidinal energies available in social groups to counteract the destructive forces which are also present in the groups men develop.[28]

Civilization is perpetually threatened with disintegration as a consequence of the mutual hostility among men.

> The interest of work in common would not hold it together; instinctual passions are stronger than reasonable interests . . . Hence, therefore, the use of methods intended to incite people into identifications and aim-inhibited relationships of love, hence the restriction upon sexual life and hence too the ideal's commandment to love one's neighbour as oneself.[29]

Freud has posited a dynamic relationship between the two sets of instinctual drives which Fromm does not seem to accept at all.

The logic of Fromm's position of lessening the role of instinctual drives in his model of man-in-society leads to a position which does justify Marcuse's criticism of him being over-sociological. Sociology needs to take account of psycho-biological drives, or givens, if it is to improve its capacity for understanding human society, how it attains cohesion, changes, socializes the young and controls deviance.[30] Marcuse's theory does link from the very outset with the psycho-biological layer in ways which much later sociology has lost.

Fromm is pushed towards being a moral philosopher, recommending men to be more moral and loving in relationships.

> Society must be organized in such a way that man's social, loving nature is not separated from his social existence, but becomes one with it.

So Fromm wrote in the *Art of Loving*.[31] This is not preaching, he claims, in reply to Marcuse's accusation in the *Dissent* article.[32] For love is the ultimate and real need in every human being, which we know to be a fact through the use of reason. Fromm may claim that he is not preaching, but he provides no analysis of why society, and in particular European and American Christian civilization, has not produced the good life, for Fromm is clear that it has not, both in *The Sane Society* and in *The Art of Loving*. Nor does he provide practical ideas about what should be done to produce more people capable of love in his sense, which is not primarily sexual love, but what Freud would have called aim-inhibited affection.[33] His work is, therefore, a form of inspirational literature rather than a very rigorous sociological or philosophical analysis. It seems to be a return to pre-Freudian thought rather than a building upon Freud, and there is seldom a carefully developed argument with Freud's insights and work.

Fromm does not discuss Freud's analysis of the people, priests and now some psychotherapists who continually reiterate the demands of the cultural super-ego, which,

> does not trouble itself enough about the facts of the mental constitution of human beings. It issues a command and does not ask whether it is possible for people to obey it. On the contrary, it assumes that a man's ego is psychologically capable of anything that is required of it, that his ego has unlimited mastery over his id . . . The commandment 'Love thy neighbour as thyself' . . . is impossible to fulfil; such an enormous inflation of love can only lower its value, not get rid of the difficulty.[34]

The role that Freud attributes to the super-ego is linked to his analysis of the way in which death instincts can be turned against the self by this element of the unconscious.[35] Ethical demands which we fail to meet induce guilt, which is destructive aggression turned against the self and which can, in varying degrees, be incapacitating for the individual. Therapy, he said, often consists in reducing the severity of the super-ego's demands on the individual. These are important points which Fromm ignores, yet he claims to be working in a Freudian framework.

So far, Marcuse seems to be closer to Freud, and to have built upon the sociological aspects of his theory more than Fromm. Before examining this aspect of Marcuse's work, it is interesting to note a point where Fromm's criticism of Marcuse's level of analysis may have some bite. Fromm argued that Marcuse's work was too removed from the empirical, and too philosophical in orientation.[36] There is something in this, if one takes the following statement of Freud's:

> Philosophy is not opposed to science, it behaves like a science and works in part by the same methods; it departs from it, however, by clinging to the illusion of being able to present a picture of the universe which is without gaps and is coherent, though one which is bound to collapse with every fresh advance in our knowledge. It goes astray in its method by overestimating the epistemological value of our logical operations and by accepting other sources of knowledge such as intuition.[37]

There are some aspects of Marcuse's thought which do approach being over-coherent on a logical basis, ungrounded in empirical research, even when the propositions are amenable to factual checks. To give just one example, Marcuse wrote:

> Beneath the manifold rational and rationalized motives for war against national and group enemies, for the destructive conquest of time, space and men, the deadly partner of Eros (i.e. Thanatos) becomes manifest in the approval and participation of the victims.[38]

Which victims, and when did they live and die? Is Marcuse claiming that all who die in wars approve of their deaths? There is some impressionistic evidence that some Japanese pilots did actively seek death in war; some evidence that some Jews passively went to the gas chambers in the Second World War. The victims of the Vietnam war, however, the peasants and children, did not participate and approve in the same sense as either of the other two cases. They were the tragic victims of a conflict which they may not even have understood in any cognitive terms, caught in a war they did not want. The failure to make these kinds of simple empirical distinction weakens many of Marcuse's generalizations.[39]

There is a prophetic side to Marcuse's writings which is out of keeping with what Freud thought was the humility of the scientist:

> ... I have not the courage to rise up before my fellow men as a prophet, and I bow to their reproach that I can offer them no consolation: for at bottom that is what they are all demanding—the wildest revolutionaries no less passionately than the most virtuous believers.[40]

Both Marcuse and Fromm seem to be offering some consolation; not much, but some. It is possible to ask how far either of these two thinkers are motivated by the need for consolation in some of their theories which suggest that things may turn out well in the end. They might, but the important issue is to be clear that all of us are seeking promises of change, and placing our faith in one political or technical idea after another, not just because they may work to achieve a desirable goal, like peace, but because we seem to need to believe that there is something available in order to console ourselves, to give us hope that human misery has limits.

All intellectuals, no doubt, tend towards the neurotic and primitive overevaluation of thought processes and other psychical acts. In discussing contagious magic, Freud wrote:

> Things become less important than ideas of things: whatever is done to the latter will inevitably also occur to the former.[41]

The work of intellectuals, especially in the areas of sociology and political philosophy, can be a form of word magic—some satisfaction is derived from manipulating ideas in a way which may not be possible in the social reality, but is possible in words. Utopian thought would seem to be the best example of this. The work of Fromm and Marcuse tends towards utopian word magic—'if only the world could be like this'—whether it be Fromm's world filled with loving persons, or Marcuse's world after the abolition of surplus repression and the performance principle. This point about the similarity of magic and intellectuals' use of words should not be taken to extremes. Just as psychoanalytic remarks about a work of art do not invalidate aesthetic judgements,[42] so the above remarks should not be seen as a judgement upon the actual content of the works of intellectuals, nor the probable necessity of such thought for any society undergoing rapid changes.

Marcuse's Use of Freud: Is a Non-repressive Society Possible?

Herbert Marcuse's contribution to the use of Freud in understanding modern society has been one of the most important to appear since the end of the Second World War. He has written specific studies of Freudian theory, but Freud, like Marx, underpins the whole of his social philosophy in subtle if not always explicit ways. His main work in this area was written during the 1950s, with some extension in the early 1960s. He was born in Berlin in 1898, and left Germany when Hitler came to power. After a year in Geneva, he went to the United States in 1934, and worked with Horkheimer in the Institute for Social Research, which had just moved from Frankfurt to Columbia. He remained in America researching and lecturing in various institutions from thereon.

The major aim of *Eros and Civilization* was an attempt to build upon Freud and to suggest ways in which his work could be useful in understanding modern, post-Second World War, societies. The book is not just about Eros, sexuality, but, as in Freud, about the complex interplay between the sexual instincts and the death instincts. In this way Marcuse seeks some understanding of the complex problems surrounding human destructiveness in the twentieth century. He wrote:

> And the fact that the destruction of life (human and animal) has progressed with the progress of civilization, that cruelty and hatred and the scientific extermination of men have increased in relation to the real possibility of the elimination of oppression—this feature of late industrial civilization would have instinctual roots which perpetuate destructiveness beyond all rationality.[43]

Unlike some other writers, such as Fromm, Holbrook and Reich,[44] Marcuse faces and confronts Freud's theory of the death instincts, and wrestles with the relationship between them and the life instincts. The reality of human destructiveness is not denied, nor is it celebrated in a philosophy of pessimistic resignation—there is some hope, because Marcuse thinks a way out of repressive domination is, at least theoretically, envisionable.[45]

Marcuse wrote that, for Freud, it is possible to say, 'Being is essentially the striving for pleasure.'[46] There is an ambivalence in Freud, which Marcuse is sensitive enough to pick up, about the ultimate pleasure for man: is it libidinal pleasure, or the pleasure of the cessation of all excitations, all tensions, the state of inorganic matter? Does Eros aim at death, as the myth of Tristan and Isolde suggests? Freud's thought moves from a monism of sexuality, to a monism of death, yet retaining a dualistic tension, so that the end outcome is still unknown.[47] As we have seen, the end of Freud's *Civilization and Its Discontents* expresses the issue clearly:

> The fateful question for the human species seems to me to

> be whether and to what extent their cultural development will
> succeed in mastering the disturbance of their communal life
> by the human instinct of aggression and self-destruction ...
> And now it is to be expected that the other of the two
> 'Heavenly Powers', eternal Eros, will make an effort to assert
> himself in the struggle with his equally immortal adversary.
> But who can foresee with what success and with what result?[48]

Marcuse retains this dualistic conception of life and death
instincts in his theory, and is concerned with the interrelationships Freud posited between them. The instincts are mutable;
as the environment of man changes, the instincts are modified
in their objectives and manifestations, although their basic
direction remains the same. The environment of man is divided
into two by Freud, the natural environment and the social
environment, and although Marcuse retains the distinction,
he is more concerned with the way in which historical changes
affect the relation of man to nature as his technology advances.
Freud certainly placed considerable emphasis on technology,
but saw nature still as a separate category which was hostile to
man.[49] Marcuse gives this latter feature much less attention
than did Freud; for Marcuse, technology can aid man to *co-
operate with* nature rather than *mastering* it.[50] So the natural
environment is very closely linked with the socio-historical
reality rather than being a highly distinct category. This is a
relatively important change that Marcuse makes, for it affects
his additions to, and extrapolations from, Freud's theory, and
illustrates the greater emphasis he gives to the possibilities of
change in history compared with Freud's less historically
orientated theory.[51]

The first additions Marcuse makes to Freud concern the
principles which govern the attainment of instinctual aims.
Originally Freud had introduced the terms 'pleasure principle'
and 'reality principle' in a paper published 1911,[52] and suggested
that the pleasure–pain principle is the primary process, in the
sense that it comes first in man's development as a genus and as
an individual as well as in the sense that it is now largely an
unconscious process. Reality testing, a secondary process,
develops to aid the pleasure principle gain satisfactions of a
more certain kind, and with less risks involved than might
occur with the direct expression of instinctual impulses. Marcuse sees not only this continuity, which Fromm argued he had
not done incidentally, but also the way in which Freud makes
the reality principle more dominant for mature adults living

in a world of scarcity (Ananke).[53] The instinctual structure of man must be modified by society if the necessary work and toil is to be done, for the energy for work to build civilization comes from unused libidinal sources. Hence, Freud thought, it was necessary for there to be repression and renunciations of sexual instinctual gratifications for such work, and also to bind together groups whose members' mutual hostility would otherwise be so great that there would be no lasting social relationships.

This is necessary, for since society 'has not means enough to support life for its members without work on their part, it must see to it that the number of these members is restricted and their energies directed away from sexual activities on to their work'.[54]

Marcuse agrees that some basic repression is necessary for civilization to be possible at all, but he argues that the amount of repression can vary from one society to another, and from one historical period to another. Freud was too ahistorical, and thought he had an explanation for all repression in any society. The key term which Marcuse introduces, to add to Freud, is 'surplus-repression'. This is in addition to 'basic' repression, Freud's own conception of repression, necessary for any civilization among humans to last, using aim-inhibited sexual energy to keep groups together and repressing destructive aggression among members of groups. 'Surplus-repression' is 'the additional controls arising from the specific institutions of domination',[55] which are to be found in a specific society with a given degree of technological development.

There is variation, too, according to Marcuse, in the specific form which the reality principle may take in a particular civilization, as distinct from civilization in general, unlike Freud's usage. Marcuse is here being more historically specific than Freud's more general theory, and he refers to the particular form of reality principle in modern capitalist societies as '*the performance principle*' '—under its rule society is stratified according to the competitive economic performances of its members'.[56] In such a society, people have to learn to renounce instinctual gratification so as to develop their capacity to give performances which are economically rewarded in the system. Rewards are not equal, but are stratified, and it is only realistic to see which types of performance carry high rewards, and to develop these at the expense of others which the person might rather develop, all other things being equal. Marcuse is aware that 'the reality' is a social construct and has changed over time, and will continue to change, and could be changed by men's deliberate action and choice in the future.

Given the increase in the possibility of change which Marcuse thinks is present in modern societies, how is Freud's theory affected? For Freud assumed that repression would have to remain if any civilization was to continue in being. Certainly there could be some relaxation in the severity with which these renunciations were introjected by many members of the educated middle classes, and this would perhaps alter life for neurotics. The renunciation of destructive aggression in terms of its outward manifestation would mean that more of this energy was available for turning on the self in the form of guilt.[57]

> The effect of instinctual renunciation on the conscience then is that every piece of aggression whose satisfaction the subject gives up is taken over by the super-ego and increases the latter's aggressiveness [against the ego].[58]

Later on Freud made the point that:

> Whether one has killed one's father or has abstained from doing so is not really the decisive thing. One is bound to feel guilty in either case, for the sense of guilt is an expression of the conflict, due to ambivalence, of the eternal struggle between Eros and the instinct of destruction or death. This conflict is set going as soon as men are faced with the task of living together.[59]

Marcuse seeks to develop Freudian concepts about the development of technology and science in modern society, which allow that change does occur in societies, to a greater extent than Freud himself did. For Marcuse, technology could eliminate scarcity (Ananke). This element is central to Marcuse's handling of the problems raised by Freud's dualistic instinct theory as applied to the development of civilization. He claims that the distinction between the phylogenetic-biological level, that is, the development of the animal man in the struggle with nature, and the sociological level, the development of civilized individuals and groups in the struggle among themselves and their environment, is blurred in Freud.[60] The necessity for the reality principle to take over from the pleasure principle in the development of the species, and of the individual, is caused by the struggle for existence in a world where resources are scarce, and wants always greater than those which can be fulfilled. This was true in the past, Marcuse can agree with Freud, but now there is a point where technology is so advanced that the necessary work could be done with less time and energy than is at present required, given the performance principle (the form which the reality principle takes in our civilization, according to Marcuse). There is now the possibility of altering the form of domination in society, and the performance principle, so that less repression becomes necessary; the surplus-repression could be less, if not removed entirely, and there could be a non-repressive development of libido.[61]

Marcuse seems to confuse the two senses of repression in this last formulation, for he had earlier accepted the need for some basic repression of libido, and of aggression, for any civilization to be possible. In the latter half of *Eros and Civilization*, he seems to forget this, and to want a self-imposed repression which would be free from external domination. This seems confusing for basic repression will be imposed on children by parents, or parental surrogates, and it may well appear to be imposed to the individual then as now. To be consistent, Marcuse can only be aiming to reduce surplus-repression as much as possible, and this can now be done, he claims, because the useful life of the performance principle is over. It has done its work for man in enabling technology and applied science to reach their present state of development. There is now a real technical possibility of reducing want and hunger in the world; the problems lie at the level of political domination.

Work, technology and mastery of natural forces can provide an outlet for destructive energies as well as for libidinal energies. On this Marcuse follows Freud; but Marcuse seems to give far more weight to the degree to which destructiveness, the energy of the death instincts, can be used for socially useful, life-affirming purposes than does Freud.[62]

The reason for this is that Marcuse seems to miss an important element in Freud's theory in his discussion of *Civilization and Its Discontents*. This is the problem of the mutual hostility among people who are working together, or living together more generally. The object of the hostility in question is other people not natural objects. Work does use destructive aggression towards natural, impersonal objects, but often creates hostility towards other people. Only in the armed forces does socially structured work sometimes allow the desire for torturing, killing and maiming to emerge.[63] Marcuse, like most other sociologists, seems to be unwilling to accept that this degree of basic sadism exists in man as one form the death instincts may take. In spite of a seeming acceptance of the death instincts, Marcuse still blocks out the full implications of what Freud wrote. It can be argued that, under different political and economic circumstances, people would not be so brutal to one another, and as was shown above, Freud would accept the point within limits. Nevertheless, these death-instinct impulses would still be present in any future society according to a consistent version of Freud's late theory.

Marcuse, to the dismay of some of his critics, such as Fromm and MacIntyre, would be willing to see more sado-masochism in *sexual life* than is thought desirable in our civilized sexual morality of the latter part of the twentieth century, and this might use some of the energy of the death instincts for erotic purposes. Would this be enough to satisfy humanity's desire for sadism? Probably not, for unless society allows real hurt on the victims, the instinct remains unsatisfied. Marcuse certainly faces the destructiveness which exists now, but seems to fail to adequately explain what will happen to it in a non-repressive society. He thinks that,

> the derivatives of the death instincts operate only in fusion with the sex instincts; as long as life grows, the former remains subordinate to the latter; the fate of the destrudo (the 'energy' of the destructive instincts) depends on that of the libido.
> Consequently, a qualitative change in the development of sexuality must necessarily alter the manifestations of the death instinct.[64]

This argument simply defines the problem away by assuming that the death instincts are subordinate to the sex instincts. The problem for Freud, and, initially, for Marcuse, was the tension between Eros and Thanatos, the life and death instincts, and one did not know which would eventually win. There is no such problem if Eros dominates Thanatos; nor equally with the opposite conclusion.

The whole point is to retain the tension between the two in any theory built upon Freud's later works, for otherwise the theory develops into a pre-death instinct theory, such as those of Reich or Fromm, and is in danger of over-optimism, or over-idealism. Alternatively, theory lapses into resigned fatalistic pessimism about man's historical future, as with some forms of Western neo-Zen and other derivatives of oriental religions. There is a danger that Marcuse is over-optimistic in assuming that a change towards less repression of sex instincts would alter the death instincts' destructiveness towards other humans, except among educated middle classes with a strong sense of guilt, and therefore with the unhappiness and tension being maintained.

However, this section of modern society, the middle classes, is undergoing changes, together with the working classes in modern industrial capitalism. Marcuse argues that the family is no longer the key institution in socialization of individuals; father is no longer the key representative figure of the reality principle, but the school, the mass media, and peer groups are more important. The significance of the father has lessened with the decline in the small business sector as the characteristic organization of modern capitalism, and the parallel growth of the large corporation, which administers people as objects. This assertion of Marcuse's is simply stated in both *Eros and Civilization* and in 'The Obsolescence of the Freudian Conception of Man', but it is not really substantiated either factually, nor, as one might expect, in terms of theory.[65] For, at first sight, there is a problem in Marcuse's assertion, namely, that the family is still the major institution concerned with the first crucial five years of life, before school starts, and before the mass media have much influence on the child. The media may influence the parents to some unknown extent through their attitudes about child-rearing, but parents, and grandparents, are still quite significant. Certainly, later on, the family is less important than it was for children of small business families, for the young child and young person can become much more independent of his or her parents.

This section of Marcuse's analysis remains too assertive and unproven, and, on the surface, simply untrue for the baby and very young child. It is perhaps worth remembering that some of Freud's patients had governors, or tutors, from a very early age, and that this altered the close interaction between mother, father and child. The modern nuclear family is in some ways more closely interactive in the first few years of the life of a baby than previous generations were, at both the top and the bottom of the stratification structure.

Marcuse continues his view of the obsolescence of the Freudian conception of men by asserting that the modern individual has less private space and time than ever before. The mass media intrude into most spaces and most moments in one form or another. The person is no longer, then, being formed along classic Freudian lines, with id, ego, super-ego and growing out of an Oedipal situation. The ego is reduced in modern people in a way that parallels Freud's analysis of the 'primitive mentality' of crowds. In modern society, the super-ego is corporate too, regulating the co-ordination of the individual with the whole.[66]

It is striking that Marcuse's impression of the lack of privacy in modern post-Second World War life, contrasts with that of Peter Berger, who sees privatization as having increased, a process in which more and more people become privatized in their concerns, the family being a prime example. Clearly, there is both an extension of the mass culture into the home itself, which is Marcuse's emphasis, but there is also an increase in the time spent in the home with the family, or on trips with the family, which is Berger's emphasis.[67] They are both part of what has happened under modern conditions, but Marcuse does seem to overstate his case about the types of changes which have occurred, in that there is still a use for the old understanding of the family as the producer of persons, as well as the new other-directed personality of the mass media culture. Both models seem useful to cope with the complexities of the types of personality which do exist. There seems to be little point, however, in overemphasizing the change from one type to another so completely that the existence of the inner-directed, Freudian man, is underestimated.[68]

In his analysis of mass media culture, Marcuse emphasizes that people,

> have dozens of newspapers and magazines that espouse the same ideals. They have innumerable choices, innumerable gadgets which are all of the same sort and keep them occupied and divert their attention from the real issue—which is the awareness that they could both work less and determine their own needs and satisfactions.[69]

The analysis he makes of leisure and popular culture is closely linked to his analysis of alienation at work, and this link enables him to see the connection between work and private time in a way which is original. For Marcuse traces the irrational sources of the increasing sexual liberalism of the post-war decades:

> Sexual liberty is harmonized with profitable conformity. The fundamental antagonism between sex and social utility—itself the reflex of the conflict between pleasure principle and reality principle—is blurred by the progressive encroachment of the reality principle on the pleasure principle.[70]

In this way, the conflict Freud saw between the individual's instinctual desires for polymorphously perverse, erotic relations, and society's restrictions of these desires being carried out in order for there to be energy available for the work of culture and civilization, appears to be lessened.

There is, however, a crucial loss, which is that erotic relations, which used to be the key sphere of private autonomy, free from social control, are now under manipulative control by the entertainment industry and commercial advertising. In the past, the body had to be non-erotic in order to perform its work duties, and for many sections of the working population this is still the case, but among the newer industries of selling, advertising and entertainment, erotic appeal is used to help the individual sell a product or themselves.

The desublimation which has developed in these sections of advanced capitalism has not led to any real gains in freedom for the sellers, nor for the consumers, but rather is a further repression: *repressive desublimation*.[71] It is repressive because it serves to maintain the existing organization of work and political domination, for people do feel subjectively happier with socially controlled desublimation. Rationally such desublimation is repressive because it masks the necessity for real changes in the organization of work in terms of less hours being spent in the production and consumption of so many unnecessary products, less unreasoned pursuit of growth at all costs no matter what it is growth of. It also is storing up troubles for individuals and communities which will have to be faced eventually. The troubles result from the lack of real instinctual gratifications being experienced, and the realization of this will be felt in ways which may release destructiveness and aggression on to the society which manipulated people into such false pseudo-gratifications.

In his lecture on 'The Obsolescence of the Freudian Conception of Man', Marcuse argues that people with 'frightful ease ... submit to the exigencies of total administration, which include total preparation for the fatal end'.[72] Further, the agression is turned outwards by the existing political rulers, away from the internal structure, and on to enemies of the ego ideal.

> The individuals are thus mentally and instinctually predisposed to accept and to make their own the political and social necessities which demand the permanent mobilization with and against atomic destruction, the organized familiarity with man-made death and disfiguration.[73]

The conflict between the pleasure and reality principles is not inevitable, for work originally began as a pleasure, a libidinally satisfying activity. Freud had seen the reality principle as a safeguard for pleasure and aiding the reduction of pain, but that the reality principle had to be accepted for growth of the individual and of humanity.[74] After the introduction of the reality principle, the unconscious activity of the pleasure principle was split off in phantasy—that is, mental activity which has no real objects in it.[75]

In the latter part of *Eros and Civilization*, Marcuse examines phantasy material in order to develop insight into the content of a non-repressive civilization, one in which the pleasure principle came into its own again, but after the work of the reality principle had been fulfilled to enable men to live satisfactorily in their environment. Such a possibility was unrealizable in Freud's theory, even though it was possible to 'expect gradually to carry through such alterations in our civilization as will better satisfy our needs and will escape our criticism'.[76] There were, nevertheless, difficulties which must be faced, over and above the tasks of restricting the instincts, which might be termed 'the psychological poverty of groups'.[77] The important point here has been commented upon above (p. 163) in relation to Marcuse's failure to take full account of hostility among human beings as a primary given of group life.

However, to return to what, in this stage of history, is the phantasy of a non-repressive civilization based on the pleasure principle. Such a civilization would retain the gains made through the reality principle, and would not return to a non-civilized state of nature. Marcuse analyses the role of the arts particularly:

> Behind the sublimated aesthetic form, the unsublimated contents show forth: the commitment of art to the pleasure principle.[78]

In a non-repressive society, the arts would no longer be so sublime, but their commitment to libidinal pleasure would find expression in actuality, in a more beautiful environment and a more aesthetic mass culture. In present society, the arts are a key element in the 'great refusal' towards existing conditions, for they combine reason and sensuousness.[79] They express a possibility for the future, not primarily a regression to the past, as is so often emphasized by Freud. This they share with philosophy, critical theory and religion.

Marcuse does not give much detailed attention to religion, but there are elements in his theory which do give it an increasing role in change, as it, too, becomes a part of the great refusal.

> Where religion still preserves the uncompromised aspirations for peace and happiness, its 'illusions' still have a higher truth value than science which works for their elimination. The repressed and transfigured content of religion cannot be liberated by surrendering it to the scientific attitude.[80]

'Illusion' is the term Freud used about religion, and some political ideologies, for ideas which are based on wishes; they may or may not be true. When, as here, Marcuse talks of religion containing truth, he means truth about values, about the real goals and ends of life, even though religion may, in large part, be believed in by people who seek illusory comforts from it.

Religion brings about a return of the repressed, it is part of the archaic heritage which links the individual to the group. In *Moses and Monotheism*, Freud analysed how the supreme crime, parricide, and the sense of guilt attached to it, is reproduced throughout history.

> The crime is re-enacted in the conflict of the old and new generation, in revolt and rebellion against established authority —and in subsequent repentance: in the restoration and glorification of authority.[81]

Christianity represents a triumph over the father—liberation. Official, institutional churches have repressed this; suffering and repression were perpetuated. Even so, Christianity as understood by some today remains potentially helpful in overcoming the present domination and repressive system.

Sexuality remains the key area for change if a non-repressive society is to be possible, for it is instinctual gratifications of polymorphous, erotic desires which would provide the deepest pleasures.

> Such regression would break through the central fortifications of the performance principle: it would undo the channelling of sexuality into monogamic reproduction and the taboo on perversions.[82]

The Oedipus complex and its associated neuroses, once so central, has already, according to Marcuse's somewhat suspect sociology of the unimportance of the family in modern societal conditions, been surpassed among the advanced sections of modern societies. Therefore the wish to fulfil childhood wishes, which would have formerly included those of the Oedipal situation, could become possible without incestous relationships as the Oedipal wishes decline with the decline of the family.

The family is an archaic institution in Marcuse's analysis, but there is some confusion between the theoretical point being made and the empirical one. It is consistent with Freud to assume that the possibility exists for the family to be less crucial at the level of theory than it was in Freud's time. Freud wrote:

> So long as the community assumes no other form than that of the family, the conflict (between Eros and the death or destructive instincts) is bound to express itself in the Oedipus complex . . .[83]

There is in the quotation the qualification 'so long as . . .' Marcuse judges that the empirical situation is such that the family is no longer the basic form in modern, capitalist sections of the world, and so seeks to develop the theory to meet the new situation. It is possible to disagree with the empirical assessment, or to qualify it, as was done above, but the theoretical issues remain distinct. The modifications made by Marcuse are worthwhile even if they are empirically premature.

Under conditions in a non-repressive society, the monogamous family would disappear, for it is required for a specific economic structure dominated by the performance principle. When this is altered, the necessity for the family will disappear. Full genital sexuality will continue, but will not be the only recognized form of sexuality. Homosexuality, in particular, is discussed by Marcuse in terms of the mythic figure Orpheus, as a symbol for the new form of eroticism, in place of Prometheus, the hero of productivity and toil. Narcissus is discussed, too, as a protester against repressive reproductive sexuality, and as an image in literature and art of a new form of Eros, not an image of stillness and death.[84] The image had been taken up by Freud in his concept of primary narcissism, which Marcuse sees as more than auto-eroticism—'it engulfs the environment, integrating the narcissistic ego with the objective world'.[85] Freud had expressed it as 'a feeling which embraced the universe and expressed an inseparable connection of the ego with the external world'.[86] This suggests to Marcuse that narcissism may contain the germ of a new reality principle:

> . . . the libidinal cathexsis of one's own body could become the source and reservoir of a new libidinal cathexsis of the

objective world—transforming the world into a new mode of being.[87]

Sublimation could be transformed, Marcuse thinks, by the reactivation of the narcissistic libido, because, as libidinal energy is withdrawn from sexual objects, it first, according to Freud, becomes narcissistic before being changed into something else.[88]

This development of ideas in Freud, beyond the point he would have wanted himself, is an interesting exercise. It is an attempt to explore, in the realm of thought and words, unconscious desires and impulses which have been explored previously in literature and the other arts. Some may prefer to explore in the aesthetic mode alone; but the work of Marcuse is in a new genre—psychoanalytic social philosophy. Some of the critics of this genre object to the whole enterprise, and therefore complain of the use of long words and a lack of empirical detail, as though the genre was to be judged by the standards of empirical science of the most elementary kind. People feel lost when reading a new type of writing and try to pull it back into something with which they are familiar.

The dénouement of Marcuse's theory has now been reached. In place of repressive desublimation, there is a hope of non-repressive sublimation, of libidinal rationality.[89] The sexual instincts are gratified, not in organized genital form, but in activities and relationships which are erotic and libidinal. The sublimations would now be chosen by individuals and groups; culture and civilization would still be built because people could obtain erotic gratification from doing such work. It is not *content* that distinguishes work from play.

> For example, if work were accompanied by a reactivation of pregenital polymorphous eroticism, it would tend to become gratifying in itself without losing its *work* content.[90]

Such non-repressive sublimation is, it is emphasized, incompatible with the institutions of the performance principle, for such libidinally gratifying work cannot be administered by élites. There do exist in this society some roles which approach being freely chosen, libidinally rewarding, work roles, but they exist only as part of an alienated minority. The majority develop hobbies and pastimes which are nearer work-play, but these too suffer from being separated off from the public, social work of the community.

Change is necessary at the institutional level before non-repressive sublimation can replace surplus repression and the performance principle. Such institutional change is not possible unless there has been some thought given to what could take its place to further the happiness of men and women. The importance of *Eros and Civilization* lies here. It is one of a small number of serious attempts to wrestle with the irrational area of human misery, and to think out what would give us a real change towards a more pleasurable life. It may appear to be phantasy, but it also has a ring of practicality in it.

NOTES AND REFERENCES

1. See D. Cooper and R. Laing, *Reason and Violence,* London, 1964. N. O. Brown, *Life against Death*, London, 1959; and *Love's Body,* New York, 1966. See also H. Marcuse, *Negations,* New York, 1968, Chapter VII, for a critical review of this latter book by Brown.
2. For continuities between Marx and Weber, see e.g. A. Giddens, *Capitalism and Modern Social Theory*, Cambridge, 1971.
3. E. Fromm, 'The Method and Function of an Analytic Social Psychology' (1932), reprinted in *The Crisis of Psychoanalysis*, Greenwich, Conn., 1970 (quotation from p. 144).
4. Ibid., p. 139.
5. B. Malinowski, *Sex and Repression in Savage Society, London,* 1927.
6. See Fromm, *The Crisis of Psychoanalysis,* Chapters 6 and 7. Bachofen's *Mother Right* was first published in 1861. It was one of the first books to discuss the newly discovered matricentric societies; mothers and women were more central to the social structure than in European society. There were different values in such cultures, especially towards nature and the earth; less intellectual and more earthy, which particularly attracted Fromm's attention.
7. Fromm, *The Crisis of Psychoanalysis,* p. 134.
8. Martin Jay, *The Dialectical Imagination*, London, 1973, p. 101.
9. There is a German version of this paper in *Sociologia* II: *Reden und Vortrage*, edited by M. Horkheimer and T. Adorno, Frankfurt, 1962.
10. Jay, *The Dialectical Imagination*, p. 104.
11. Ibid.
12. Ibid., p. 105.
13. H. Marcuse, *Eros and Civilization*, New York, 1955, 1956; London, 1969 (references to the British edition).
14. E. Fromm, *The Sane Society*, New York, 1955. E. Fromm, *The Fear of Freedom*, London, 1942.
15. Fromm, *The Crisis of Psychoanalysis,* p. 31.
16. Ibid., p. 36. (Also his books mentioned in n. 14 above.)
17. Ibid., p. 36.
18. Marcuse, *Eros and Civilization*, p. 202.
19. S. Freud, *Civilization and Its Discontents* (1930), Standard Edition, Vol. 21. References to the revised edition, London, 1963, p. 71.
20. S. Freud, *The Ego and the Id* (1923), Standard Edition, Vol. 19. In this work 'ego' is not identified as consciousness; it is in part unconscious.
21. Fromm, *The Crisis of Psychoanalysis,* p. 37.

22. Ibid., p. 38.
23. See, e.g. E. Fromm, *Marx's Concept of Man*, New York, 1961.
24. Fromm, *The Crisis of Psychoanalysis*, p. 40.
25. S. Freud, *Five Lectures on Psychoanalysis* (1909), Lecture IV, reprinted in *Two Short Accounts of Psycho-analysis*, Harmondsworth, 1962 (quotation from p. 69).
26. See Fromm, *The Crisis of Psychoanalysis*, p. 25. Fromm also makes the point that Marcuse does not stress full genital sexuality in the way Freud did, but rather non-reproductive sexuality. This is to miss the weight Freud gave to non-genital stage sexuality in the development of symptoms. Marcuse develops the aspect of Freud which thought that too much could not be expected of every person in the area of full genital sexuality and that more 'perverse' sex should be tolerated by some people (see Freud's paper 'Civilized Sexual Morality and Modern Nervousness)'.
27. See, e.g. J. Robinson, *Christian Freedom in a Permissive Society*, London, 1970. And D. Mace, *The Christian Response to the Sexual Revolution*, London, 1971. M. Schofield, *The Sexual Behaviour of Young People*, London, 1965.
28. See esp. Freud's *Civilization and Its Discontents*. And *Group Psychology and the Analysis of the Ego* (1922), Standard Edition, Vol. 18. For a discussion of death instincts, see E. Fromm, *The Heart of Man*, New York, 1964; and *The Anatomy of Human Destructiveness*, London, 1974 (esp. the Appendix).
29. Freud, *Civilization and Its Discontents*, edition cit., p. 49.
30. Marcuse, *Eros and Civilization*, p. 24.
31. E. Fromm, *The Art of Loving*, London, 1957, p. 94.
32. Reprinted as the Epilogue in *Eros and Civilization*.
33. Fromm, *The Art of Loving*, p. 65. Freud's notion of aim-inhibited libido, called 'affection', can be found in *Group Psychology and the Analysis of the Ego*, p. 71.
34. Freud, *Civilization and Its Discontents*, edition cit., p. 80.
35. See Freud, *The Ego and the Id*, edition cit., p. 43.
36. Fromm, *The Crisis of Psychoanalysis*, 1970, p. 25.
37. Freud, *New Introductory Lectures*, Lecture 35 (1933, first English translation, 1964). Reference to Penguin edition, Harmondsworth, 1973, p. 196.
38. Marcuse, *Eros and Civilization*, p. 55.
39. See, for instance, MacIntyre's criticism in *Marcuse*, London, 1970, Chapter 4. See also H. Marcuse's essay, 'Aggressiveness in Advanced Industrial Society', first published in *Negations*, New York, 1968, which is more specific, being written during the Vietnam War.
40. Freud, *Civilization and Its Discontents* edition cit., p. 82.
41. S. Freud, *Totem and Taboo* (1913), Standard Edition, Vol. 13, Chapter 3 on 'Animism, Magic and the Omnipotence of Thought'. Reference to Routledge & Kegan Paul edition, London, 1960, p. 85. (This is an important paper ignored by Marcuse!)
42. See, e.g. A. MacIntyre, *The Unconscious*, London, 1958, pp. 75–6.
43. Marcuse, *Eros and Civilization*, pp. 80–81.
44. See D. Holbrook, *Human Hope and the Death Instinct*, Oxford, 1971. Also W. Reich, *The Sexual Revolution*, 1929, 1935.

45.   Marcuse, *Eros and Civilization*, p. 126.
46.   Ibid., p. 106.
47.   Ibid., p. 40. See also D. de Rougement, *Passion and Society*, London, 1956. A brilliant analysis of Tristan and Isolde myth.
48.   Freud, *Civilization and its Discontents*, edition cit., p. 82. See also Freud, *Beyond the Pleasure Principle*, edition cit., p. 93.
49.   See Freud, *The Future of an Illusion*, edition cit., 1927, p. 14:('The gods retain their threefold task: they must exorcize the terrors of nature, they must reconcile men to the cruelty of fate, particularly as is shown in death . . .').
50.   Marcuse, *Eros and Civilization*, p. 97.
51.   For this reason Freud is in part a conservative thinker in political matters.
52.   Freud, 'Formulations Regarding the two principles in Mental Functioning' (1911), available in P. Rieff (ed.), *General Psychological Theory*, New York, 1963.
53.   Marcuse, *Eros and Civilization*, p. 31. And Fromm, *The Crisis of Psychoanalysis*, p. 27.
54.   Marcuse, *Eros and Civilization*, pp. 32–3. Quotation from Freud, *A General Introduction to Psychoanalysis*, New York, 1935 and 1943: p. 273. (Entitled *Introductory Lectures on Psychoanalysis*, London, 1929.)
55.   Marcuse, *Eros and Civilization*, p. 46.
56.   Ibid., p. 50.
57.   Freud, *Civilization and Its Discontents*, edition cit., pp. 60–61.
58.   Ibid., p. 66. Marcuse quotes a different translation of the same passage in *Eros and Civilization*, p. 75. The English version is used here from the Hogarth Press edition.
59.   Freud, *Civilization and Its Discontents*, edition cit., p. 69.
60.   Marcuse, *Eros and Civilization*, pp. 113–14.
61.   Ibid., p. 118.
62.   Ibid., pp. 79–80.
63.   See Freud, *Civilization and Its Discontents*, edition cit., pp. 47–9.
64.   Marcuse, *Eros and Civilization*, p. 118.
65.   Ibid., pp. 86–7. See also his lecture on 'The Obsolescence of the Freudian Conception of Man' (1963), to be found in English in H. Marcuse, *Five Lectures*, Boston, Mass., 1970.
66.   See ibid., p. 49. See also *Eros and Civilization*, p. 91.
67.   P. Berger, 'Towards a Sociological Understanding of Psychoanalysis', in *Social Research*, 1965, pp. 26–41.
68.   For distinction between other-directed and inner-directed, see D. Reisman, *The Lonely Crowd*, London, 1950.
69.   Marcuse, *Eros and Civilization*, p. 89.
70.   Ibid., p. 85.
71.   Marcuse, 'The Obsolescence of the Freudian Conception of Man', in *Five Lectures*, p. 57.
72.   Ibid., p. 50.
73.   Ibid., p. 51.
74.   Freud, *Formulations Regarding the Two Principles in Mental Functioning* (1911), reference to Collier Books edition, New York, 1963, p. 26.
75.   Ibid., p. 24.
76.   Freud, *Civilization and Its Discontents*, p. 52.

77. Ibid., p. 52.
78. Marcuse, *Eros and Civilization*, p. 151.
79. Ibid., p. 147.
80. Ibid., p. 70.
81. Ibid., p. 68.
82. Ibid., p. 162.
83. Freud, *Civilization and Its Discontents*, edition cit., p. 69.
84. Marcuse, *Eros and Civilization*, p. 137.
85. Ibid.
86. Ibid. (quoting Freud's *Civilization and Its Discontents*).
87. Ibid., p. 138.
88. Ibid.
89. Ibid., p. 168.
90. Ibid., p. 172.

9 Summary and Conclusion

Freud's scheme for the understanding of man-in-society, which has been outlined in the preceding chapters, is an interconnected whole which was developed and revised by him during the course of his working life. The interconnections are extremely important for a proper understanding of Freud, and it is not possible to isolate some parts and treat them as separate from the rest of the theoretical scheme. This summary will, therefore, stress these interrelationships.

First, there is the relationship between the individual and the social group. The focus on the individual, however valid and useful it may be in therapeutic work, is unviable as a way of understanding human action. Freud's theory is not a theory of individual personality systems seen in abstraction from groups. As was suggested in the discussion on the concept of the super-ego, there is a strong emphasis on internalized values derived from the surrounding culture. The whole dynamic of the personality theory rests on the conflicts between wishes and impulses produced by the body's instinctual energies and the values which have been internalized by the person from the external social environment. To understand Freud as a psychologist who simply focused on the individual is to make a serious error. His was a *sociological* understanding of the development of persons.

It was a sociology with a difference—it was linked quite systematically with the biological organism of human beings, via the notion of instincts. In this lies its importance for contemporary sociology and social psychology, for it provides a way of avoiding the over-socialized conception of man which has become so dominant in these disciplines. As Dennis Wrong and Alex Inkeles, among others, have pointed out, some conception of human *nature* is necessary in any sociological theory.[1] The human body sets limits, although wide ones, to the activities of human societies. An adequate supply of food, and adequate shelter from the elements are basic prerequisites in every society. Reproduction and socialization of the next generation are equally fundamental. Regular periods of relaxation and sleep are essential. Finally, ways must be found to handle the illnesses and deaths of a society's members. These basic elements of human living have often been seen as too biological to deserve serious attention by many sociologists, but that does not alter the fundamental part the human organism plays in societal life and in social change.

Freud's stress lay on additional features of human nature, namely, on the relatively free-floating character of human sexuality, which is not biologically programmed into a clear-cut mating season, as it is in some other species. It affects areas of experience and parts of the body which superficially appear to be far removed from genital reproduction, as in anal erotism, for instance. The notion of the polymorphously perverse nature of human sexuality is fundamental to the understanding of the development of character in societies, as was seen, for example, in relationship to the anal character. This idea of sexuality had arisen from Freud's work with patients, both those who developed symptoms in place of acting on the strong instinctual impulses to indulge in practices they thought disgusting, and those who did practise sexually perverse acts. The notion of sexuality in children was checked, in a somewhat haphazard fashion, through observations of children and infants, in the first instance by Freud, and then later by other analysts in a more reliable manner. The point seems to be well established: human sexuality is much more free-floating, in terms of aims and objects, than has until recently been accepted in Western culture. There is still doubt about the precise pattern that infant sexuality follows in different human cultures, and it could differ from one culture to another in terms of the stress which socializing agents place on various aspects. The anal phase, which follows the first, that is, the oral phase, may well be different in Western capitalist cultures from others, but it is doubtful that it would not exist at all. All infants learn what their culture prescribes about urinating and defecating, and act accordingly.

One of Freud's assumptions is that human beings are constitutionally bisexual, although the predominance of masculinity or femininity may vary from individual to individual. This assumption is important in relation to the Oedipus complex, for there are masculine parts of girls, which means some girls could experience Oedipal wishes as do boys. The female elements of girls and boys would experience the converse Electra complex. However, it is important to bear in mind that Freud thought the phallus was the part of the body of most interest to both boys and girls at this stage. The sexes are not highly differentiated at this age, three or four years; this occurs later, after the Oedipal stage is resolved.

The Oedipus complex, which occurs in this third stage of growth, the phallic stage, has interconnections with other parts of psychoanalytic theory than just that of the development of children. It has a key importance in the account Freud gives of religion, and of the arts, both of which play a fundamental part in his understanding of the sociology of the unconscious archaic heritage. As was shown in the main chapters of this book, the theme of *parricide* features over and over again in Freud's theories.

A major advantage with Freud's speculative theory of parricide is that it begins to provide a description, and even an explanation, of the actual content of Christianity, and of Judaism especially. The associated theme of *longing for the father*, and for parental protection, occurs in many other religions too, such as Islam, and in parts of Buddhism, especially in the popular devotion to Buddha. There are parallels between the relations of a person to their father, or equivalent figure, and their relation to religion, as Freud found in his analysis of the wolf-man. Religion does not only derive its emotional attraction from the individual's development, for Freud is quite clear that there is a basic unconscious guilt in men and women which religion handles. The guilt is a left-over from the primal parricide, and it draws on energy from the death instincts.

Freud's arguments for the death instincts in *Beyond the Pleasure Principle* were obscure at times, and were based on poor biology. This particular set of arguments seem unnecessary to establish the fact that human beings *know* that they will die in a way in which other species do not. This knowledge has to be handled in some way, and societies have to find ways of alleviating the feelings which arise, both as a result of the knowledge of death and of those ambivalent emotions of guilt and pleasure which Freud pointed out exist after the death of some close person.

There is also the assumption, which Freud made, that there is a basic element of destructive aggression in human beings which derives from the death instincts. The energy of the death instincts seems to aim at a return to quietude, Nirvana, a tensionless state of non-stimulation. In the process of moving towards this goal, and because the energy of the death instincts can become entangled with other unconscious elements, the death instincts may appear as destructive action on the outer world, or as masochistic self-destruction. This latter may be expressed as suicide, ill-health, melancholia and depression, or as sexual masochism. The super-ego derives some of its energy from the death instincts. This appears as an over-severe super-ego, making impossible demands on the ego and the id. The result is a state of tension between the ego ideal and the ego, a sense of failure, inadequacy and guilt.

One solution to this is for the person to join a crowd. Here, a new ego ideal can be found, and tension can be lessened, or eliminated altogether. Being taken over in this way, by the crowd and its leader, is an attractive alternative to many, for it does reduce the severity of the strain from the super-ego. Crowds loosen normative controls, and actions which would normally be forbidden by the person become possible in a crowd situation. This is especially true of destructive action towards people and property. On the other hand, the ego ideal which members of a crowd internalize, may be culturally more advanced, and in this way change and forward movement can take place.

The later theoretical work of Freud was concerned with working out the implications of the dual instinct theory: sexual instincts and death instincts, or Eros and Thanatos. Freud asks how far civilization is successful, or how far it produces so many discontents among its members that it will probably come to be rejected by them. Civilization, or, in other words, advanced modern societies, represses instinctual impulses, both of sexuality and of the destructive death instincts, and uses the energy to build both technology and modern social institutions. The repression of libidinal energy is necessitated by the mutual antagonism which exists among groups of humans living and working together. The libidinal energy is then available to enable groups to hold together over time to accomplish their tasks. Religion and morality, *the archaic heritage* of mankind, are used for the purpose of repressing sexuality and developing commitments to the values and activities of civilization. For some people, science, of which psychoanalysis is a critical part, performs this function instead. Political ideologies, such as socialism or nationalism, may achieve a similar thing for others, with religion and traditional morality continuing for many others.

Civilization advances at a cost. The cost is an increased amount of guilt among more and more people, produced by their rejection of the destructive energy of the death instincts, and by their turning it inwards on themselves. Sexual morality could be relaxed in some ways, Freud thought, thereby allowing more instinctual gratification without guilt. There would need to be considerable use of libidinal energy, however, for the work of civilization to continue and advance. This sets limits to the degree to which sexuality can be freely expressed among the majority of people. The direct gratification of instinctual impulses offers people the surest form of happiness and pleasure. Repression, sublimation and rejection of instinctual impulses is necessary, however, for civilization to develop and continue. The increase in civilization has not led, therefore, to the hoped-for increase in happiness. Instead, there is more security from destruction of natural forces, and from the sadism and destructiveness of other people. Increasing security *versus* decreasing happiness: this is the fundamental dilemma in Freud's later theory.

The ways in which the Frankfurt School developed Freud's thought and linked it with a sociology derived from Marx and Weber were examined, for it is here that some of the most fruitful uses have been made of psychoanalysis as a theory of social man. Marcuse has made the most consistent developments of Freudian theory, retaining, as he does, both the sexual and the death instincts in his thought. However, he does not stress the role of the archaic heritage enough, especially in relation to the continuing importance of the institutions of the family, and of religion, in the United States and in Europe. Freud's own theory gave a much greater emphasis to the part the archaic heritage plays in modern societies, and to the difficulty man has in moving away from it. The sins of the fathers, who were once murdering sons, still haunt contemporary man.

This concludes the brief summary of the theory, and hopefully the interconnections of the different sections are a little clearer. No mention has been made of the criticisms of Freud which were discussed in the earlier chapters. This reflects the fact that the book as a whole has been relatively sympathetic to Freud. A number of times I have been struck by the immensity of Freud's theoretical structure, and the way in which he had anticipated many of the criticisms which would be made of his work. First, for example, people sought to argue that sexuality was not as important as he held, and some claimed that he over-emphasized it. The result of losing the emphasis Freud gave to sexuality is that it gets ignored, as in the work of Fromm and Jung, for example. Similarly with the death instincts, and the assumption of an instinctual destructive urge in man, Freud anticipated that this view would also be rejected, in favour of the more usual views of human beings—'they are not so bad after all'. Psychoanalysts, like Fromm and Reich, who have tried to move away from a death-instinct theory did not produce theories which are any advance on Freud. On the contrary, they lead to new illusions—that all that is required is that sexual morality be reformed or abolished, as Reich held, or that we should be more loving towards one another within a socialist society, as Fromm held, and then destructive violence will disappear from human life. The dual-instinct theory is central, as Marcuse understands. Once any aspect of it is lost, the originality of Freud's theory is undermined.

Sociologists have tended to lose the element of conflict, so basic to psychoanalytic theory, by over-concentrating on the ego and the cultural elements which the super-ego internalizes, and under-emphasizing the role of the instincts. Certainly the instincts are malleable by social and cultural conditions, as Freud understood. This point is taken by many therapists and sociologists to mean that there is nothing else left, no instinctual energy in the body, quite independent of its social and cultural expression. It is one thing to assert that instincts are affected by culture in the way they are expressed, and quite another to assert that culture obliterates the biological organism's impulses altogether. Once the assumption of instinctual impulses arising independently of culturally derived material is lost, then the element of change and conflict is lost too.

Freud's superiority in the realm of theory, in sociology and social philosophy, came as a surprise to me. I did not set out to vindicate Freud against all his critics, but to examine the usefulness of his work for building upon as another alternative base for modern sociology.

The available bases of sociology, although often powerful in some areas—in the way that phenomenological approaches have been in the sociology of deviance, for example—seemed to leave something out. Phenomenological approaches have moved too far away from the human body as a point of reference, and have gone too much into the realm of consciousness. Constructions of reality seem to be capable of being built up by groups in human society with no reference to any physical reality at all, in the view of phenomenologists. Such a complete cultural relativism may appear tolerant, and un-prejudiced racially, religiously and politically, but, by accepting all points of view as equally possible, all come to be equally legitimate. The criterion for assessment is only that they give a social construction which is meaningful to those who live within it, but which could be false or evil. It is this consequence which is of concern. There is something 'out there', which means that some views of reality will turn out to be closer to a true picture of the 'out there' than others. This is not meant to be a state-ment of the correspondence theory of truth, but something less grand. Simply, that some ways of constructing a bridge, for instance, are more successful than others. The way they are built reflects the picture of reality on which they are based. Those which stay up, under a variety of weather conditions, are more successful than those which collapse. This seems to be some sort of test of a picture of reality.

It is this connection with reality which seems to disappear in phenomenological sociologies. Not that sociological theory needs testing in the way that bridge builders' theories are tested. This is not possible. Rather the point is that these sociologies make no allowance for such testing of theory, even within natural science and technology. Freud did make such an allowance in his theory, and it affected his own theoretical work in relation to magic, for instance. Judgements have to be made about the degree of rationality of a belief system by the sociolo-gist in order to know what type of explanatory scheme to use. Non-rational, and irrational, belief and value systems need a different type of explanation than do more rational ones. Freud does operate with a theoretical standpoint which allows this distinction to be made, and he often did make such judgements himself. He assumed that magical thinking was not as rational as technological thinking, which checked its conceptions and ideas against 'reality'. He therefore described and explained magical thought and practices as based on wishes, and upon an irrational belief in the omnipotence of thought processes. Freudian theory has distinct advantages over the relativism prevalent in some sociology, in the way in which it sees rational thought and action as an important human attribute. Con-sequently, it also avoids relativism vis-à-vis ethical and political values.

Freud shared the common assumption about the value-neutrality of science, and claimed he was not producing a new value system. He confused value-relevance, value judgements

and objectivity within a scientific analysis. He did not understand that a scientific analysis can be done as objectively as
possible, free from bias stemming from values, but nevertheless
be value-relevant. The problems chosen for investigation will
reflect a value standpoint, and the conclusion may well have
value implications. This need not affect the relative objectivity
of the analysis. Freud certainly chose problems from a value
standpoint—that of a doctor interested in relief of unnecessary
suffering, and of a rationalist interested in the further development of technology and the movement away from infantile
religiosity. These values were not unrelated, however, to his
findings in psychoanalysis. Freud thought that his research
work with many of his patients justified his conclusions about
the advantages of rational thought processes for the person, as
well as for society. Similarly with religion, he thought that his
psychoanalytic researches justified the conclusion that religiosity
was almost always based on infantile feelings and wishes, and
that people were better off without religious attachments if
they were to further their own well-being and happiness, and
that of other people. The value standpoint is affected by the
research, and research problems are chosen for their relevance
to the value standpoint Freud held.

This close relationship between values, and research and
theory, is one which Freud did not express in his own writings
on the philosophy of science. His own philosophical position
was too tied to materialism, and to a natural-science model as a
basis for his epistemology, to be adequate to cope with the
actual work he did in the human sciences. There is no reason to
suppose that someone who makes an original contribution to
any science must also provide an adequate, let alone a definitive,
account of the consequences for philosophy of the new dis-
coveries. Freud certainly did not have a proper understanding
of the logical differences between human sciences, concerned
with language and the communication of meanings, and the
natural sciences, where meaning never enters into the material
of research at all. This did not fundamentally affect the way he
did his psychoanalytic work with patients, or his writing of
theoretical books and papers, for his errors were on the secondary level, that is, they were statements *about* what he did.

Jurgen Habermas has given the best account, at the philosophical level, of how Freud's psychoanalysis is to be understood. Habermas's account sees the therapeutic process as a
communication process, and sees the analyst as helping the

analysand to decipher distorted communication material within himself, and between himself and other people.[2] It was also noted, in Chapter 2, that Freud was a *theoretical* thinker, and understood the importance of theory and speculation in the development of science. A rather surprising parallel was noted between Popper and Freud here, for Popper also argues for the importance of *theoreticism* as a viable type of work within science. Popper's point that some Freudian propositions are irrefutable, and therefore not strictly part of a science, is only true in relationship to a bowdlerized version of Freudian theory, which is adhered to as a closed-belief system. This is not really how Freud operated. He made a number of revisions to his instinct theory, for example. At first there were sexual instincts and self-preservative or ego instincts. It was only later that he introduced the death instincts in order to handle some findings, and the technical problems which then arose within psychoanalytic theory in the light of the empirical findings.

Psychoanalytic theory did break new ground in the human sciences, and there seems, as yet, to be no philosophy complex enough to give a thorough account of what has been achieved. To some people this way of putting things will appear absurd, for they may assume that philosophy of science, or methodology, should be able to guide theory construction and help to sort out the wheat from the chaff within social science. The assumption made here, however, is that sometimes fundamental changes occur in science first and later philosophy and methodology provide an account of what has happened. This is a claim that can be made about psychoanalysis. The achievements in both practice and theory are reasonably established, not as absolutes, but certainly as novel and useful theoretical conceptualizations. Methodological principles which have been developed to cope with changes in physics, biology, mathematics or other natural sciences cannot be assumed to be applicable to an area as complex as that of a discipline concerned with human emotions. To have applied such criteria to psychoanalysis, and to find it wanting, was the height of dogmatism. The intellectual atmosphere has loosened up more recently, at least in sociology, and humanistic modes of approach are now more firmly established.

It is because Freudian theory has not been examined, nor assimilated, into sociology in any depth that an analysis of Freud seemed to be called for, so that he can be re-examined in the new atmosphere prevailing in sociology. Old dogmatisms having died, new ones may be emerging. But the new ones are not as dogmatic as the old. There is an acceptance of the difficulties involved in understanding people in society, and the old models, whether Marxist, neo-Marxist, functionalist or structuralist, seem less adequate than they did to an earlier generation of sociologists.

The older models in sociology seemed to leave something out. That 'something' seems to me to lie in the area of the human body and the unconscious processes which occur not just within people, but between them when they interact in groups. Psychoanalysis provides a method for handling these matters in a way that no other theory does. It provides a language for describing the feelings and processes, a method of working with small groups and individuals, and a larger theoretical framework in which to place smaller-scale social changes and events. There are undoubtedly elements of dogmatism in psychoanalysis, but we have to accept that such dogmas are the *sine qua non* of work which moves beyond empirical description. For this latter type of research merely reflects the dogmatisms of the common-sense framework of the time, place and groups on which it reports. To move beyond this descriptivist approach is to enter a more dangerous area, for a new theoretical framework becomes necessary to move outside the area of a prevailing 'common sense'. Such theoretical frameworks have to be based on something themselves, and the best point of reference would seem to be the human body and its emotions, for there is an element of the universal about the body and its basic processes. This universal element allows the sociologist to escape cultural relativism.

Cultural relativism, which is implied in many of the phenomenological sociologies, will be found inadequate by both sociologists and those who look to it for guidance and help with their situation in modern society. Psychoanalytic theory has such a great importance for the future of sociological understanding of modern societies because it is not built on relativistic assumptions. Relativism is very seductive, for it can appeal to the values of tolerance and claim to be unprejudiced. There is a cost, however, and this is that relativism in the social sciences becomes more than a methodological assumption which could be justified for some, but not all, problems, and turns into a general outlook. The logical consequence of relativism is that value judgements cease to be made by anyone at all. If there is no rational basis for value judgements, then values will simply be a reflection of a person's socialization and their personality. If values can be rationally chosen, then this will have to affect the way in which the social sciences describe and explain human actions.

In the last of his *New Introductory Lectures* (1933) Freud wrote:

> There have certainly been intellectual nihilists ... in the past, but just now the relativity theory of modern physics seems to have gone to their head. They start out from science, indeed, but they contrive to force it into self-abrogation, into suicide; they set it the task of getting itself out of the way by refuting its own claims. One often has an impression in this connection that this nihilism is only a temporary attitude which is to be retained until this task is performed. Once science has been disposed of, the space vacated may be filled by some kind of mysticism, or, indeed, by the old religious *Weltanschuung*. According to the anarchist theory there is no such thing as truth, no assured knowledge of the external world.[3]

This type of muddled epistemology which Freud encountered in his time among nihilists has now entered some sociology.

Freud's attitude to Marxism was more sympathetic than it was to nihilism and anarchism, the political form of intellectual nihilism. The problem with Marxism was that it promised what it could not offer, for destructiveness between people did not derive just from property relations, but from more basic instinctual sources. There was a danger that Marxism could be turned into another 'illusion' to replace religion. Nevertheless, Freud retained a respect for the men of action who had begun an experiment in Russia which might achieve real changes in the economy and begin to meet the material needs of the people more adequately than had been done before. The element of relating to real material needs of people, which Marxism possessed, did appeal to Freud more than the religiosity of many American and European public figures.

> At a time when the great nations announce that they expect salvation only from the maintenance of Christian piety, the revolution in Russia—in spite of all its disagreeable details— seems none the less like the message of a better future ...[4]

As has been shown, the Frankfurt School writers have sought to link the thought of Freud and Marx more systematically. The marriage has not always been successful. In Marcuse's work, for example, there is a difficult relationship between the social philosophy based on Freud, and Marxism. The difficulty stems from the different conceptions of man-in-society in the two theories. For Marx, the technology and the economic relations of a society are fundamental, whereas for Freud it is the cultural repression of instinctual energy which is fundamental. Marcuse has seen the key area of interconnection between the two to be in the area of work, and this is surely correct. Further development of the theory can only be made now in relation to actual praxis; that is, in attempts to change something in the social world, guided by theory. Modern technology may offer the possibility of breaking out of the past patterns of work, dominated by the Protestant work ethic and by fears of unemployment. With real change in the way work is viewed, societies could, and would, begin to change the type and degree of cultural repression. It may well be that this is in fact beginning to occur now, only we are too close to it to see the change which is going on in this period.

Freud would still warn us against new illusions, and having too high hopes. If he is right, then some repression of sexuality is necessary under any set of economic arrangements, to counter the fundamental mutual hostility of people towards one another. Nevertheless, there is going to be change; indeed, there has been change since Freud wrote. His work remains outstanding in providing us with a means of understanding the key areas of our lives to which we should look for the basic changes.

Sociology has concerned itself with ideological meaning, it needs now to take unconscious meanings into account too. The claim advanced here is that only by integrating Freud's conceptualizations of unconscious processes that occur between people can sociology hope to develop an adequate understanding of change in modern societies.

NOTES AND REFERENCES

1. D. Wrong, 'The Oversocialized Conception of man in Modern Sociology', *American Sociological Review*, Vol. 26 (1961), pp. 183–93. A. Inkeles, *What is Sociology?*, Englewood Cliffs, N.J., 1964, Chapter Four.
2. J. Habermas, *Knowledge and Human Interest* (1968), London, 1972.
3. S. Freud, *New Introductory Lectures on Psychoanalysis* (1933), Standard Edition, Vol. 22. References to Penguin edition, Harmondsworth, 1973, p. 212.
4. Ibid., p. 218.

Bibliography

1. Bibliography of Freud's Works

(A.) Books
There are a number of bibliographies of Freud's works which are readily available, the most complete being in Volume 24 of the Standard Edition of Freud's works. The books given below are those consulted for the purposes of this book on the sociology in Freud. References are to *The Standard Edition of the Complete Psychological Works of Sigmund Freud*, edited by James Strachey, published by the Hogarth Press, London, in 24 volumes.

(In collaboration with Breuer, J.) *Studies in Hysteria* (1893–5), Standard Edition, Vol. 2.

The Interpretation of Dreams (1900), Standard Edition, Vols. 4–5.

The Psychopathology of Everyday Life (1901), Standard Edition, Vol. 6.

Three Essays on the Theory of Sexuality (1905), Standard Edition, Vol. 7.

Five Lectures on Psycho-Analysis (1910), Standard Edition, Vol. 11.

Leonardo da Vinci and a Memory of his Childhood (1910), Standard Edition, Vol. 11.

Totem and Taboo (1912–13), Standard Edition, Vol. 13.

Introductory Lectures on Psycho-Analysis (1916–17), Standard Edition, Vols. 15–16.

Beyond the Pleasure Principle (1920), Standard Edition, Vol. 18.

Group Psychology and the Analysis of the Ego (1921), Standard Edition, Vol. 18.

The Ego and the Id (1923), Standard Edition, Vol. 19.

An Autobiographical Study (1925), Standard Edition, Vol. 20.

Inhibitions, Symptoms and Anxiety (1926), Standard Edition, Vol. 20.

The Question of Lay Analysis (1926), Standard Edition, Vol. 20.

The Future of an Illusion (1927), Standard Edition, Vol. 21.

Civilization and Its Discontents (1930), Standard Edition, Vol. 21.

New Introductory Lectures on Psycho-Analysis (1933), Standard Edition, Vol. 22.

An Outline of Psychoanalysis (1938), Standard Edition, Vol. 23.

Moses and Monotheism (1939), Standard Edition, Vol. 23.

Psychoanalysis and Faith. The letters of Sigmund Freud and Oskar Pfister (1903–39), translated by E. Mosbacher, London, 1963.

The Freud/Jung Letters, edited by William McGuire, London, 1974.

(B.) Articles
References are given to the Collier Books Edition of *The Collected Papers of Sigmund Freud*, edited by Phillip Rieff, 1963, Collier–

Macmillan, New York. The coding used for the volumes in this edition is as follows:

S.E.C. = *The Sexual Enlightenment of Children*
S.P.L. = *Sexuality and the Psychology of Love*
C.C.   = *Character and Culture*
G.P.T. = *General Psychological Theory*
T.T.   = *Therapy and Technique*
H.P.M. = *The History of the Psychoanalytic Movement*
T.C.H. = *Three Case Histories*
D.   = *Dora—An Analysis of a Case of Hysteria*

Pre-1910
'Obsessive Acts and Religious Practices' (1907), *Collected Papers* (C.C.).
'Character and Anal Erotism' (1908), *Collected Papers* (C.C.).
'Civilized Sexual Morality and Modern Nervousness' (1908), *Collected Papers* (S.P.L.).
'On the Sexual Theories of Children' (1908), *Collected Papers* (S.E.C.).
'Analysis of a Phobia in Five-Year-Old Boy' (1909), *Collected Papers* (S.E.C.).

1910–19
'A Special Type of Object Choice Made by Men' (1910), *Collected Papers* (S.P.L.).
'Observations on "Wild" Psychoanalysis' (1910), *Collected Papers* (T.T.).
'Formulations Regarding the Two Principles of Mental Functioning' (1911), *Collected Papers* (G.P.T.).
'The Most Prevalent Form of Degradation in Erotic Life' (1912), *Collected Papers* (S.P.L.).
'The Dynamics of the Transference' (1912), *Collected Papers* (T.T.).
'Recommendations for Physicians on the Psychoanalytic Method of Treatment' (1912), *Collected Papers* (T.T.).
'The Theme of the Three Caskets' (1913), *Collected Papers* (C.C.).
'From the History of an Infantile Neurosis' (1918), Standard Edition, Vol. 17; *Collected Papers* (T.C.H.).
'The Moses of Michelangelo' (1914), *Collected Papers* (C.C.).
'On Narcissism: An Introduction' (1914), *Collected Papers* (G.P.T.).
'Instincts and Their Vicissitudes' (1915), *Collected Papers* (G.P.T.).
'Reflections Upon War and Death' (1915), *Collected Papers* (C.C.).
'Repression' (1915), *Collected Papers* (G.P.T.).
'The Unconscious' (1915), *Collected Papers* (G.P.T.).
'A Case of Paranoia Running Counter to the Psychoanalytical Theory of the Disease' (1915), *Collected Papers* (S.P.L.).
'Metapsychological Supplement to the Theory of Dreams' (1916), *Collected Papers* (G.P.T.).

'On the Transformation of Instincts with Special Reference to Anal Erotism' (1917), *Collected Papers* (C.C.).
'Mourning and Melancholia' (1917), *Collected Papers* (G.P.T.).
'The Taboo of Virginity' (1918), *Collected Papers* (S.P.L.).
'Psychoanalysis and Religious Origins' (1919), *Collected Papers* (C.C.).
'The Uncanny' (1919), Standard Edition, Vol. 17; *Collected Papers*.

1920–29
'Certain Neurotic Mechanisms in Jealousy, Paranoia and Homo-sexuality' (1922), *Collected Papers* (S.P.L.).
'Remarks upon the Theory and Practice of Dream Interpretation' (1923), *Collected Papers* (T.T.).
'The Libido Theory' (1923), *Collected Papers* (G.P.T.).
'The Infantile Genital Organization of the Libido' (1923), *Collected Papers* (S.P.L.).
'Neurosis and Psychosis' (1924), *Collected Papers* (G.P.T.).
'The Economic Problem in Masochism' (1924), *Collected Papers* (G.P.T.).
'The Passing of the Oedipus-Complex' (1924), *Collected Papers* (S.P.L.).
'The Resistances to Psychoanalysis' (1925), *Collected Papers* (C.C.).
'Some Psychological Consequences of the Anatomical Differences Between the Sexes' (1925), *Collected Papers* (S.P.L.).
'A Religious Experience' (1928), *Collected Papers* (C.C.).
'Dostoevsky and Parricide' (1928), *Collected Papers* (C.C.).

1930–39
'Libidinal Types' (1931), *Collected Papers* (C.C.).
'Female Sexuality' (1931), *Collected Papers* (S.P.L.).
'Why War?' (1932), *Collected Papers* (C.C.).
'The Acquisition of Power over Fire' (1932), *Collected Papers* (C.C.).
'Analysis Terminable and Interminable' (1937), *Collected Papers* (T.T.).
'Splitting of the Ego in the Defensive Process' (1938), *Collected Papers* (S.P.L.).

2. Supplementary Bibliography of Writings by Other Authors

Adorno, T., and Horkheimer, M., *Aspects of Sociology* (1956), London, 1973.
Althusser, L., *Lenin and Philosophy and Other Essays*, translated by B. Brewster, London, 1971. (See the Appendix: 'Freud and Lacan'.)
Berger, P., *The Social Reality of Religion*, London, 1969. (Published in the U.S.A. as *The Sacred Canopy*, New York, 1967.)

Berger, P., 'Towards a Sociological Understanding of Psycho-analysis', *Social Research*, 1955.

Berger, P., and Luckmann, T., *The Social Construction of Reality*, London, 1967.

Bottomore, T., and Rubel, M., *Karl Marx, Selected Writings in Sociology and Social Philosophy*, London, 1956; paperback edition, Harmondsworth, 1963.

Bronfenbrenner, U., *Two Worlds of Childhood: U.S.A. and U.S.S.R.*, London, 1970.

Bettleheim, B., *Symbolic Wounds*, New York, 1954; revised edition, 1962.

Brown, Bruce, 'Marx, Freud and the Critique of Everyday Life', *Monthly Review of Books*, London and New York, 1973.

Brown, N. O., *Love's Body*, New York, 1966 and 1968.

Brown, N. O., *Life Against Death*, London, 1959; paperback edition, London, 1968.

Budd, S., *Sociologists and Religion*, London, 1973.

Cohen, P., 'Theories of Myth', *Man*, Vol. 4, No. 3, September 1969.

Durkheim, É., *Sociology and Philosophy*, translated by D. F. Pocock, London, 1965.

Erikson, E., *Childhood and Society*, New York, 1950; London, 1951; paperback edition, Harmondsworth, 1965.

Fletcher, R., *Instinct in Man*, London, 1957 and 1968.

Fletcher, R., *The Making of Sociology*, Vol. 2, London, 1971.

Fox, R., 'Totem and Taboo Reconsidered,' in E. Leach (ed.), *Structural Study of Myth and Totemism*, London, 1967.

Fromm, E., *Sigmund Freud's Mission*, London, 1959.

Fromm, E., *The Anatomy of Human Destructiveness*, New York, 1973; London, 1974.

Fromm, E., *The Crisis of Psycho-analysis*, Connecticut, 1970.

Gerth, H., and Wright Mills, C., *From Max Weber. Essays in Sociology*, London, 1948.

Giddens, A., *Capitalism and Modern Social Theory. Analysis of the writings of Marx, Durkheim and Max Weber*, Cambridge, 1971.

Habermas, J., *Knowledge and Human Interests*, London, 1968 and 1972.

Habermas, J., *Theory and Practice*, London, 1974.

Halmos, P., *The Faith of the Counsellors*, London, 1965.

Holbrook, D., *Human Hope and the Death Instinct*, Oxford, 1971.

Homans, G., 'Bringing Men Back In', *American Journal of Sociology*, Vol. 66, 1960–61.

Jay, Martin, *The Dialectical Imagination (Frankfurt School 1923–50)*, London, 1973.

Jones, E., *Sigmund Freud: Life and Work*, 3 vols., London and New York, 1953, 1955, 1957.

Jung, C., *Psychology and Religion*, Yale, Conn., 1938 and 1970.

Laing, R., and Cooper, D., *Reason and Violence*, London, 1964.

Lee, R. S., *Freud and Christianity*, London, 1948; paperback edition, Harmondsworth, 1967.

Lévi-Strauss, C., 'The Sorcerer and His Magic', in *Structural Anthropology*, London, 1963; paperback edition, New York, 1967.

Lichtheim, G., 'Freud and Marx' in J. Miller (ed.), *Freud*, London, 1972.

Lowen, A., *The Betrayal of the Body*, New York, 1967.

MacIntyre, A., *The Unconscious—A Conceptual Study*, London, 1958.

MacIntyre, A., *Marcuse*, London, 1970 (Fontana Modern Masters series).

MacIntyre, A., *Against the Self-Images of the Age*, London, 1971.

Malinowski, B., *Sex and Repression in Savage Society* (1927), Part I: *Description of Childhood and Puberty in Our Society and Melanesia*, London, 1953.

Marcuse, H., *Eros and Civilization*, New York, 1955; paperback edition, London, 1969.

Marcuse, H., 'Freedom and Freud: Theory of Instincts', in *Five Lectures*, New York, 1970.

Marcuse, H., 'The Obsolesence of the Freudian Conception of Man', in ibid.

Marcuse, H., 'On Science and Phenomenology', in A. Giddens, *Positivism and Sociology*, London, 1974.

Mead, G. H., *On Social Psychology*, Chicago, 1934 and 1956.

Mitchell, J., *Psychoanalysis and Feminism*, London, 1973.

North, M., *The Secular Priests*, London, 1972.

Parsons, T., 'Psychoanalysis and Social Structure', in *Essays in Sociological Theory*, New York, 1949.

Parsons, T., 'The Father Symbol: an Appraisal in the Light of Psychoanalytic and Sociological Theory', in *Social Structure and Personality*, New York, 1964.

Parsons, T., 'Social Structure and the Development of Personality: Freud's Contribution to the Integration of Psychology and Sociology' (1958), in ibid.

Parsons, T., 'The Superego and the Theory of Social Systems', in *Psychiatry*, Vol. 15 (1952); reprinted in P. Roazen, *Sigmund Freud*, Englewood Cliffs, N.J., 1973.

Popper, K., *Conjectures and Refutations*, London, 1963.

Reich, W., *The Mass Psychology of Fascism* (1934), London, 1946; New York, 1970.

Reich, W., *The Sexual Revolution*, Part I (1929); Part II (1935).

Reik, T., *The Ritual*, New York, 1946.

Rieff, P., *Freud: the Mind of the Moralist*, London, 1959.

Roazen, P., *Brother Animal. The Story of Freud and Tausk*, New York, 1969; paperback edition, Harmondsworth, 1973.

Roazen, P., *Freud: Political and Social Thought*, London, 1968.

Robinson, P., 'Marcuse', in *The Sexual Radicals*, London, 1969. (Published in the U.S.A. as *The Freudian Left*, New York, 1972.)

Roheim, G., *The Origin and Function of Culture*, 1943, 1968 and 1971, New York.

Roszak, T., *The Making of a Counter Culture*, London, 1968.

Rougement, D. de, *Passion and Society*, London, 1956.

Rycroft, C., *Reich*, London, 1971 (Fontana Modern Masters series).

Scharf, B., 'Durkheimian and Freudian Theories of Religion: the Case of Judaism', *British Journal of Sociology*, Vol. XXI, No. 2, June 1970, pp. 151–63.

Schofield, M., *The Sexual Behaviour of Young People*, London, 1965; paperback edition, revised and rewritten, Harmondsworth, 1968.

Segal, H., *Introduction to the Work of Melanie Klein*, London, 1964.

Steiner, F., *Taboo*, London, 1956; paperback edition, Harmondsworth, 1967.

Szasz, T., *The Myth of Mental Illness*, London, 1961.

Wollheim, R., *Freud*, London, 1971 (Fontana Modern Masters series).

Worsley, P., 'Groote Eylandt Totemism and le totemisme aujourd'-hui', in *The Structural Study of Myth and Totemism*, London, 1967.

Wrong, D., 'The Over-socialized Conception of Man in Modern Sociology', *American Sociological Review*, Vol. 26. 1961, pp. 183–93.

Index

In order to enable the reader of this book to gain a more rigorous under-standing of Freudian theory, Freud's own psychoanalytic concepts are printed in bold type in this index. The more important page references are also printed in bold type.